Body and Emotion

University of Pennsylvania Press
SERIES IN CONTEMPORARY ETHNOGRAPHY

Dan Rose and Paul Stoller, General Editors

A complete list of books in the series is available from the publisher.

Body and Emotion

The Aesthetics of Illness and Healing in the Nepal Himalayas

Robert R. Desjarlais

PENN

University of Pennsylvania Press

Philadelphia

Library of Congress Cataloging-in-Publication Data
Desjarlais, Robert R.
  Body and emotion: the aesthetics of illness and healing in the Nepal Himalayas / Robert R. Desjarlais.
     p.   cm. — (Series in contemporary ethnography)
  Includes bibliographical references and index.
  ISBN 0-8122-3166-X — ISBN 0-8122-1434-X (paper)
    1. Shamanism—Nepal—Helmu Region.   2. Sherpa (Nepalese people)—Religion.
  3. Helmu Region (Nepal)—Religious life and customs.   I. Title.   II. Series.
  BL2033.5.S52D45   1993
  299'.54—dc20   92-23545
                                                                            CIP

If we had a keen vision of all ordinary human life,
it would be like hearing the grass grow or the
squirrel's heart beat, and we should die of that
roar which lies on the other side of silence.
George Eliot *Middlemarch*

sdod na sems pa tsher ka
'thon na rkang chung na tsha
rkang chung na gi gi 'dug
su shi gang la bshad byung

If we stay our hearts will ache,
If we go our little feet will hurt
the sorrow of little feet hurting,
to whom can we tell?

Yolmo "Song of Pain" (*tsher glu*)

Contents

Illustrations

Acknowledgments

The present study owes itself to the combined support of many teachers, friends, colleagues, and institutions; I am grateful to have the opportunity to thank them. In Nepal, Lopsang Bombo, K. B. Gurung, Latu Lama, Dawa Lama, Karma Gyaltsan Lama, N. R. Nepali, Mukta Tamang, Khrishna Pradhan, and Lal Bahadur Tamang all offered not only their assistance to this project, but, perhaps more importantly, their friendship. *Ga ler phebs*, "go carefully," to all.

The United States Educational Foundation, Action Aid Nepal, and Tribhuvan University offered their assistance and support while I was in Nepal. The field research from which the book draws received financial support from the Wenner-Gren Foundation for Anthropological Research, the Program for Psychocultural Studies and Medical Anthropology at the University of California, Los Angeles, and the Department of Anthropology, UCLA. A postdoctoral fellowship from the National Institutes of Mental Health enabled me to write the final drafts of the manuscript while a fellow in the Department of Social Medicine, Harvard Medical School. I would like to thank the above institutions, the participants in the Program in Medical Anthropology at Harvard University, and my postdoctoral colleagues (Ladson Hinton, Roberto Lewis-Fernandez, Cheryl Mattingly, A. David Napier, Jonathan Sugar, and Donald Vereen), for their support.

Warm cups of salt-butter tea to Byron Good, John G. Kennedy, Arthur Kleinman, Nancy Levine, and Kenneth Lincoln, all of whom have enriched the book with their masterly, selfless efforts. Thanks also to the anonymous scholars who offered invaluable advice on the papers and drafts that led to the final version. Portions of the work benefited from presentations to the Workshop in Religion and Psychotherapy, University of Chicago, the Workshop in Psychological Anthropology, Harvard University, and the Department of Anthropology, University of California at Berkeley.

Carole Browner and Ernestine McHugh offered their thoughts on the manuscript at the most helpful of moments, and Vincanne Adams, Naomi and John Bishop, Donald Brenneis, Marcia Ellison, Bonnie Glass-Coffin, Mary-Jo Good, Devon Hinton, Douglas Hollan, Allen Johnson, Matthew

Kohrman, Lewis L. Langness, Charles Leslie, Robert Lipton, Gregory Maskarinec, Molly McGinn, Brinkley Messick, Theresa O'Nell, Herbert P. Phillips, Stacy Pigg, Fitz John Porter Poole, Douglass Price-Williams, David P. Smith, Barbara Tedlock, Nancy Warwick, Jane Wellenkamp, and Gary Wintz were kind enough to comment on all or parts of the manuscript in its various incarnations. If the ear listens closely, it can hear the whispered voices of these many friends and colleagues.

I am grateful to Graham E. Clarke for his kind help with comments and for his permission to use his writings on Yolmo social history and political organization. My historical account is based largely on his work, and readers interested further in the history and social organization of Yolmo society are directed to his work on the region, and to that written jointly by him with Thakurlal Manandhar, details of which are given in the References. Michael Aris and John Donne helped to translate my unorthodox Yolmo phrasings into Tibetan script. Michael Desjarlais offered his darkroom expertise in developing the photographs herein, and Binney Hare penned the maps and illustrations. Paul Stoller, Dan Rose, and Patricia Smith have served admirably as editors, readers, and friends.

Without the love and encouragement of Tracy McGarry, this work would not have been written. Special thanks to my family, who encouraged my travels through the years. Lastly, the residents of Helambu, particularly those of Gulphubanyang, welcomed me into their homes, listened to my garbled questions, and taught me much. The book is dedicated to these remarkable people.

*   *   *

Portions of the following include revised and expanded versions of two published essays of mine: "Poetic Transformations of Yolmo 'Sadness,'" in *Culture, Medicine and Psychiatry* 15:387–420, and "Yolmo Aesthetics of Body, Health, and Soul Loss" in *Social Science and Medicine* 34:1105–1117. I am grateful to the editors and publishers of *Culture, Medicine and Psychiatry* (Kluwer Academic Publishers, P.O. Box 17, 3300 AA Dordrecht, the Netherlands), and *Social Science and Medicine* (Pergamon Press Ltd., Headington Hill Hall, Oxford, OX3 OBW, United Kingdom) for their permission to draw from this work.

Note on Transcription

Yolmo wa, or "the Yolmo people," speak the national language of Nepali, as well as the distinct Tibetan-derived language of Kagate, a Bodic or Tibeto-Burman dialect that acquired this name by first having been recorded as spoken among a group of "paper-makers" in Eastern Nepal, this being the literal sense of the Nepali term *kagate* (Clarke 1980a). I spoke with villagers in both these languages, but primarily in Nepali at the beginning of my field stay, and more in the Yolmo language (Kagate), which I was less competent in, toward the end of my stay. Yolmo wa rely on both languages in everyday conversations (using Kagate among themselves and Nepali among non-Yolmo peoples), and talk in either is often interspersed with phrases from the other.

I transcribe Nepali words cited in the text (e.g., n. *chhornu*, "to separate") according to Turner's (1965 [1931]) method. Most Yolmo words (such as *tsher ka*, "pain of separation") are transcribed according to Wylie's (1959) system of Tibetan orthography. I have offered glossed meanings to these terms and, when appropriate, the rough sound of the word as it appears to the English ear. The exceptions to these Tibetan words are local phrases that do not appear to have direct Tibetan correlates (e.g., *tashing nashing*, "hair-pain") or that have taken on unique meanings in the Helambu region (e.g., *bombo*, "shaman," from the Tibetan *bon po*, practioners of the Bon religion). These unorthodox words are written according to the English ear and, unlike the Tibetan words, are not divided into distinct syllables. When possible, I have tried to link these latter words to their Tibetan origins (e.g., lama, t. *bla ma*). All of the key Nepali and Tibetan words are listed, along with their rough sounds and glossed meanings, in the glossary.

Part I

Loss

1. Imaginary Gardens with Real Toads

While conducting fieldwork in the late 1980s among Yolmo Sherpa, an ethnically Tibetan people who live in the Helambu region of northcentral Nepal, I participated in some twenty-odd healing ceremonies as the shamanic apprentice to a veteran "grandfather" healer called Meme (t. *me me*). Barefoot, illiterate, sporting ragged farm clothes and a scruffy beard beneath an angular face, the sixty-seven-year-old Meme possessed a wealth of sacred knowledge. In everyday conversation his uncouth speech and manners told of the low-status family from which he came. But when healing, this dignified *bombo* or "shaman" (t. *bon po*) could communicate with the gods, divine the mysteries of illness, joke at timely moments, and shamanize till dawn. Due to these talents, neighboring families frequently asked him to perform curing rites.

Throughout my stay, I accompanied Meme Bombo when he was called to heal. Meme's house, an old but sturdy structure, with a drum hanging from the rafters and fleas treading the mud-washed floors, lay on the southern fringes of Chumdeli, a hillside hamlet surrounding a Lamaist temple and populated by farmers, some of whom claim to be Yolmo and others Tamang people (this being a social division that locally can be represented in ethnic terms), and those *'dres pa* "mules" of mixed Tamang-Yolmo descent. Son of a Tamang mother and Yolmo father, Meme himself was of the latter lineage, but as he studied under a Yolmo shaman from the northwest, his craft fell along Yolmo lines.

On the afternoon of a healing, I would climb through the dense forest that separated Chumdeli from my home in the village of Gulphubanyang and walk down a zigzag trail through terraced fields of wheat and maize until I reached Meme's farmstead. After sipping tea with his family, I would tag along as Meme ambled in the twilight shadow toward his patient's house. Until early morning, when I usually fell asleep, I assisted Meme in the limited ways I could, helping him to "play the drum," sacrifice chickens, and beseech the gods to enter our bodies. Footsore, smoke-eyed, I approached these evenings with a combined sense of apprehension, fatigue,

Photo 1. Meme Bombo.

boredom, and wonder. During many of the ceremonies, I entered into a "trance state" that was entirely convincing to me, though undoubtedly distinct from what Yolmo shamans themselves experience when gods "fall" into their bodies. The trances took place when the shaman performed an oracular divination (*mo*): playing his drum methodically while facing the sacred altar (composed of twenty-five rice-dough *gtor ma* cakes representative of, and offerings to, various deities), Meme would soon begin to "shake" as a deity's "breath" entered his body to speak of hitherto unknown causes of the patient's malady.

My own trance paralleled the descent of Meme's gods into his body. Taking the role of shamanic initiate, I would sit in a semilotus position to the right of my "guru" and attempt to follow the curing chants. In time, Meme would begin to feel the presence of the divine, his body oscillating in fits and tremors, and my body, following the rhythm of his actions, would similarly "shake." Tracked by the driving, insistent beat of the shaman's drum, my body would fill with energy. Music resonated within me, building to a crescendo, charging my body and the room with impacted meaning. Waves of tremors coursed through my limbs. Sparks flew, colors expanded, the room came alive with voices, fire, laughter, darkness.

To demonstrate an ability to host the gods in one's body is the entrance exam, of sorts, into Yolmo shamanism, and my apprenticeship with Meme formed the cornerstone of a research project (see Figure 1). The main thrust of this study focused on incidents of illness and healing among Yolmo villagers. Yolmo (sometimes locally pronounced "Yermu") is the traditional Tibetan name of the Helambu region, from which comes the name Yolmo wa for the people. (The historical and political account in the next section is based on the work of Clarke, some of which still remains to be published.)[1] The dominant groups are also known simply as Lama, and on the male side are descended from Tibetan priests. In the central upland area, many of these religious masters also used to own temples near Kyirong, an area to the northwest of present-day Tibet. In the seventeenth century, they had the right to land of the Yolmo temples confirmed in the name of Newar and then Gurkha kings, that is, by the Nepalese state.

Annual pilgrimage turned into migration, and some of the religious virtuosi settled at these temples to be joined in marriage by the offspring of the local "Tamang" elite of their tenants and congregation. These people were little different from the Tamang from whom in recent times "Lamas" have often taken care to distinguish themselves. In this way, in the eigh-

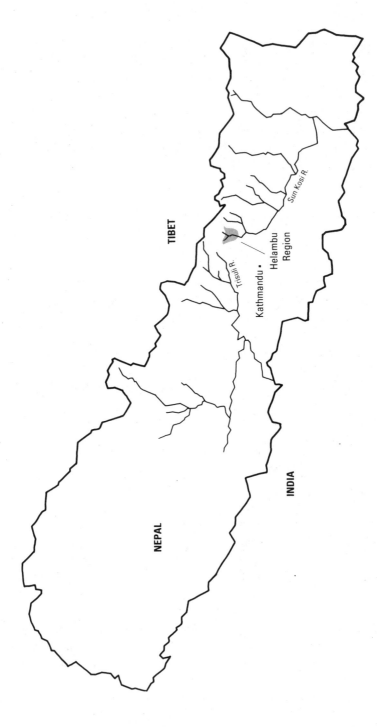

Figure 1. Location of research area in Nepal.

teenth and nineteenth centuries, villages grew up on the crests of the ridges that expressed their dominance as well as their beliefs through their temples and Buddhist religious practice. In secular terms, the priests had an economic role as landlords and a political one as representatives of the state. This is the particular cultural development that has given rise to the "Lama People," the "Lama-Tamang," and the "Lama-Sherpa," as Yolmo wa can also be known. The main term of this conjunct is the Tibetan word "lama" (t. *bla ma*), which has the sense of "priest" or "higher-one"; this contrasts the elite from neighboring, low-status families, who eventually came to be known simply as Tamang.[2]

The diffuse, interactive, and interdependent quality of Yolmo identity is characteristic of many groups in Nepal.[3] In fact, Yolmo wa are one of several Tibeto-Burman–speaking peoples who inhabit the midhills of the Nepal Himalayas. The cultures of these distinct groups, which include (ranging roughly from west to east) Gurung, Tamang, Yolmo, Sherpa, and Limbu clans, are shaped by the two great traditions bordering them. To the north dwell the Tibetans, a devoutly Buddhist society now controlled by the Chinese government. To the south lie the Hindu populations of the Kathmandu Valley, the Terai basin, and the Indian plains. While Yolmo wa, like their Himalayan neighbors, evince religious institutions descendant from Tibet, Nepalese society has influenced their language, customs, and sociopolitical workings.

One way in which national politics has shaped Yolmo culture has been in the reworking of an ethnic identity. Although Yolmo wa now often identify themselves as "Sherpa" to outsiders, the term is a relatively new addition to their ethnic lexicon. Previously, they called themselves "Lama" to distinguish themselves ethnically from Tamang clans who neighbor Yolmo wa on the southern and western sides of the Helambu Valley. But with the increasing international renown of their cultural cousins (the Solu-Khumbu Sherpa of the Mount Everest region), Yolmo wa have aligned themselves with this prestigious group in the last three decades and now refer to themselves as "Sherpa" to outsiders. While Yolmo wa have begun to form political contacts and to intermarry with Sherpa groups to the east, in many ways they hold closer cultural affinities with neighboring Tamang families.[4] Economic exchanges between Yolmo families, who live "above," and Tamang families, who live "below," are often asymmetrical; Tamang sharecrop lands owned by Yolmo wa and often work as day laborers for the wealthier "priests."[5]

Geographically, the Helambu Valley, as it is known in Nepali, consists

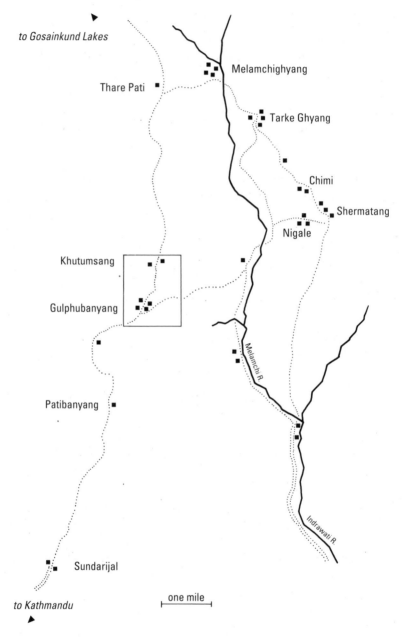

to Gosainkund Lakes

Melamchighyang

Thare Pati

Tarke Ghyang

Chimi

Shermatang

Nigale

Khutumsang

Gulphubanyang

Melamchi R.

Patibanyang

Indrawati R.

Sundarijal

to Kathmandu

one mile

Figure 2. Map of Helambu.

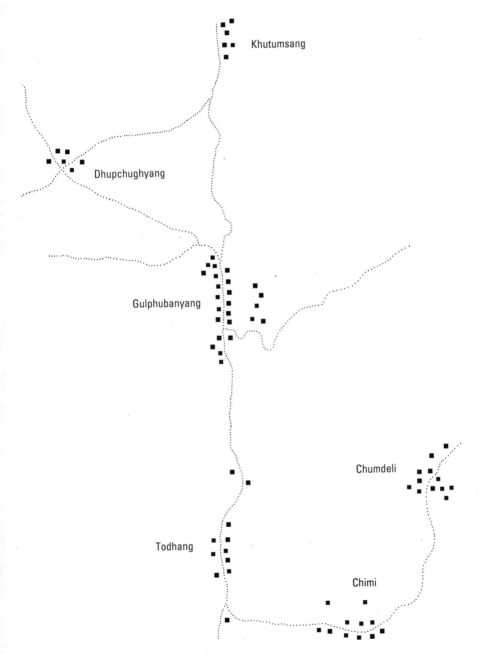

Figure 3. Map of Gulphubanyang region.

of two mountain ranges that ascend north from the Kathmandu Valley to the Himalayas, with foothills radiating east and west off these ranges.[6] The northern crest of this horseshoelike ring consists of two broad peaks that separate Yolmo from the Langtang region and Tibet and thus account for its name, for in religious texts *Yol mo gangs ra* denotes "place screened by snow mountains/glaciers."[7] Between the two limbs of the mountainous arch flows the Melamchi River. Brahmans and Chhetris, two Hindu castes, live at the lowest elevation of the valley, cultivating rice, fruits, and other tropical crops alongside the river. People locally known as Tamang reside higher up,[8] above the Hindu population but below the wealthier "Lamas," who themselves reside within fifty to sixty villages lining the forested crests of the hills between seven and ten thousand feet elevation.

Within these villages, commerce, land rentals, pastural grazing, and the farming of maize, potatoes, and other high-altitude crops provide the main sources of food and income, although recently tourism and "factory" employment in Kathmandu and India have brought additional material wealth. Until 1991, the national *Panchayat* system of Nepal officially set political agendas by regulating district elections, but village politics were often defined by local power structures of wealth, status, and kinship. As for kinship, as with other cultural practices, there has been a great deal of particular local variation, but one widely found local preference (also common elsewhere in the Nepal Himalaya region) is for a combination of patrilineal descent and residence, together with cross-cousin marriage.[9] Though devout practioners of the Nyingmapa or "Ancient School" of Mahayana Buddhism, Yolmo villagers with whom I lived (of the southwestern side of the valley) also turn to local shamans in times of physical and spiritual distress.[10]

While the oldest and most prestigious Yolmo villages cluster around temples along the northeastern rim of Helambu's crest (e.g., Melamchighyang, Tarke Ghyang, Churyegyang), settlements have developed in this century along the western perimeter as new village-temples have been established by offshoots of Lamaist lineages from the north (see Figure 2).[11] Several of these small villages (such as Chumdeli, where Meme lives) now populate the southwestern edge of Helambu, around seven thousand feet above sea level, in the vicinity of Gulphubanyang. The latter settlement is a burgeoning bazaar with a row of homes, tea shops, and small stores straddling the Nuwakot-Sindhu Palchock district line (Bagmati Zone) two days' walk north of Kathmandu, the capital of Nepal.

From February 1988 to March 1989, I lived in Gulphubanyang, work-

Photo 2. Gulphubanyang, 1986.

ing with Yolmo wa there and in several neighboring hamlets. Perched atop a windy knoll, the chain of mudstone, tin-roofed houses hugs both sides of a trail (and, lately, trekking route) leading to northwestern Helambu and the Gosainkund Lakes. The second part of the village name, *banyang*, denotes a saddlelike ridge (*Gulphu*, where cattle are sheltered), and the name suits the place well, for the village sits atop a steep ridge set between two larger crests running to the east and west. To the north and south range forests offering lumber, firewood, and grazing fields; to the east and west, steeply terraced fields of wheat, millet, and corn line the eroding hillside until it drops into the basin below.

Developed in the middle of this century by two enterprising Gurung brothers, Gulphubanyang now houses Gurung, Yolmo, and Tamang shop-keepers, priests, and farmers (including some who have built second homes to reap the benefits of its market economy). The village is also home to a medical clinic, a trekking lodge, and a British-run development project staffed by college-educated Nepalis. An extensive network of footpaths link Gulphubanyang to a universe of neighboring hamlets, such as Chumdeli to the southeast (see Figure 3). Tamang and a few Gurung lineages (a distinct ethnic group which, in the Helambu region, practices Hinduism) live below and to the south; Yolmo settlements, including a Lamaist "temple" (*dgon pa*, "gonpa") in the hamlet of Dhupchughyang a mile away, populate the wooded lands to the north.

Many of these outlying hamlets maintain strong economic, political, and kinship ties with Gulphubanyang. Several families, in turn, have built or rented houses in Kathmandu, where family members work or are en-gaged in business. A migration of residents throughout the year, but primarily during the trekking seasons, has resulted from the demands for labor in the tourist and other industries. This rapidly changing, multiethnic community, with strong ties to the central Nepalese government and a steady stream of tourists trickling through, continuously shapes the form and history of Yolmo life as it exists in this locale. For instance, in contrast to the original Lama villages on the ridge of central Helambu, where Clarke has identified a cultural history based on a corporate social life among households in close relation to village-temples,[12] Yolmo villages on the southwestern slopes indicate more dispersed, loosely structured kinship networks; these networks are tied less to a central temple polity than to distinct, household-based economies. In turn, whereas the Lamaist tradi-tion has progressively overlayed and usurped local shamanic practices in the highlands of eastern and central Helambu (as it has among Sherpa of the

Solu-Khumbu region),[13] Yolmo wa who reside on the western slopes continue to stress shamanic rites as a system of healing—the result, perhaps, of the limited influence of temple life and the prevalence of Tamang shamanism in the region.[14]

It is within this complex local context, as it took form in the last decade, that Meme walked at dusk to local households to perform shamanic healings. In 1988, he was often accompanied by an American ethnographer intent on studying his craft. The nature of this apprenticeship took several forms. Along with attending Meme's healings, I spoke with healers and patients in the days and weeks following a ceremony. With Meme and a few younger shamans, I inquired into the subtleties of their *bidyā* or "learning," from divination and demonology to the exorcistic "throwing" of ghosts and witches. With patients, I asked them to tell of their experiences of illness and healing. Other villagers were queried on more general themes, such as notions of body, emotions, gender, and pain. Eventually, Karma, a young, gifted bachelor from a Lama family in eastern Helambu who taught English in a Kathmandu boarding school, moonlighted, during the latter part of my stay, as a translator and key informant. In all, by living with villagers primarily on their own terms, more bumbling initiate than intrusive, elite stranger, I felt that my body developed a partial, experiential understanding of their world, from the ways in which they held their bodies to how they felt, hurt, and healed.

One of the major domains of pain in Helambu is a kind of malaise that can be glossed as "soul loss." While this illness can take several forms, villagers typically suffer from it when a sudden fright causes the *bla* ("la") or "spirit" to leave the body and wander about the countryside, prey to malevolent ghosts, demons, and witches. If the spirit is lost, the body feels "heavy" and lacks energy and "passion." The afflicted person does not care to eat, talk, work, travel, or socialize. Thoughts become "dull," unbalanced. One has trouble sleeping, witnesses ominous dreams, and is prone to further illnesses. If a person falls sick in this manner, his or her family summons a *bombo* such as Meme; the shaman divines how the spirit was lost, where it has wandered, and how best to retrieve it. He then ritually searches for and attempts to "call" the lost life-force back into the body of his patient.

This book is an account of Yolmo souls: how and why they are lost, how healers return them to their owners, and why incidents of "soul loss" occur so frequently in certain parts of Helambu. I specifically wish to examine the play between cultural sensibilities and emotional distress, from the cultural forces that mold, make sense of, and occasionally exacerbate feelings of loss, sorrow, and despair to the social institutions that assuage the pain and anxiety often bound within these sentiments. How do local ways of being, feeling, and knowing tie into experiences of illness and healing? Of chief concern here is the "aesthetic" nature of everyday life: the common graces and embodied values that govern how villagers go about their lives, walk down a hillside, or talk with neighbors; the forms and sensibilities that contribute to the sensory grounds of an aging body, a lost soul, or a healthy person. Since these ways of being are not free-floating but are driven by social dynamics that influence the very marrow of experience, their political underpinnings must be assessed. At the same time, the accent on the sensory leads me to go beyond a symbolic analysis, for I want to understand something of what it might feel like for Yolmo wa to grow old, to suffer grief, to lose and regain their souls. And finally, I ask how someone from a distant land (like myself) can come to comprehend such experiences. To what extent, and through what means, can we grasp the emotional and sensorial life of another person or people? How, in turn, can an author best arrange words on a page to pass this knowledge on to a reader?

*   *   *

My experiences of trance might help us to begin to answer the latter queries. When I returned to the United States fifteen months after arriving in Helambu, I learned that a handful of anthropologists have written of trance states similar to my own but interpreted them in a slightly different fashion. Maya Deren and Larry Peters experienced music-induced "possession" on several occasions (Deren in Haiti, Peters among Tamang of Nepal),[15] and Michael Harner and Michael Taussig comment on drug-induced hallucinatory states encountered while participating in South American shamanic rituals.[16] In reading these accounts, one gets the sense that the visionary world of the native can be that of the anthropologist: what the outsider experiences of trance reflects what local healers or participants experience, as if the ethnographer's imaginings produced the photographic equivalent of the natives' own histories. Deren, for instance, suggests that her identity as an artist privileges the nature of the insights she can make; her "acute sensitivity to form" ultimately enables the "they" (the Haitians) to become a "we."[17] Peters, on the other hand, develops an "experiential approach" to ethnographic fieldwork, delving into shamanic trances in the faith that "a more complete knowledge would result if I experienced what my informants said they did."[18] Peters finds it difficult to go native during the trances; the difficulty appears to be chiefly a personal one—arising from his inability to shed his "cultural and intellectual biases"—rather than one occasioned by the nature of the situation. However, as with Deren, the "they" ultimately becomes a "we": Peters concludes, upon thinking for a moment like a Tamang, that "I stepped across cultural boundaries and was freed of my previous intellectual inflexibility."[19] Harner and Taussig give less introspective accounts of their trance experiences, but for them, too, the trance state, as a means toward understanding the indigenous worldview, seems unproblematic. Indeed, Taussig develops a theory of Peruvian healing (as working through a principle of "montage" akin to Brechtian notions of the theater) based on what he perceives of *yage*-induced hallucinations.[20] As he writes, "Somewhere you have to take the bit between your teeth and depict yage nights in terms of your own experience."[21] Harner, in turn, decides to learn shamanism "firsthand" after realizing the dragonish creatures he met upon consuming *ayahuasca* were "already familiar" to a Jivaro healer—"known to him from his own explorations of the same hidden world into which I had ventured."[22]

The trance states that I knew of, in contrast to these reports, suggest that the process of cultural conversion or translation is not so clear-cut. The hidden worlds were not the same. Though I would "shake" in time with Meme, suggesting a physiologic baseline to trance, it quickly became clear that what I experienced and demonstrated of trance behavior was far from identical to what my neighbors were familiar with. My ceremonial duties soon lent me the nickname of "grandfather shaman" (*Meme Bombo*), but, unlike that of the elderly Meme, the name was partly in jest. Unlike Yolmo shamans, who use crossed legs as a springboard on which their torsos bounce up and down, my body shook more like a piece of Jell-o, wavering from side to side. Children giggled at the strange contortions my body would make and adults chuckled at my reports of what I saw when I was "shaking" (though the sheer fact of my trance seemed to reaffirm for villagers the reality of their gods, and my ability to host them). "As it is, the quickest of us walk about well wadded in stupidity," quips George Eliot in the sentence following this book's epigraph, and I certainly waded in cultural ignorance in Nepal. During the first healings, my body felt like an "unworkable monstrosity," to borrow Clifford Geertz's tag for that impossible creature, a human being without culture.[23]

In reality, of course, my culture had not preconditioned me for trance,

Photo 3. The author, in "trance."

and I experienced my "shamanic" existence as an uncontrolled ganglion of nerves, a loose hodgepodge of unsystematized sensations. While divine words flowed from the shaman's mouth in trance, I encountered a montage of storied images (wandering through a cave, bumping into transformative tigers, talking with my own rendition of the *ri bombo*, a local gnomish "forest shaman"). And when I shared with Meme the content of these trance visions, he quickly dismissed their relevance, suggesting that I only saw images of an epiphenomenal nature.

"Meme," I asked him one day as we basked in mountain sunshine outside his home, "these visions I have, of caves, tigers, and elfin creatures, what do they mean?"

"Nothing," he said with a flurry of bony fingers. "When you shake, the gods are gazing into your body to see if you are pure or not. But since you don't know our language well, and do not know what the gods look like, you only see lightening flashes in the dark, as when a man is knocked on the head."

My initial ritual incompetence and the cultural irrelevance of my "shamanic" visions lead me to question the ease with which anthropologists have assessed foreign realities based on what they have experienced of trance. I feel, for instance, that Taussig errs in basing his innovative analysis on what he experiences of drug-induced trance states, for the hallucinations of an American intellectual (shamanism in an age of mechanical reproduction) must be quite different from what a local healer or patient envisions. Similarly, Deren's fearful encounters with a "white darkness" seem to speak more of her own personality than that of Haitians, Harner's visions refer more to the Book of Revelation than to the local mythology, and Peters's failure to go native undoubtedly owes itself to the cultural baggage he carried to Nepal. This is not to say that there is little to be learned from these reflexive accounts; they can offer valuable insights into the healing process. But we must bear in mind that subjective experiences of this sort are deeply patterned by the long-standing cultural context forming and informing one's identity. I found that one cannot adopt cultures as readily as one puts on clothes.

Yolmo initiates themselves experience trance quite awkwardly at first. One night I watched a part-time apprentice host the gods within his body with a knee-jerk frenzy of movements, a range of syllabic fits and starts, with his torso chugging along like a backfiring diesel engine. But even this clumsy display had its rhyme and reason; there was a culturally patterned way to be a shamanic initiate, a proper, sensible way to confront the divine. Unlike Yolmo apprentices, then, who knew how to become a shaman even if they weren't one yet and so did not risk laughter when they sat by the altar, I first had to learn something of the basic tenets of Yolmo experience, ways of using the body and interacting with others, that would then enable me to learn how to be a proper shaman. This learning how to learn, or "deutero-learning," as Bateson puts it,[24] lies for me at the heart of the ethnographic enterprise. I learned to enter into trance not solely by attending Meme's séances, but by frequenting the teashops and porches of Gulphubanyang, walking with Meme along the trails leading between villages, and by sensing the sounds and smells of the terraced countryside. By busying myself with these activities, gleaning how to eat a bowl of rice with style or greet an elder with grace, I learned how to use my body in a way that was conducive to my more ritualized efforts.

All this suggests that my trances did not involve a template that recorded, like a photograph, what Yolmo shamans experience of trance. Instead, my memory of the trances should be taken as a sensory transcript of a conversation between cultures, with my experiences marking the crossover between American and Himalayan ways of being.[25] The trances thus reflected more my idiosyncratic attempts to conform to and make sense of Yolmo society than they did any Yolmo intimacies. At the same time, as my comprehension of Yolmo society gradually developed in the months after the initial trances, my experiences of trance, patterned by the context in which I found myself, slowly began to compare more to (and comment on) what the shamans seem to experience. Bateson has argued, in line with his theory of deutero-learning, that distinct "paradigms" of Balinese experience (from body image to kinesthetic principles) enable Balinese to learn how to undergo trance.[26] Similarly, while my experiences never escaped the prism of my own cultural reality, I felt as if I became partly "socialized" for Yolmo trance, an acculturation which Meme gradually seemed to take note of; he more readily placed his drum in my hands. My understanding of cultural ideas of the body facilitated the approach and strength of trance states, for a local view of the body as a collection of marionettelike parts enabled the "shaking" to come on more powerfully. In turn, my sensitivity to cultural imagery channeled the symbolic character of my visionary experiences. In the first months, I experienced visions akin to what Mary Watkins calls "waking dreams"[27]—in my case, an episodic montage of imaginative scenarios loosely bound together into a narrative, storybook frame. But during the last few healings, the visions became more controlled, centered, steadied: timeless meditations on the (culturally constituted) homologies of altar, body, and geography—as expressed in some field notes recorded on the night of an October healing, six months after arriving in Helambu:

> The images arrive very focused, concentric: an awareness of a landscape outside, hills and green pastures. A sense that the *gtor ma* cakes represent spiritual forces from this geography. Hence a parallel between the landscape and the altar, and another (metaphoric) parallel between the altar and my body. A focused, relaxed meditation on the five colored directions: yellow, white, red, green, blue. A sense of the five colors flowing from the altar through my body, like a rainbow, from my buttocks up along my spine— flowing in rhythm with my breath. Metaphoric parallels pass quickly, simultaneous awareness.

But to me, the isomorphism that developed between my trances and Yolmo aesthetic forms does not suggest that I became, either in trance or everyday life, a Yolmo wa, or that I experienced what Yolmo experience. Rather, I became a strange hybrid, caught in a no-man's-land betwixt and between cultures, learning something of a visited way of life yet relying heavily on my own. But perhaps it is precisely in the clash between worldviews, in the tension between symbolic systems (how reality is defined, the body held, or experience articulated), that some anthropological insights emerge. One learns of another way of being and feeling through contrast, noting the differences that make a difference. By participating in the everyday life of a society distinct from one's own, an ethnographer confronts and slowly learns (often tacitly but always partially) patterns of behavior previously unfamiliar to his or her body. In my experience, it is through this behavioral reworking that the differences characterizing two forms of life become most apparent; novel ways of moving, talking, and interacting contribute to a visceral appreciation of the forces that occasion those actions. This book, then, is a meditation on Yolmo forms of life as I came to understand them, with the tools I had on hand: a mix of shamanic practice, embodied knowledge, and persistent note-taking. Through this meditation, I wish to advance a way of writing ethnography that includes the reader's body as much as the author's in the conversation at hand.

*　*　*

Reflecting on my trance experiences and the images that flowed from them, I am reminded of Marianne Moore's definition of poetry's subject matter. Poets, for Moore, need to be "literalists of the imagination," presenting for inspection "imaginary gardens with real toads in them."[28] Like Moore's poetry, the nature of my trances seemed to be a paradoxical mix of symbolic fictions and familiar realities. The imaginary trance gardens, populated with fierce tigers, dark caves, and archetypal old men, were fertile and febrile. I played a Bergmanesque game of chess with Death in May (with black and white *gtor ma* cakes); flew eaglelike above the Himalayas in June (an account of which drew peels of laughter from the festive audience: "Tell us again, Meme Bombo, where you went to!"); and walked a parched wasteland in July. The latter vision quest, which occurred on the occasion of a healing for Mingma Lama, a frail old man who lost several of his "life supports" (*srog*) after the death of two close friends, began as follows:

> From the beginning, a sense of walking in a wasteland. A desert, parched, dry. A dead fish rotting in a dried-up river bed. A burnt tree, ash-covered. A bird hangs upside down on one limb; on closer inspection I see it is stuffed, fragile, held to the tree by cheap metal wires. The air is very hot, but no direct sunlight, only haze. A half moon seen, waning. I am alone, wandering.
> Yet a sense that ahead in the distance there is a mountain; trees, flowers, water. It is as if I need to go to this mountain, a domain of life.

> I now notice that in the wasteland there are underground pathways of energy; I am reminded of the aboriginal "songlines" of Australia. I understand that these pathways are of symbolic energy, of a special type of music (rhythms of vitality). These pathways are the antithesis of earthquakes, for they integrate rather than destruct the earth.

Despite the phantasmagoric nature of these visions, with their wastelands and personalized symbols, a few toads apparently revealed themselves. The first "real" toad was the imaginary garden itself. The trances, facilitated through driving, repetitive music, induced a mode of consciousness in which mythopoeic, image-based thought predominates, a dreamlike process linked to altered and "shamanic" states of consciousness in both Western and non-Western contexts. In this instance, thinking worked through analogy, metaphor, and metonym, a form of experience that often has therapeutic import.[29] Western therapists employ similar techniques in what is called "guided imagery" or "active imagination."[30]

On reflection, many of the images did serve to represent, capture, and illuminate psychological dimensions of my life at the time, possibly engaging a therapeutic, "transcendent" function, as Jung put it.[31] The wasteland, for instance, seems to have charted the burdens of fieldwork. In several caves, in turn, I happened on a skeleton devoured by a fierce tiger but then reassembled into a tiger or an old man.

> In the front of the cave, there are scattered bones. In the back, a tiger transforms back and forth into a decrepit old man. This creature tells me the bones are mine, while numerous tigers, ghost-like, devour them.
> Just inside the cave, on the left side, a leopard's skin hangs from the wall. Bones lie in a pile below this. Next to the bones is an extinguished fire. Ashes.
> Sitting, shaking, a sensation that I am part tiger, possessing a tiger's tail.

The "corporeal dismemberment" might have symbolized the transformative nature of my ongoing shamanic initiation,[32] as well as the liminal death and rebirth process of the fieldwork endeavor itself.[33] Perhaps more significantly, however, the newfound self-awareness seemed complemented by "insights" into my cultural hosts, for the trance states offered uncertain commentary on the psychosocial dynamics of illness and healing; they apparently functioned in a manner comparable to Meme's divinations. Less than one month after arriving in Helambu, I attended the healing ceremony for Sumjok, a quiet married woman who fell seriously ill after a miscarriage. Tense, withdrawn, silent, Sumjok lay on a cot as Meme divined the causes of illness (the assault of the *ri bombo*, the "forest shaman" who often inflicts madness). As the gods "fell" onto Meme, I likewise entered into a trance state, the visual content of which I later jotted in a notebook.

> The first images involve the patient: she transforms into an outline of white stripes—or bars, as in a jail cell. She is hollow inside save for a small white dove. I sense the dove is trapped inside her "cell," but there is no opening. A lock appears at the top of her head. This lock is to be opened by a *gtor ma* cake, thus letting the dove free. The dove would then flutter around the room, visiting the heads of all the family members, connecting them all with a vibrant thread.
>
> Image of the woman clasping her hand over her mouth while the family members, looking on, hold hands over eyes.
>
> Image of a tree (of life), rich and vibrant, beside a cemetery marked by tombstones. Leaves fall from the tree and land in the cemetery grounds. A shaman, dressed in full regalia, appears on a swing which extends down from a branch of this tree. As he swings, he scoops up leaves which have fallen on the cemetery grounds and affixes them back on the tree.
>
> When turning to the altar, a sudden burst of energy, of light, explodes from the *gtor ma*, pushing my body back as a strong wind will do, making me shake fiercely. A bolt of energy experienced—of energy, of color, ecstasy and health, of a need to connect everyone together through "threads," of flowers expanding and emmanating color, energy, and health.

The images focus on the scene of healing, as actively imagined by me: Sumjok lying on her cot, transformed into various, isolated identities; a tree in a distant cemetery supporting a mythic healer; and my ecstatic sense of various colors and energies enlivening the dark room, although I took what I saw to be imaginary, not ontically real. Yet despite their "illusory" nature, a series of motifs emerged from the stream of images, each giving crystal form to Yolmo lives as I later came to understand them and shall explore in depth below: a tense duality between corporeal body (*lus*, "li") and spiritual *sems* or "heartmind" (a dove trapped inside a hollow body); the need for social integration (threads tying family members together); the shaman as mediator between life and death; the aesthetic sensibilities of Yolmo healing (energy, renewal, balance); and cultural constraints on emotional expression and empathy (Sumjok, hand over mouth; her family, hands over eyes).[34]

The last pair of images alludes to an ethos and epistemology prevalent in Helambu. Briefly, and at the risk of simplifying the discussion to be developed below, the body, like a house, hides its contents from the eyes of others, and villagers generally find it difficult to know what another person is thinking or feeling. As neighbors often responded to my inquiries, "How can we know what is in another's heartmind [*sems*]?" In turn, villagers typically strive to maintain an equilibrium in their social lives by controlling the expression of personal desires that may run against the social grain. They therefore feel it inappropriate to let others know what they are feeling, and villagers often find it necessary to control or "hide" sentiments of grief or anger from others. The net sum of this ethos is that, despite a culturally recognized need to "cleanse" one's heart, those suffering distress often find it difficult to communicate their plight to others.

Although the "local rationality"[35] generally fails to note the link between illness and emotional distress in the everyday life of Yolmo wa, emotional tensions often seem to relate to incidents of "soul loss," for culturally shaped sentiments of grief, sadness, anxiety, and despair tend to lie at the causal root of this dysphoric illness. Shamanic healing, in turn, appears to offer an indirect medium through which this private distress is voiced, fashioned, and potentially transformed. The main evidence for this idea was found in several shamanic divinations I observed: deities speaking through Meme commented on and gave discursive form to the emotional distress of his patients. A young Yolmo bride whom I shall call Yeshi, for instance, lost her "spirit" (*bla*) in late spring and so lost her strength and volition to eat, work, and engage with others. While Yeshi's family said they did not know why she fell ill, I found her to be uncommonly lifeless, perhaps due to the apparently untenable living situation she faced at that time. During an October healing, Meme divined that her illness was caused by "many tears falling from her eyes," deep feelings of "confusion" and "anxiety," and an inability to "hold" her heart—an etiology that lifted the blame off Yeshi for her despair, gave meaning to her tears, and conveyed her plight to others.

As the shaman divines, so the anthropologist imagines: I experienced my own "divination" of Yeshi's troubles two months after my arrival in Helambu, on the night of a May healing performed on her behalf.

> Everything becomes very cold, frozen. The door is blown open, broken down. Snow shoots in, crashes down from the roof, collapsing the stairs in the weight of its descent. Everything—people, plants, altar—are frozen, iced-over. A vacant wind blows. I realize the falling snow means we are on top of the Himalayas, but only the shamans know this. The laymen are oblivious to the snow.
>
> A complementary battle occurs between the snow and the hearth fire, the struggle forming a circle of energy.
>
> I get the message the healing "powers" transform people, removing their old skins, receiving new ones. Especially people's eyes are made new, their perception renewed. Everything is renewed.

> The hearth is cracked. An imbalance in the fire (between the male and female sides) cracks the hearth, the floor. Healing patches up the cracks, but does not repair the imbalance.

While this trance linked Yeshi's spiritlessness to familial conflicts, as imagined by the cracked hearth and warring fire and ice, subsequent "visions" of the Yolmo elder Mingma, engaged on the night of his July healing, hinted at his physical decline. After walking through my private wasteland, I returned to the scene of healing, where Mingma lay close to the fire.

> I see the patient composed of fibers, yet these fibers are not integrated, making him weak and tired. A result of a long life. Through healing the fibers will be integrated, sown, woven together. I wonder how the shamanic altar will be used. The answer: to "turn over" energy, moving from weakness to strength.
> I sense the *gtor ma* altar is a fire, radiating warmth and vitality. The altar sends out blue and red filaments. Combined with the drumming music, the strings of energy go to the patient, wrapping gently around him, integrating his "fibers," giving him strength and vitality. Yet I am also aware he is slowly getting old, losing his strength, dying.

For Yeshi's family, healing proposed a renewal of eyes, skin, and hearth; for Mingma, it required a reintegration of his waning "fibers." Although I imagined Mingma to be strengthened by the healing process, I sensed that his illness related to the aging process and that he was slowly dying. In the meantime, a salubrious energy radiated from the shaman's altar.

The "revelatory" quality of these visions intrigues me. I experienced the three trances relatively early during my fieldwork, at a time when I could articulate little of Yolmo villagers and their ways of healing. And yet a handful of vivid images presaged much of what I later learned in other ways and try to convey in these pages. The mute woman and blind family embody the Yolmo ethos, Mingma's fibrous body portrays the aesthetics of illness and healing, healers see what laymen cannot, the imbalances in Yeshi's hearth reflect culturally patterned tensions between men and women, and the irreparable nature of these imbalances suggests that healing is often more salve than solution. At the time, I understood little of the import of the images. Only after living in Helambu for over a year, attending further healing ceremonies, talking in depth with patients and healers, translating shamanic divinations, and, upon returning to the United States, dusting off my notes from those sleepy nights, did I learn of their cultural relevance. That the "divinations" were later borne out by systematic ethnographic inquiry lends credence to the idea, discussed elsewhere, that oracular divinations enable Yolmo healers to tap into tacit realms of knowledge. The imaginary gardens of shaman and anthropologist, envisioned quite differently, may harvest comparably real toads.

And so if the healer is part anthropologist, perceptive of and attentive to local meanings and tensions, then the anthropologist can become part shaman, delving behind the "local rationality" to divine the causes and nature of human suffering. Some readers might find this statement a bit disingenuous, considering my critique of earlier accounts of ethnographic trances. Yet while my "divinations" were of a soundly subjective nature, arising out of the constraints of my own experience, they apparently did realize some sort of tacit knowledge. And I take this knowledge to have dealt less with some hidden world on the other side of silence than with my own mundane involvement with the everyday lives and concerns of Meme's clients. I do not find much that is mystical in the process: while the revelations took a vivid form in my case, I believe they probably occur in most successful ethnographic endeavors. Ethnography is divinatory by nature. Pierre Bourdieu and Renato Rosaldo contend that the anthropologist is a "positioned subject" in the social structure, holding a point of view that both fosters and inhibits particular kinds of insight.[36] But I want to stress that the ethnographer's vision is both structured and hindered by local systems of knowledge. The field researcher connects with the same communicative pathways that her informants use; her blindspots and insights form part of the cultural cybernetic, her subjective position influences the interpretation of local sensibilities, and she is affected by similar cultural paradoxes and pathologies of knowledge. The anthropologist becomes part of the system being studied, and most tools of inquiry must conform to the features of this system. Yet in the long run, these constraints—or, better, an understanding of them—can occasionally facilitate, rather than impede, ethnographic insight. While we can never get beyond the muck of our daily interactions, a sensitivity to the pitch and tenor of these interactions can tell us much.

In Helambu, the system is one of shut doors and closed mouths, and these constraints shaped the nature of my research. As I neither worked with a field assistant nor knew the languages well my first months in Helambu, I spent much of my time participating on a low-key level in everyday life. Sharing small talk and salt-butter tea with the likes of Meme and Mingma, I sat in local tea shops, attended healings and funerals, and developed a tacit sense of the mundane features of Yolmo lives. In casual, porchside chats with Nyima, a middle-aged woman with long, coal-black hair bound beneath a brilliantly colored scarf, I learned how to avoid leeches and the ways to dance at a funeral. But when I asked Nyima direct questions, such as how many life-forces she possessed or how she felt when she lost them, she claimed not to know. If I persisted, she would light up a cigarette with shaky hands and speak in an increasingly high-pitched tremor.

"Why ask me? I haven't learned this. Go ask a shaman or lama," she chided.

I heard these words many times in Helambu. Many of the secular population (particularly women) prefer not to advance their opinions on cultural beliefs, based on the notion that there is a right answer to which they are not privy.[37] Nor do most villagers wish to divulge information, for they have a strong regard for privacy; it is considered rude to inquire about personal matters and unworthy to reveal one's "heartmind" to others. There is also the fear that if others know too much, they may take advantage of this knowledge (through witchcraft, business affairs, etc.). I therefore found many of the usual inroads to anthropological understanding (life histories, clinical data, residence patterns, personal narratives) to be hindered by local constraints on social communication. I was restricted, much like Yolmo wa, to glimpses through my neighbors' "windows" to interpret the shadowplay within.

How can an anthropologist transcend the limits to social knowledge and so gain insight into the "unknowable"? In my study of Yolmo souls, I have relied on an archaeology of meaning, making sense of Yolmo experiences through its artifacts, sifting through the images and sensations permitted to me, the dreams and ghosts that haunt local memories.[38] Despite recent endeavors to study the "lived experience" of cultural selves,[39] I found I could only poke into the wispy traces of meaning left, like footprints in the sand, in the wake of my neighbors' actions. Yet perhaps we can best approach the subjective realities of others by attending to the imaginative forms that course through, and ultimately define, those realities.

If this archaeology offers any insights, they have been uncovered through both "rational" and "intuitive" means. Observations on Nyima's anxiety the day after her uncle died, followed by the debilitating loss of her "spirit," led me to question the link between illness and emotional distress; shamanic reflections on a mute woman hinted at the nature of this link. As the "divinatory" images suggest, much of my understanding of local dynamics was obtained through—and crystallized by way of—avenues outside of conscious, conceptual thought. An observation by Bateson on the epistemology of the self has helped me to frame the nature of this process. "The total self-corrective unit," Bateson wrote in 1971, "which processes information, or, as I say, 'thinks' and 'acts' and 'decides,' is a *system* whose boundaries do not at all coincide with the boundaries either of the body or of what is popularly called the 'self' or 'consciousness.' "[40] In other words, I find that the anthropologist's "self-system" can know more than his conscious self, and his imaginary gardens, like the shaman's revelations (waking dreams, nightly visions), can tap into and cultivate tacit knowledge. Like Meme and his patients, I turned to divination to find out why souls are lost, where they wander, and how best to recall them. By delving into the local system of knowledge, working within its constraints, I learned to learn (and rely on) the constraints and loopholes of that system.

*   *   *

The reader may well imagine that the shamanic visions, whatever their source, are at best a suggestive example of what and how I came to know of Yolmo lives. I would not feign to portray Yeshi and Mingma by drawing on the visions alone, nor would I attribute much significance to them if they did not correlate with other forms of knowledge. Yet I believe they reflect the learning processes involved when a person participates in a series of rituals, frequents a tea shop, listens to a story, and so begins to embody cultural practices. In my experience, much of this learning occurs tacitly, at the level of the body; the trance images, as I read them, crystallized embodied forms of knowledge. Meaning, patterned within the body, took form through images, which were then absorbed anew by the body. This was an ongoing process throughout my stay, for when a fieldworker begins to participate in the myriad of moments that make up the practice of everyday life, these interactions soon shape his or her understanding of local values, patterns of action, ways of being, moving, and feeling. Whenever I exchanged sips of tea, caught the gist of a joke, heard the guttural sounds of a lama's chant, or felt the loss of a villager, I was participating in my share of life in Helambu, and my body assimilated such experiences within its fund of meanings. It is out of that fund of knowledge that my understanding of Yolmo lives begins, and the trance imagery probably emerged. As I see it, the trances gave imaginal form to my body's conversation with the other bodies stepping about Helambu.

Perhaps a tangible image will help to clarify what I mean by embodied knowledge. In Nepal, I found that "knowing through the body" often centers on knowledge of the body, for how I came to hold my limbs in Helambu led to a tacit assessment of how villagers themselves experience somatic and social forms. Yolmo men, when smoking a cigarette in a half-plowed field or exchanging words along a sodden trail, customarily crouch close to the soil, feet flat on the ground, knees bent, head low, buttocks touching heels, hands close to the chest, with fingers cupping a cigarette. At times, when I moved to join a conversation or warm my hands by a fire, my limbs reflexively approximated the coiled position, though the soles of my feet never touched the earth and my knees elbowed out in awkward angles. Despite these handicaps, the position offered an orientation toward the sensory grounds of my experience distinct from what I was familiar with. My body soon took on the air of a dynamic whole, compact in space and energy, centered at the chest, and head close to heart. The mandala-like parts of my body, distinct in themselves, worked toward this center, with the embodied awareness achieved more earthly than astral.

Through time, experiencing the body in this manner (including the residual, intermingling effect it had on how I stepped through a village, climbed a hill, or approached others) influenced my understanding of Yolmo experiences; it hinted at new styles of behavior, ways of being and moving through space that I did not previously have access to. By using the body in different ways, I stumbled on (but never fully assimilated) practices distinct from my own. Touching head to heart merged thinking and feeling (two acts unsegregated in Yolmo society); a sense of the body as a vessel dynamically compact led me to see Yolmo forms as vital plenums of organ and icon; and my loose assemblage of bent knees and jointed bones contributed to the springboard technology that gradually brought some force and ease to my shamanic "shaking." In turn, as the workings of the body often reflect the physiology of a society,[41] the latter view soon led to the realization that a Yolmo household or village seems put together much like a farmer is: as a collection of distinct and jointed parts loosely bound into a unified whole. Wielding the body in a particular manner in daily activities thus led to a visceral appreciation of how villagers themselves seem to engage in those activities.[42]

The appreciation could have gone further. As a Yolmo shaman acquires his *bidyā* or "learning" without the use of books, villagers were perplexed by my preference to record Meme's teachings in cassettes and notebooks, rather than to set them directly within my "heartmind." I

Photo 4. Feet flat, knees bent, head low.

explained that, since we in the West had forgotten how to memorize, I would lose the specifics of what I learned unless I jotted them down on paper. This did not get me very far. "How can you play the drum if you have to refer to a book?" a group of young men scoffed one evening outside my cabin. When I joked that I planned to tack the chants onto the drum's surface like a musical score, they laughed, but walked away unsatisfied. I would never be a "true shaman," one novice healer said, shaking his head, unless I knew everything "by heart." For quite some time I took this man's response at face value: one must memorize the shaman's songs in order to perform effectively. Yet now, months away from Helambu, I hear, with some regret, a subtler message: it is the music as much as the surface meaning of the shaman's repertoire that one must engage within the flesh. By incorporating a mantra's magic within his heart, throat, and limbs, a melody echoing others through its sinewy folds and assonant rhymes, an apprentice healer begins to incarnate a sensibility that goes beyond the linguistic. The play of the drum quickens into a kinesthesia of curing, a mumbled mantra summons the presence of the sacred, rhythms of healing grow more tactile than cerebral: if I had better realized this chemistry while in the field, I might have gone about my apprenticeship differently, danced to another tune, and so expanded my field of awareness. I footnote my oversight here because, for me, it reflects a tendency in contemporary anthropology to privilege the linguistic, the discursive, and the cognized over the visceral and the tacit.[43] Largely neglected has been the realm of the senses, the sufferings of the flesh. We have lost an understanding of the body as an experiencing, soulful being, before and beyond its capacity to house icon and metaphor. A less cognate, more sensate treatment now seems needed.[44]

Whatever its limits, the sensibility cultivated by my physiology in Nepal remained for the most part unarticulated while I was banging on a shaman's drum. Only after I returned my body to a desk, began to use its anatomy in yet another way, and set fingers to keyboard did I begin to flesh out its links to the more tangible bits of data that filled my notebooks. Indeed, I find that a significant amount of what I learned in Helambu occurred through visceral, sensory means; this knowledge has deeply influenced later assessments of Yolmo lives, including the writing of this account. When I reviewed my field notes on returning to the United States, I was surprised to find they did not embody the more intangible dimensions of what I had learned—the tacit "habitus" of Yolmo actions—so much as my body had noted them, viscerally, as a sponge soaks up displaced water.

*   *   *

The book is an attempt to squeeze that sponge for the inner moisture. I find myself writing from a position neither within Yolmo sensibilities nor singularly detached from them, but with one foot outside and the other entangled within their webs. This interactive stance, with neither foot on solid ground, forms the essence of the present inquiry. My understanding of the leitmotivs of this work—homeless souls, sentient bodies, the specters of loss—has been shaped by Yolmo aesthetics and epistemology, as has been my grasp of these systems of value and knowledge. Windowed houses, restricted purviews, and shamanic revelations mark the limits of what I can know, and write, of Nyima, Yeshi, and Mingma.

The question remains, then, through what means can an ethnographer write about (express, communicate, re-present) tacit knowledge? How can we translate the complexities of everyday life into the fixity of a few words? For me, the sense that much of my understanding of life in Helambu lingers on "the hither side of words"[45] influences how I write of Yolmo souls, and I attempt to work with and through a poetics of culture to better illuminate the gist of these unshapen understandings. For his *Mythologiques*, Lévi-Strauss developed a mythopoeic stance, expressed through the metaphor of musical leitmotivs, to write "the myth of mythology."[46] Here, I seek to develop an "argument of images,"[47] constructed of ghosts, souls, and dreams, to approach the play between image, feeling, and experience. Since some ethnographic understandings came to me by way of images, I try to communicate this knowledge through images.[48] Local metaphors, idioms, and poetics grace the narrative in order to give a feel for the cultural reality in question. My intent is to convey something of the give-and-take of Yolmo life such that the reader, when actively reading or "rewriting" this account,[49] will more vividly sense the heaviness of a spiritless body or the dark presence of a hungry ghost. "I hold," T. S. Eliot wrote, "that the world is something more than the noise it makes; it is also the way it looks on a page."[50] If this is so, then I suppose the task is to pack the noise of the world into the words of a page so that a reader can hear it anew.

An imaginative inquiry seems especially suited for Yolmo realities, for local experiences seem to be grasped and expressed through images. Illiterate villagers like Meme and Nyima tend not to tell full-fledged stories much, nor, I believe, do they see life through the same narrative lens that my American colleagues do.[51] For instance, while dreams in the West work by way of storied narratives ("I was walking down a road . . ."), Yolmo reveries involve a handful of simple snapshots (a ghostly graveyard, a burning house). Perhaps related to what Anthony Marsella deems an "imagistic mode" of representing reality common to several non-Western societies,[52] what a resident of Helambu remembers and tells another of a dream are usually a few, select images known to bear prophetic meaning. Similarly, in conveying suffering to others, villagers tend not to tell sequential accounts of how they hurt or heal, but rather to "tell images" that portray their plights: a witch's bloody assault, the "casting" of grief from the body. The prose of this book attempts to retain a bit of this image-based reality.

The main risk involved in such a narrative experiment is that it can stumble into what Geertz calls "ethnographic ventriloquism": "the claim to speak not just *about* another form of life but speak from within it"[53]— blindly "doing" the natives in different voices. The potential gain is to more richly describe the experiential fabric of another way of life, conveying through the magic of indirect speech ("show, don't tell") dimensions of cultural experience often neglected in ethnographic writing. Much of culture-as-practice occurs in the varied events, dialogues, and habitual exchanges of daily life; the building blocks of vivid prose necessarily rest on these events. This is the nonlinear complexity that scholarly writing, by its analytic nature, has such a hard time pulling together, but that storytelling, with its technology of open synthesis, can orchestrate so well.[54]

What we need is a reading that hovers close to the body. My grasp of the shamanic fell short of incarnating the music of the body; it would be a comparable mistake to content ourselves with a symbolic analysis of Yolmo experience. By "symbolic analysis" I have in mind an approach that would treat Meme's body like a suitcase of texts and symbols that he—the true actor—lugged around wherever he went. In contrast, I wish to propose, in following the German phenomenologist Helmuth Plessner, that Meme not only "has" a body, but "is" a body.[55] And since the body that Meme "is" feels, knows, tastes, acts, and remembers, I find it necessary, if I wish to understand how this physiology heals or falls ill, to consider Yolmo experiences from the plane of the body: to consider a villager's "ego" or consciousness not as somehow distinct from the body, but positioned within a larger sphere of life—that of sensory experience. A concern for "discourse," "symbols," and "practice" is in vogue of late in anthropology. This book wagers, in contrast, that we can best make sense of the pains of Meme's clients by attending to the felt presence of those pains.

All this bids for a new tack toward ethnography, a style that seeks to touch on and work from within the plane of the body, a syntax that reaches for the sensory, the visceral, the unspoken.[56] Yeats tells us that "art bids us touch and taste and hear and see the world, and shrinks from what Blake calls mathematical form, from every abstract thing, from all that is of the brain only, from all that is not a fountain jetting from the entire hopes, memories, and sensations of the body."[57] Is it possible that art of this ilk has value for the social sciences? There is much to experience that eludes the logic of signs, and a key mandate of future ethnographies will be, in my opinion, to evince the felt immediacies that mark songs of grief, rhythms of healing, divine presences. Several recent studies stake out what an anthropology of the senses could entail;[58] my hope is that the present work advances this orientation. The trick in all this is to translate the felt, the immediate, into words. How can we approach this? My guess is that the sting of a wound or the comforts of healing can be engaged through a narrative blend of dialogue, texture, rhythm, and silence.

The work is phenomenologic and interpretive. I aim to give a sense, as far as I understand it, of what it feels like to grieve, to lose one's spirit, to be healed in Helambu. We also need to sketch out the political tensions and social formations that give rise to these bodily experiences. Yet rather than begin with analytic categories foreign to Yolmo realities (the "id," "primary guilt"),[59] the initial focus is on local forms of experience in order to sketch out their influence on moments of illness and healing. A major but often quiet concern is with how certain forms of social life shape the bodily and "mental structures," as Bourdieu puts it, through which that life itself is apprehended.[60] We study Yolmo lives from the ground up, delving first into the "basic orientations" of cultural experience,[61] including notions of body and soul, the embodied "aesthetics" of everyday life, Yolmo epistemology (how one goes about knowing of self and other), and the local ethos (the dominant cultural styles of experiencing and expressing felt experience). The central chapter to this book, entitled "Soul Loss," integrates these themes to account for the nature and prevalence of this illness among the residents of southwestern Helambu. In the final chapters, we move from illness to healing to explore Meme's craft, unraveling the ritual process to examine the aesthetic, sensory, epistemic, and psychosocial dimensions of Yolmo shamanism. The work thus implies a narrative progression, taking the reader through the "story" of illness and healing. My hope is that the various strands of this tale, diverse on the page, will come together in the body of the reader.

As with all ethnographies, the present story is thus, at best, a translation of—or conversation with—native voices. More "map" than "territory,"[62] it engages a geography that represents the hilly terrain of Yolmo experience. There are, of course, many ways to make a map: scholars concerned with the translation of cultures have typically focused on the problems involved in assessing different beliefs, concepts, "rationalities," and "social logics."[63] Yet as the concerns of this book have more to do with the somatic sensibilities of certain Yolmo wa, a study of those sensibilities might require a different method, a method that seeks to convey something of the felt quality and "imaginative force" of Yolmo lives. W. S. Merwin uses the latter phrase in suggesting that the translation of a poem inevitably fails if one merely looks for direct word-for-word correspondences in a second language.

> A single primary denotation may be shared; but the constellation of second-ary meanings, the moving rings of associations, the etymological echoes, the sound and its own levels of association, do not have an equivalent because they cannot. If we put two words of a language together and repeat the attempt, the failure is still more obvious. Yet if we continue, we reach a point where some sequence of the first language conveys a dynamic unit, a rudiment of form. Some energy of the first language begins to be manifest, not only in single words but in the charge of their relationship. The surprising thing is that at this point the hope of translation does not fade altogether, but begins to emerge. Not that these rudiments of form in the original language can be matched—any more than individual words could be—with exact equivalents in another. But the imaginative force they embody, and which single words embody in context, may suggest convocations of words in another language that will have a comparable thrust and sense.[64]

My handling of ethnography calls for a comparable craft. Rather than graph a concept-for-concept translation onto the original context ("depression" for "soul loss," "the unconscious" for "divine knowledge"), we must work within the cultural reality in question, sketching out the rudiments of form that compose it. By the latter term, I loosely mean the basic, socially derived images, schemas, and structures that help to animate cultural experience. In the translation of poetry, rudiments of form concern linguistic structures, metaphoric valences, similes of sound; with an interpretation of cultures, they involve patterns of relationships, aesthetic sensibilities, rhythms of experience. Rudiments of form inform for a people how pain is felt, space imagined, evil exorcised, and death achieved. Body and house as permeable membranes, body and village as mosaic, and a cadence of loss and fragmentation are a few of the cultural forms we shall encounter here. Cognitive scientists hold that these forms register within the brain, but I would like to imagine that they also course through the body and the play of children. Wherever their locus, the ethnographer must search for a language that illuminates their combined thrust and sense as they relate in the original context. An ethnographer's convocations of words, if woven together like the chords of a sonata, can offer an experientially rich sense of what it may be like to grow old in a distant village. This is the working hypothesis to be tested here: by grasping the charge of the relation between different cultural forms, between ways of feeling, hungry ghosts, and the subtle play of images, we can better realize the imaginative force, if not the specific territory and content, of Yolmo experience.

But I hasten to note that translation of this sort remains forever uncertain. Like the "shamanic" visions, my rough map of Yolmo experience is hedged in by the limits of my purview, and so lies at best in a no-man's-land, betwixt and between cultures. As this cannot be otherwise, I agree with Jackson and Stoller that anthropologists must cultivate, with pen as with thought, a certain "negative capability."[65] The term comes from Keats, who claimed that Shakespeare, in contrast to Coleridge, possessed the capacity of "being in uncertainties, mysteries, doubts, without any irritable reaching after fact or reason."[66] With ethnography, such a philosophy applies to the recipient as well as the author of uncertainties. Every social situation brings with it (perhaps necessarily so) an air of flux and ambiguity, and it is the responsibility of ethnographers to carry this ambiguity over into the world of the reader such that he or she begins to embody (like the fieldworker) some of the forms and sensibilities common to a village. Indeed, students of narrative tell us it is the artfully undetermined story, latent with possibility and meaning, that is the most memorable.[67] Perhaps it is with images, intractable, irreducible, palpable, that such engagement begins.

And so a way of knowing melds with a way of writing. A reader's orientation toward an ethnography compares to the interactive stance of its author (both struggle to make sense of cultural complexities); the following pages try to bring the reader's body into the ethnographic endeavor through the presence of closed doors, dark descents, and waning moons. Ethnographers often chorus that good writing makes for a better "read," but they have typically overlooked the fact that how one writes about an alien way of life can contribute to a reader's implicit understandings of that life. Sounding a score of words engages a way of being in the world. Again, it is the body, not simply the intellect, that I am most writing for and from. "If I read a book," Emily Dickinson wrote, "and it makes my whole body so cold no fire can ever warm me, I know that it is poetry. If I feel physically as if the top of my head were taken off, I know that is poetry."[68] An ethnography might not produce the seismic tremors that a poem can, but its consequences can activate nerve endings and touch the body in comparable ways. My body began to feel differently while it was walking around Helambu. Will the reader's after stepping through this book?

In the end, we return to the question of empathy. To what extent can a person participate in another's feelings or ideas? How can we best render this knowledge to others? Clifford Geertz claims that we can understand another way of life not through a process of empathy but "by seeking out and analyzing the symbolic forms—words, images, institutions, behaviors—in terms of which, in each place, people actually represent themselves to themselves and to one another."[69] Yet my sense is that empathy, which is at work, arises from a visceral engagement with symbolic form. If this is so, how can a storyteller's words assist in the act of "vicarious introspection" (as Kohut defines the process)?[70] Whatever the answers (and novelists certainly have their own), the ethnographic entails special constraints. Empathy rides on the faith that the grounds of experience between two people are similar, such that we can "know" what another is feeling based on what we ourselves would feel in that situation. But when the grounds between reader and "character" are significantly at odds, it is necessary to first spell out their contours. Unless we can achieve a basic understanding of how another person makes sense of the most elemental aspects of their being—how he or she experiences body, pain, or gender—any efforts toward empathy with that person will run aground, particularly when this involves cultural lands as distant as Helambu and the United States. To learn something of the lives of Meme, Nyima, and Yeshi, then, we must first consider how they construe the everyday, how their bodies make sense of their surroundings, and how they view their passage through the karmic cycle of life, death, and rebirth. Here, phenomenology reads as a narrative strategy.

2. Body, Speech, Mind

One drizzly September morning, Meme and I walked a mile west of Gulphubanyang to a small hamlet populated by low-status Tamang and Yolmo families to pick up a shamanic drum I had ordered from Rinchen, a local craftsman. I found the descent along the mountain path to be a slow one, with Meme's bare feet stopping before each twig to brush it off the damp trail. Upon arriving within the cluster of homesteads that made up the hamlet, Meme and I sat on straw mats outside Rinchen's house as he and his sons plowed a plot of land on a hillock above. When the sons finished their work, they returned to their homes and Rinchen invited us inside his. We entered a cluttered, dimly lit room where chickens stepped through a dirt floor in search of stray corn kernals and a young woman sat mending the loose strands of a straw winnowing tray. Rinchen told Pasang, the wife of his second son, to reheat some cornmeal and lentils and prepare bowls of corn beer.

With the smell of damp hay wafting through the air, we sat on mats before the hearth as Pasang rekindled the fire, heated the food, and served it to us on aluminum plates. We ate, then discussed the price of the drum. After selling us his ware, Rinchen, a shaman himself but years younger than Meme, asked his senior to "see" the pulse of his daughter-in-law. Pasang, no more than eighteen and perhaps a newlywed to the house, had not been feeling well for some time. She came out from the shadows of the hearth with unkempt hair and a faded red sweater. Meme hunched over to feel her pulse, and her father-in-law gestured with his hands to narrate a geography of discomfort on his own form—a piercing "pain" (*tsher ka*) in the shoulders, blood racing from the heart, dreams of darkness. Pasang sat passively on the floor as Meme divined that a particular type of ghost (*shi 'dre*, "shindi") was afflicting her. Soon the two healers nodded their heads in agreement, and Pasang, apparently unmoved by their diagnosis, sat back down, smoothed out her apron, and returned to the torn winnowing tray.

We begin with this image of Meme hunched over Pasang, fingers touching wrist, because it presents some of the basic concerns of our study:

the realities of Yolmo women, the embodiment of pain, and a shaman's ability to divine (and potentially remedy) the sources of this pain. The image also conveys something of the presence of bodies in Helambu and the role that tacit, embodied knowledge plays in this land. Indeed, if we are to grasp what ghostly pains mean to Pasang, why Nyima and Yeshi lose their spirits, or how Meme heals, we must first consider how Yolmo construe and experience their bodies in everyday life. What meanings and sensibilities do local anatomies embody? How do these sensibilities reflect pressing social and political concerns? What, in sum, are some of the key forms and tensions marking Yolmo experience, social history, and moments of illness?

To begin to answer these questions, we need to concern ourselves with the imaginative structures that animate the language, actions, and dispositions of Yolmo villagers—the rudiments of form that pattern how space is imagined, bodies experienced, and conversations transacted. These forms are not the binary oppositions of Lévi-Straussian structuralism, which emmanate from the neurolinguistic contours of the human brain and so transcend cultures.[1] Rather, they relate to the basic filaments of a given cultural tradition, derive from the way in which social interactions occur, and give form to the most visceral of bodily experiences. In many ways, they constitute the grammars of cultural experience.[2]

My attention to Yolmo "grammars" of experience might surprise some readers. Where are the traces of pain, the heavy bodies, the scents of healing, promised above? Not so fast: we need some context first. So-called experience-near ethnographies, which quickly jump into the muddy terrain of lived experience and paint the tastes and odors of a Third World bus stop, for example, are now in demand in the United States.[3] The reader gets the sense that she is sitting inside the bus stop, drinking coffee alongside the anthropologist, and feeling what the bus driver feels. But my guess is that many of these studies simply reiterate what any tourist might get wind of. They often do not explain, in any significant way, how cultural categories shape the form, tenor, or meaning of bodily experience and so contribute to potentially vast cultural differences in the smells and senses of a cup of coffee shared between friends. There is also the idea that, while sensory experiences may have different meanings for diverse cultural actors, the experiences themselves are somehow precultural, exquisitely natural, an Esperanto of lived experience.[4] As I suggest above, we need to question that assumption. Rather than merely calling out the sights and sounds of Yolmo lives, then, I want to sketch out how the social formations that prevail in Helambu mold the very essence of sensory experience. Once we learn something of the grammars of Yolmo experience, we can enter into a much richer conversation between cultural traditions (with our bodies serving as vehicles of reflection). In so doing, it will become clear how my concerns differ from ethnopsychological studies of self and personhood,[5] for the term "ethnopsychology" implies that distinct psychological dynamics can be dissected away from a cultural system and so be considered apart from larger social and political concerns.

Mark Johnson comes close to my considerations of the rudiments of form in his recent book *The Body in the Mind*.[6] Johnson, a cognitive scientist, attempts a "geography of human experience" that "seeks to identify the chief contours (structures) and connections that our experience and understanding exhibit."[7] Through this geography, Johnson tries to understand the basic, nonpropositional dimensions of human imagination and finds that certain "embodied schemata" help to structure human experience. These schemata, which range from the sense of bodily force to the "experiential gestalt" of containment, stem from how we make sense of felt experience. The senses of bodily force, gravity, and kinesthetic balance that we carry with us, for instance, influence which metaphors we find salient and define our understandings of logic, rationality, and narrative closure. Above all, Johnson's point is that many of our basic orientations toward the world derive from tacit bodily orientations (the visceral *sense* of force) rather than from the seemingly objective, propositional categories of human reasoning (rational *ideas* of force and logic).

Like Johnson, I feel the need to get at the rudimentary forms and schemas that animate cultural experience. Yet while we must certainly consider bodily experience in itself, we must also take into account experiences between bodies and between diverse cultural forms (anatomies, buildings, social gatherings). For Johnson, "embodied schemata" arise from physical experience and so apparently transcend diverse cultural traditions. In a discussion of the "logic" of one American law clerk's view of possible motives for an imagined but unrealized rape, for instance, Johnson proposes that "certain aspects of the meaning of 'sexuality' are culturally, and perhaps humanly, shared dimensions of our experience *at the preconceptual level*."[8] One such aspect is, for Johnson, the notion that "physical appearance [attraction] is a physical force." Yet if "realities" of this sort are humanly shared, how are we to account for the vast differences between Yolmo and American bodily orientations and symbolic forms? As it stands, Johnson's study lacks an appreciation of the busy interchange between bodily experience and cultural forms. Pasang's physiology might influence the language she uses and the images she dreams with, but could the language and images she relies on also influence her physiology? I believe so. The ways in which a given people build houses, conduct rituals, and tell stories influence the ways in which they experience their bodies. For this reason, we need to situate Yolmo experiences of body and soul within the larger context of social formations and political history. This formal prelude will then enable us to appreciate the aesthetic sensibilities that provide the moral template for so much of Yolmo life and help to make sense of the pungent sights, sounds, and smells of Meme's healings.

Spaces of the Body

We begin with the body (*lus*, "li") because, for Yolmo wa, it is the primary means of giving form and meaning to experience. In Helambu, the body both embraces and engenders significance. It is a dynamic whole, a corpus of space and meaning. The body is a corpus of space, for it possesses finite spatial dimensions and maps experience—knowledge, morality, feeling— into spatial form. And it is one of meaning, for Yolmo bodies are replete with significance; icons and images course through Yolmo forms as much as cells and organs constitute Western physiologies.

Much of this imagery reflects religious motifs that lend the body an aura of patterned sanctity. Pasang's fingers, for instance, are said to index the gods of the five directions: east, south, west, north, center. The syllables of the Buddhist prayer *om mani padme hum* register metonymically within her forehead, shoulders, navel, genitals, and feet, while the Buddhist invocation of deities *om a hum* (body, speech, mind) sounds through her *rtser tshugs* ("tsertshug"), voice box, and stomach. The incorporeal *rtser tshugs*, an entryway into the body just above the fontanel, houses protective gods. Deities also defend the other eight "gates" to the body: the eyes, nostrils, ears, mouth, and anus. When a person dies, the "soul" (*rnam shes*, "nam-she") departs from one of these orifices; the higher the opening on the body, the better a person's rebirth will be in his or her next reincarnation.[9]

Of the many loci of the body, several include forms of knowledge difficult to fathom. Meme taught that a body's veins or "rivers" (n. *nadi*) beat smooth and rhythmical when healthy, but when the body is sick, a ghost causes the pulse to "come out," strike erratically, sometimes fast, sometimes slow. "The mirror of life," engraved with a person's fate, shines in the forehead. The appendix stands for one's "life span" (*tshe*)—straight and white, when healthy; crooked and red, when diseased. A palm's lines prophesy the number of years and children one will have; these lines change each day. Wrinkles around the eyes bear specific divinatory knowledge: one kind of crease foretells of material wealth, another suggests familial strife.

Notice that the body pinpoints each image in a specific locale: deities and knowledge inhabit an anatomy much as villages lie at specific sites along a pilgrim's route. This iconographic mapping is founded on a more pervasive spatialization of the body, for Yolmo wa imbue their forms with highly significant spatial dimensions and representations. The form of these representations derives, I believe, from a particular metaphysics of space.

In reading Tibetan tantric texts, variants of which Yolmo lamas recite, one often encounters a particular treatment of space. Within the context of meditative ritual, religious mendicants imaginatively fill space with a host of spiritual beings. Here, the tantrist imagines that "all around and in the spaces between, like a gathering of clouds, there are dakas, dakinis, protectors and guardians of the Law." There, he conjures a scene of "mothers, filling all of space." Elsewhere, he visualizes that "the empty space between the two pavilions is filled with full-blown blue lotus flowers."[10] In reading these incantations, we are left with the impression that all of space becomes, or can become, filled with images—to the extent that interstices cease to exist.

I believe the capacity for space to become filled with meaning suggests a metaphysics significantly at odds from that currently dominant in the West. Western philosophers posit that "space must be filled to be visible; empty space is an abstraction."[11] Yolmo space seems less abstraction than a tangible entity in itself. It appears more as plenum than as vacuum, full rather than empty, less intangible absence than a thick, image-rich ether. As within the plane of a Lamaist *thang ka* portrait of Buddhist deities, each point in space seems graced with color, meaning, and geometric significance.

Evidence suggests that the repletion of space is a valued and aesthetically pleasing quality for Yolmo wa. A successful festival is one in which "many people come"; the walls and cupboards of a prosperous house are lined with photos, kitchen utensils, and bottles filled with colored waters; and a guest, on leaving a home, should not empty a teacup served to him for this would suggest that his hosts are either stingy or unprosperous. The interior of a Yolmo Lamaist "temple" (*dgon pa*, "gonpa") presents a similar appraisal of space. On entering this sacred domain, one confronts a sen-

Photo 5. A Lamaist *thang ka:* Mahakala with five *khyung*.

sorium of images. The entryway hosts fierce guardian deities who protect the temple from malevolent intrusions; pillars and beams are carved and painted with deep blues, reds, and golds; the walls and ceilings show paintings of the Buddha in his many manifestations. Padmasambhava, one of these incarnations, sits in gold cast above the decorous altar; red, green, and white banners, suspended from the ceiling, hover in mid-space; the pungent scent of butter candles and salt-butter tea wafts through the air. Villagers add to this rich iconography whenever a ritual or funeral occurs, for legs, sandals, and coats blanket the surfaces of the floor. The seating arrangement is not without its hierarchy: lamas, ranked by age, seat themselves adjacent to the altar, other men sit "below," and women and children crowd around the door and windows.[12] At times, I found the crush of bodies to offer a sense of *communitas*: arms intertwine with arms, heads lean against shoulders, a low chant reverberates through the single-chamber room.

Yolmo bodies, like the temples of lamas, are dense with meaning. Understood to be finite vessels bearing dimensions of depth, width, and length, they imply value schemes predicated on motifs of interior and exterior, left and right, high and low. This is partly evident in the multitude of "geographic" representations the body assumes. Yolmo bodies represent a microcosm of the universe, the five directions, and the pantheon of gods charted by these cardinal points. Celestial measures of high and low, as with other aspects of Yolmo culture, find their way into the body. This bodily topography compares to that expressed in a Tibetan folk song, which equates bodily parts with cultural objects:

> The feet are two pouches of flesh,
> the knees are the wheel of the law,
> the testicles are two bags joined at the top,
> the waist is the *dorje* [ceremonial bell],
> this miserable belly is a red sack,
> the chest is like the upper rafters of the house,
> the hands are like the wings of [birds],
> the face is a [door] with nine holes[13]

From the crest of the head to the soles of the feet, Yolmo bodies imply a value scheme with purity waning and pollution waxing the further one descends human anatomy. It is a major insult to pass one's (soiled) feet over another's frame, a risky joke to steal a schoolboy's hallowed cap. To defer to

Photo 6. Karma's drawing of a shamanic healing.

an honored friend or elder, the head should bow to his feet. While the right hand is pure, the left pollutes. Similarly, the moral topographies of body and cosmos compare to one another. Most villagers know of a tripartite division of the universe, with a heaven (*lha yul*, "land of gods"), a land of humans (*mi yul*), and a hell (*dmyal ba*). The body maps morality, for heaven and hell span the body high and low, with "bad talk" emmanating metonymically from the lower torso. Following this moral slide from face to foot, nosology mimics cosmology. Celestial gods (*jo, jomo*) harm the eyes, telluric ghosts (*shi 'dre*) spawn stomach aches, and subterranean serpent-deities (*klu*) afflict the skin of (mostly) the legs and feet.

A dense imagery, a hierarchical structure, a repletion of space—these are some of the common qualities of Yolmo forms, be they of a temple, a shaman's drum, or a human body. Another quality equating many Yolmo forms is the play between interior and exterior, ingress and egress, inclusion and exclusion. This play derives from the houselike architecture of many Yolmo forms. To wit, the structure of the body mirrors that of a house, with the physiology of one forming and informing the other. Pierre Bourdieu suggests that the "inhabited space" of an Algerian house provides the symbolic vehicle par excellence for the body's "em-bodying of the structures of the world": the archetypal spatial divisions generated in the house (outer/inner, male/female, social/private) pattern the mappings of the body (right/left, male/female, moral highs and lows).[14] For Yolmo wa, a person similarly reads the "book" of structured space with the body. Clarke writes of Yolmo houses, "There is a very clear and precise symbolic division along the long axis of the house through the hearth: domestic activities are to the inner side, religious activities are to the window side. . . . This division corresponds to that between male and female."[15] As Yolmo houses engender binary domains of sacred/profane, outer/inner, high/low, male/female, so does the body. Motifs of inner/outer, closures/openings, right/left, and purity/pollution course through Yolmo bodies male and female.

It is not surprising, then, that villagers liken the human body to a house with personal life-forces dwelling within. I once asked Nyima's husband Latu, a wealthy, witty, handsomely dressed folk philosopher of forty years, why dreams of burning houses presage illness. Analogies consumed this village lama like Flaubert's flies, but his lively tongue always taught me something.

"Because our body is like a house," he replied, tapping fingers to his chest, "with our breath [dbugs], our soul [rnam shes], living inside this house. Just as a family will move from one house to another, so our soul leaves our body when we die, and moves, life after life, from one body to another. And just as a house can wear down and collapse, so can our body."[16]

Less articulate than Latu, other villagers tacitly liken the body to a house, for it bears basic structural affinities with it. Founded on the Buddhist notion of "the residence and its residents" (the corporeal lus and its various vitalities),[17] the body houses the soul of man. Like a house, a body protects and segregates. If we consider how Tibetans construe their dwellings—"as a microcosm, as a secure enclosure, in contrast to the space outside, which is the playground and hiding-place of countless, omnipresent powers continually threatening to ambush him"[18]—we gain a sense of how Yolmo wa similarly blueprint the body: as a bounded shell that protects and separates self from environment, much like a hut's mud-and-stone walls.

A view of the body as structured like a house bears several consequences for the way in which Yolmo wa make sense of the everyday. Motifs of inner and outer, depth and surface, and openings and closures pervade Yolmo understandings of psychology, knowledge, and medicine. Yolmo society itself divides into "inside" and "outside" people: close intimates and suspicious strangers. The body's architecture segregates thought/emotion into "inner" and "outer" talk: while outer talk is "thinking out loud," inner reveries refer to what one privately "thinks inside, in the heartmind [*sems*]." For the most part, society sanctions those who cannot "hold" their thoughts within the heart.[19] Gossip, in turn, harkens to a somatic rift between private and social knowledge: women "cannot keep secrets within" because they themselves claim not to possess a *phodo*, or Adam's apple. Matching this rift between social and private musings is a notion of "inner will" (n. *bhitra icchā*) signifying those sentiments kept to oneself. When expressed to another, a person's affections move from the heartmind out of the body.

Inner depths contribute to Yolmo medical discourses, for illness often results from malevolent intrusions into corporeal interiors—ghosts, gods, and demons invoke pain by entering into the flesh. As one man explained, "Once a ghost [*shi 'dre*] gets inside our body, we are sick. When you're eating delicious food, the ghost gets into your body, and then starts eating that food." The further this illness penetrates the body's "inner flesh," the more difficult it is to heal. As one sickly woman put it, "When illness comes, it affects the body's inner flesh. When inside the flesh, we feel pain. If it reaches the bone, there will be a long sickness, and it cannot be cured." Thus while a Yolmo shaman can cure surface or "outside" (*phyi*, "chhi") illnesses, he has difficulty healing when the inner "engines" (*nang gi engine*) are "broken." For that, the afflicted must enter a hospital. Finally, as the defensive boundaries of children, women, and the aged are weaker than those of the strong, they fall sick more easily.

As the body is a permeable membrane with forces flowing in and out, villagers take great pains to protect their forms from harmful interlopers. The body needs to be protected. Deities guard the nine "gates" of the body to fend off the otherwise facile invasion of malicious spirits. Meme magically "binds" (*mthud ge*, "tumge") his body at the commencement of the healing ceremony to defend against intrusive witches. Children carry protective amulets (*srung ga*) about their necks to cast an impenetrable "wall of fire" around their forms and so ward off ghosts and demons (*shi 'dre* and *sri*). And since ghosts "touch" or influence the body mostly through the middle finger, adults sport rings there "to close the door."

Illness frequently results from the pathologic invasion of spirits, ghosts, and malignant forces into the body; healing works to "throw" demons from the body's depths. If a ghost penetrates into the body to "dwell" within it, villagers try to exorcise it—through bribes, threats, or entreaties. "A *shi 'dre* is driven off," one young healer explained, "like one chases animals from a field." Such oustings of harm explain the belief that if a sick person dreams that she gives birth, vomits, bleeds from the body or doles money out to another, health is imminent, for such images forecast that illness is leaving the body. And in more metaphoric terms, Yolmo healings purport to "cut," "separate," or "untie" spiritual "harms" (*nad pa*, "nepa") from the body.

While it is crucial to defend the body from foreign entrées, Yolmo wa simultaneously strive to prohibit spiritual substances from leaving it. Illness haunts a body if it loses vital life-forces, and death occurs when the "soul" (*rnam shes*) vacates its residence. Dreams, which often bear divinatory knowledge, likewise comment on the motif of vital substances leaving the body: if a villager dreams of a lake with water flowing out, he will fall sick soon; if the lake bears no outlets, money will fall into his hands.[20] Seminal ejaculations, finally, drain the body of energy and stamina, making a man prone to illness.

Yolmo bodies, in essence, are plenums of significance, with felt experience framed on a culturally specific architecture. Yet while the Yolmo body is like a house, the windows remain open and a slight draft stirs throughout. Yolmo souls are not embodied in homes unto themselves; they reside in busy neighborhoods of social and symbolic interactions. This leads to a tension between two complementary patterns of bodily experience: despite the somatic partition between interior and exterior, there is considerable trafficking over the threshold of the two realms—ghosts, sentiments, and life-forces continuously traverse corporeal boundaries. At the same time, there is a strong motivation to block this flow and separate a body's interiors from its outer environment through various magical means.

Autonomy and Interdependence

The tension between Pasang's body as a mediating, relational process on the one hand and as a bounded, private whole on the other can be better understood by contemplating Yolmo social life, particularly as it has recently taken form in the vicinity of Gulphubanyang. In Helambu, village, familial, and bodily politics can be read, to some degree, as the history of tension between two contradictory cultural values: those of independence and interdependence. Yolmo wa, though deeply communal beings, also profess a strong notion of individuality, with this dialectic fostering a conflict between the desire for autonomy and the need for interdependence. This tension is not unique to the residents of Gulphubanyang: variations on the theme have been identified among Gurung of north-western Nepal and Solu-Khumbu Sherpa and Limbu of northeastern Nepal, suggesting it derives from sociocultural dynamics common to Tibeto-Burman peoples of the Himalayan region.[21] In Helambu, the tension can be traced to contradictions inherent in Yolmo social organizations. In recent years, the crystallization of these contradictions has taken a particular turn among Yolmo wa of Gulphubanyang, a turn which might help to explain the nature of felt experience among these people.

Graham Clarke, a British ethnographer who worked in Helambu from 1974 to 1977, and again in Helambu and surrounding areas in 1985–1986 and 1990, found that Yolmo villages there were based on a corporate life organized around two principles: first, kinship, marriage, and extended families; and second, ties between households through the village-temple. A history of competition between various interest groups, of early social fusion between Tibetan and Tamang to form the original Lama villages, and of subsequent lineage fission and expansion over the region, lies behind the current social organization.[22] The development of the earliest Yolmo villages (primarily in the original ridge of central Helambu) related to the founding of temples controlled by different lineages. In time, the fission of lineages led to the creation of other village-temples in different locales. Historical records indicate that, in the eighteenth and nineteenth centuries, the social order of these villages was chiefly based on kinship, with social organization based on the political significance of distinct clans and lineages of agnatic descent.[23] In recent years, however, economic and political changes have provoked a shift from a social order based on kinship to one based on the temple and the village, in which distinct households contribute resources to maintain the economic stability of the temple (itself the political center of a village). With this shift, a household's place in a lineage has gradually become less important than its rank in the status hierarchy of the village.[24]

In 1988, I found that the proliferation of market economies further advanced this shift: Yolmo society presently consists of a set of collectivities, with the members of some groups related through kinship and others through social affiliations. These corporatelike groups, which together form a series of concentric circles, include the household (with immediate family as members); the extended family (with households as members); the village (with households and extended families as members); and Yolmo society itself.[25] Within each of these groups, members relate to one another in terms of exchange, hospitality, mutual support, and relative status within a social hierarchy. Status hierarchies, acts of inclusion and exclusion, and the threat of fission shape the workings of each group.

A Yolmo "household" (*trongba*), for instance, consists of a house-father, a house-mother, and other immediate family members, including affines such as a son's wife.[26] Built into a household is an implicit hierarchy, with members ranked according to gender, relative age, and, in the case of affines, the status of the woman's family within the village hierarchy. The hierarchy of a household manifests itself in the customary seating arrangements of a family: men sit in terms of relative age to the right of the hearth (as one faces the hearth), toward the window, with the house-father below the altar, while women sit to the left, where kitchen utensils are kept (with affines usually closest to the door). The members of a household function together as a corporate group: they coordinate labor and resources in the work of farming, business, and child care. Because a household consists of individuals, however, the potential for fission exists in each household: sons can become house-fathers on their own or break completely from the household in disputes over inheritances.

While a Yolmo household is a relatively bounded group, composed of immediate family members and affines, a "family" (*mes mi*, "memi") is a more loosely defined organization. An extended family often consists of households related by agnatic descent but can also include various affines, uterine descendants, and neighbors. Latu's family, for instance, includes (at least) his father, wife, and adopted daughter; his brothers and their wives and children; his sister and her family; his wife's brother and his children; and several Yolmo neighbors with whom he has close ties. In essence, a family consists (as Clarke observes) of "those who regularly and informally help each other and exchange hospitality."[27] A family can therefore include nonrelated neighbors and at the same time exclude agnates. Two brothers who have a history of conflict, for instance, might refer to themselves as being in different "lines." Each family, in turn, has its own hierarchy based on relative age, gender, and wealth. Since a family is not bound by direct agnatic ties (as a lineage is), households attempt to increase their rank within the village hierarchy by allying themselves with households of higher status.[28] The latter households can then move to either include or exclude the former households within their "family."

The competition between households suggests that a village itself has its own organizational structure, with the households of a village relating to one another in terms of status. As Clarke notes, the hierarchy is evident in the seating arrangements for religious rites held in the temple: a person's position in space denotes his or her relative status in the village hierarchy.[29] A household's rank within the village hierarchy is determined by an array of factors, including clan lineage, wealth, involvement in the temple, and relative age of the household father. While some villages have strict "membership" criteria, with legal membership to the village-temple limited to a certain number of households,[30] others (such as those around Gulphubanyang) are loosely bound, with inclusion in the village based on the purchase of property within the area. Village politics often relate to attempts by households to maintain or increase their status within the village hierarchy through increased wealth and beneficial marriages and exchanges. Consequently, while a Yolmo village consists of a network of households tied to different patrilineal and exogamous clans, the significance of a household's place in a local lineage has become less important than its place in the village hierarchy. Indeed, as Clarke points out, the social mobility on which a village hierarchy is based may lead to conflicts over local interests, the fission of local lineages, and migrations out of villages; this was a major factor in the expansion of Lama villages downhill and outward from these initial high ridge villages throughout the region in the nineteenth century.[31] Kinship groups thus have the potential to fragment into separate households and lineages.

A Yolmo village, then, like a household or family, exists as a corporate group and distinguishes itself, as a group, from other villages. This corporate-based village order can lead to the sense among villagers that they are "all one family."[32] A more inclusive, larger "family" is that of Yolmo society itself; this group is distinguished from neighboring ethnic groups, such as Tamang and Gurung who were from outside the region and who were not included by virtue of a communal linkage to the temple and Lamas. Within Yolmo society itself a hierarchy exists, yet when this society is compared with (or unites in opposition to) other ethnic groups, each household is seen as equal.[33] Similarly, while the members of a household, family, or village relate to one another through notions of hierarchy, an egalitarian ethos applies when each of these groups is compared to another, and, as

Clarke notes, the members of a group are characterized by "unity in opposition to outsiders."[34]

It is evident that, along with notions of hierarchy and equality, acts of inclusion and exclusion define the workings of Yolmo households, families, and villages. Another characteristic of these groups is that fission and fragmentation constantly threaten their integration. The threat derives from the specific configuration of Yolmo society, relates to conflicting values of autonomy and interdependence, and shapes the actions of the likes of Meme and Pasang.

The dilemma, as I understand it, takes the following form. Yolmo society consists of a set of groups, in which members form a polity (for example, a household) that, however, is part of a larger group, such as a family (see Figure 4). A household is a collectivity unto itself, with its own boundaries, hierarchy, and criteria for inclusion. It works as an autonomous, self-serving system, with the financial and political resources of its members contributing to the welfare of the group. Yet a household is also part of a larger group, the "family," which has its own boundaries, hierarchy and criteria for inclusion. Like a household, a family works as an autonomous, self-serving system, with the financial and political resources of its members contributing to the welfare of the group. Indeed, by definition a family is composed of households that regularly and informally help each other and exchange hospitality. Consequently, a household, though autonomous, is also interdependent with the other households that make up a family. A dilemma ensues: while a household strives to maintain wealth, resources, and status within its own boundaries, it is also expected to share wealth, resources, and status with the other households of the family to which it belongs. Always in question is the degree to which a household should keep resources to itself or share them with others. A parallel tension is at play, albeit to a lesser degree, in the composition of villages and Yolmo society as a whole, for families, while autonomous, need to contribute to the welfare and status of the village, and villages to that of the society.

The individuals who make up households and families are similarly caught up in dilemmas of inclusion and exclusion, autonomy and interdependence. To some extent, a son, like a household, is understood to be both autonomous and interdependent (women are bound more by the constraints of dependence). While cultural values motivate the son(s) to increase his own wealth and status, he is also expected to contribute to the welfare of his parents' household (and, consequently, to the larger family).

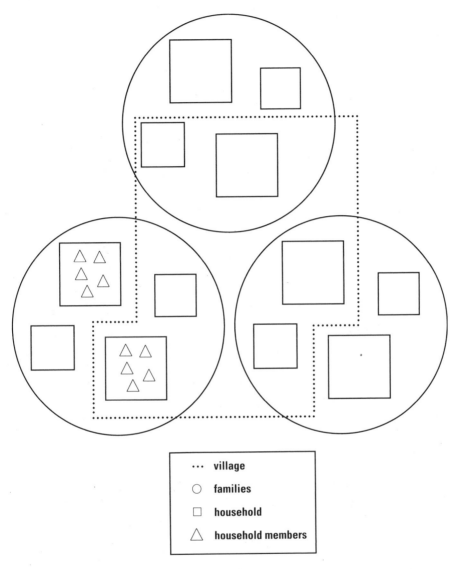

Figure 4. A model of Yolmo society.

Members of a household typically try to relate to one another in a way that benefits individuals as well as households—or, at least, maintains surface harmony. On occasion, however, contrasting values spark tensions and social fission. Any marked asymmetry between brothers within a household (or households within a lineage) can lead to conflict and the splitting of different family "lines." The threat of fragmentation exists at other levels of Yolmo society as well: since Yolmo groups are composed of distinct factions bound into a loosely unified whole, the potential for fragmentation always exists within a household, a family, a lineage, or a village. Indeed, Clarke has found that the evolution of Yolmo society has often pivoted on the fission of Lamaist lineages and the establishment, by lineage offshoots, of new village-temples in different locales.[35]

The Corporate Body

Yolmo history, with its tale of unity and fission, corresponds to the physiology of a body such as Pasang's. Yolmo society consists of groups that relate to one another through networks of kin, status hierarchies, and reciprocal exchanges of hospitality and resources. For the most part, Yolmo experience seems founded on these relations, be they between kindred bodies or distant villages. This embedded communality fosters what may best be called a "relational self"—a sense of personhood, that is, conceived and experienced through social relations.[36] By definition, a person in Helambu is enmeshed in a social network made up of family members, relatives, neighbors, "insiders" and "outsiders"; much of subjective experience seems to draw on this network. This does not mean that Yolmo wa lack a sense of individuality or uniqueness. Rather, the body is always experienced in relation to others. In Helambu, a person cannot exist without a familiar context, a ranked hierarchy, and culturally specific ways of relating to others. These ways of relating typically involve exchanges of hospitality, kinship ties, and mutual assistance, from the movement of women in marriage to the sharing of tea and cigarettes. Yet, as with other corporate groups in Helambu, they also include competition for status and resources. A villager sees himself as an interest "group" unto himself, with body, speech, and mind working together for the benefit of the somatic whole. Yet that person is also part of a household, a family, a village, and is expected to contribute to the welfare of those groups.[37] As with a household or family, the elements of a body are caught up within the contradictory values of autonomy and interdependence.

A villager's basic concern for what lies within and without her body mirrors the principles of inclusion and exclusion that characterize Yolmo households, families, and villages. In turn, a Yolmo body itself possesses a hierarchy of varied organs and values. Like the geography of a village, a body assumes a collage of brain, stomach, and foot that, ideally, works together as a unified whole. Indeed, in a very real sense, Yolmo wa take their bodies to function like the other corporate groups with which they are familiar: as a hierarchical assemblage of disparate "organs" loosely bound together into a somatic whole. The Lamaist paintings (*thang ka*) that adorn temples, for instance, figure divine bodies as a collage of jointed bodily parts: forearm, fingers, and torso appear as distinct entities proximate in space to one another. Intrinsic to these conceptions of the body is a dialectic of unity and difference, fragmentation and integration. This dialectical body largely forms and informs village politics and the physiology of a healthy person. The different bodily organs must work together to achieve health; if they cease to coordinate or communicate their actions, the body falls ill.

Conflict

The conflicts that can arise from the contradictory values of autonomy and interdependence influence local imageries of illness—imageries, such as Pasang's ghosts, that often reflect problematic social relationships. Tied to Yolmo relationality, one common illness among the Lama people is *dasa graha* or "astrological plight" (literally, "ten planets"). This pan-Nepali malady occurs when an inauspicious alignment of planets bears detrimental consequences for the unlucky. *Dasa graha*'s prime symptom is the disruption of social relations between the afflicted person and others. Here a person does not suffer physical pain so much as anger, quarrels, and bad business. During my stay, one man found himself losing money and in a quarrelsome mood, arguing with his wife and neighbors. "I'm suffering from *dasa graha*," he concluded with the divinatory aid of a shaman.

The tussles commonly caused by *dasa graha* reflect the dangerous liaison between illness and social conflicts. The health of a person often reflects the quality of his or her relations with others. Patients often fear that their pain results from the harmful actions of others. "The arrow [*bān*] of some people got into me," explained one woman, who now wears a protective amulet (*srung ga*): "Whatever the people do, it won't harm me now."[38] "The shaman divined," another villager recalled of a recent sickness, "and he told me that it was the effect of two people against me." "Sometimes if people are together," yet another deduced, "and one envies another's eating food, then those bad thoughts can affect the other through illness." The harmful gossip of "human talk" (*mi kha*) causes illness by "drying up" the prosperity, wealth, or business of its victims. And the status of one's well-being often relates to another's in an image of limited health: if, in a dream, snowflakes fall not on the dreamer but on another, the dreamer's life-sustaining "life span" (*tshe*) will decrease while the other's will increase.

Hence a deep ambivalence scars Yolmo "togetherness": it is better to be with people than without, but one's neighbors can be dangerous. Such tensions reveal that Yolmo villagers, while members of social groups, are also individuals, guardians of their own corporate forms. Yolmo photographic aesthetics portray this fact. When having their picture taken, Yolmo wa prefer to pose not by themselves but with friends, family, or a larger group. Yet they stand, stiff and somber, one by one, some distance apart. Only after the photographer asks them to bunch together do they do so.

So while villagers wish to be together, and to be portrayed as such, they also desire to be represented as unique individuals: interrelated, yet autonomous. We can readily predict that the tension between personal and social identities sparks conflicts between self and society. Indeed, Yolmo concepts of personhood (and, often, experiences of illness) seem to be founded on such tensions. As one boy urged when I tried to get him to draw a picture of a person by sketching one myself, "You should make another man—make two—and have them fight each other!" The imagery of conflict also characterizes the afterlife at times. Yolmo lamas, in speaking of rebirth, sometimes refer to the six realms of the Buddhist "wheel of existence" (*srid pa'i 'khor lo*) rather than the tripartite cosmology that laymen generally speak of.[39] Within this circular "wheel," those dwelling in the second realm are said to harvest the fruits of a tree growing in the realm below it. "Yet everyone living in the second," one lama said, "has to fight over the fruit, claiming it for themselves. There is much anger, always fighting, no peace."

I once observed an unusual, comic interaction that occurred during an otherwise somber funeral. Two men paired off and theatrically engaged in a joking match of sorts. One prestigious man approached another and humorously tried to drag him off, pulling him by the arm. The second (of slightly lower status) responded by yanking his arm out from the first's grasp, declining to accompany him. Bantering of this sort went on for ten minutes to the apparent delight of the gathering crowd. While participants claimed that they were "just joking" here, it struck me that the comic relief, which took a similar form at two other funerals, dramatized the nature of social events in Helambu. When partaking of large communal gatherings, villagers appear to be uneasy about their social roles (smaller affairs, meanwhile, seem more relaxed).

The implicit sentiment here is that a villager is coerced into acting in a socially appropriate manner and must sacrifice personal desires that fall against the grain of the social fabric.[40] The corporate needs of the individual body must defer to the collective demands of the household or the village. Although villagers experience personhood via social relations, they encounter moments when conflict characterizes these relations more than harmony does. Social conflicts spark illness, antisocial behavior characterizes drunkenness, knowledge divides into private and social realms, and many life histories note tensions between personal desire and social propriety.

Brain and Heartmind

The contradictory values of autonomy and interdependence course through the very tissues of a villager's body; this is most evident in the relation between the "heartmind" (*sems*, "sem") and the "brain" (*klad pa*, "lepa").

The *sems* or "heartmind" lies at the heart of Yolmo understandings of thought and emotion. "Without *sems*," Karma once said, "it seems we wouldn't be human." Distinct from, but often said to lie within, the organic "heart" (*snying*, "nying"), *sems* is cognate with the *citta* or "mind" of Theravada Buddhism: "The core of personality, the center of purposiveness, activity, continuity, and emotionality."[41] It also compares, in form and function, to the Nepali *man*.

Sems, defined by Chandra Das as "soul; as power of perception, moral volition, spirit," plays an important role in the transcendental aims of Buddhist religion.[42] Less technical than Tantric adepts, Yolmo villagers take *sems* to form the basis of memories, dreams, and desires. Villagers often told me that *sems* was like one's "imagination" in the sense of conceiving of what was possible—the mind's fanciful eye. If a woman daydreams about her childhood, or imagines some future event, it is the work of *sems*. The heartmind is also the locus of emotional needs and drive. Its function is to desire and want; personal volition emanates from the *sems*. As Latu told me, "When you wish to go somewhere, do something, say something—it is *sems*. You do something because you have thought it in the *sems*." If a villager wishes to move a body part, the heartmind wills it and "tells" the brain (*klad pa*), which then commands the body to act.

Emotions are the domain of the heartmind. "If there is no *sems*," Latu said, "there is no emotion. *Sems* is like a seed; if there is no seed, there is no plant: the emotion." *Sems pa sdug po, sems pa tsher ka*, and *sems la skyid po 'dug* are a few expressions suggestive of this emotional process: "Sorrow, pain, and happiness (comfort) arise within the heartmind."

Though emotions "arise" within the *sems*, the heartmind leaves the body at will. When a villager dreams, the *sems* travels to the place and time envisioned; the images encountered constitute a dream. A similar flight of fancy holds true for waking thought. When the heartmind thinks of a distant place, it travels there like a bullet of light. Once, sitting deep in thought outside my house, I was asked, "Is your *sems* in America?" As I understand it, the heartmind's flight of fancy occasionally appears as a metaphoric journey (as with the American idiom, "My heart is with you"), but it also exists for villagers as an ontic reality, with the heartmind traveling to the space-time imagined.

Sems is the locus of personal knowledge, for a person's stream of consciousness flows through the heartmind. Like emotions, memories are held by the *sems*. When a man cannot remember something, he might report "*sems la bzhag mi 'dug*": "It cannot be put into the *sems*." When one recalls an image but not its name (as with the American expression, "It's on the tip of my tongue"), it dwells within the *sems* but fails to reach the mouth. Forgetfulness, in turn, results from an inability to retain things in the *sems*. To think, in sum, is to "see" or "know" with the heartmind.

The heartmind is subtly but firmly interwoven into the experiential fabric of Yolmo life. As Latu expounded one day, "When in the mother's womb, you don't know anything, you don't have *sems* [as there is no stimulus and so no experience]. After birth, you have *sems*, and have to worry about everything. Wanting to save or waste money, it is *sems*. Wearing good clothes, or not caring: *sems*. Wanting to die alone, without others, it is *sems*." Notice how the heartmind relates to individual desires.

A villager's heartmind develops through life; the "bigger" the *sems*, the stronger, more courageous, and less overtly emotional a person is. A strong *sems* is one that can contain or "hold" emotions within. Consequently, as children, women, and the elderly are believed to have smaller "heartminds" than an average adult male, they are said to be more emotional and frighten more easily. *Sems* also relates to notions of morality. Once, when someone stole a tape recorder from my hut, villagers suggested that it was taken by children who didn't know better. "They don't have *sems* like we do," they advised, inferring that children do not possess the developed sense of right and wrong that adults do. Morality and affect, thought and imagination—such is the work of *sems*, the heartminds of the Lama people.

Sems works in tandem with the *klad pa*, for the "brain" regulates the fancies of the heartmind. While the *sems* desires, the brain commands. While the heartmind wills actions to be performed, the brain carries out these actions; it strives to find ways to actualize desires—albeit only those deemed appropriate. Similar to the psychoanalytic notion of the superego, the *klad pa* functions to control what the *sems* imagines. "If someone does a bad thing to us," one low-status man suggested, "then our *sems* wants to do something bad in return. But the *klad pa* orders us, the *sems*, what is best to do. The *klad pa* makes 'control'; it says you mustn't do that." Of interest here is that while everyone's brain is thought to be the same—"about what to do and what not to do"—each person's heartmind is thought to be different, as if the *klad pa* represented collective mores and the *sems*, individual desires. Significantly, the brain stands "above" the heartmind.

The conflict between "brain" and "heartmind" reflects a core tension between the corporate body and social groups. Personal desires can be at odds with collective needs; the notion of a bounded body fosters a climate of privacy and individuality. Two parallel tensions thus form the basis of Yolmo experience: one between the body's solubility and boundaries, the other between the person and the social milieu through which it is defined.

Fragmentation

While the above tensions occur throughout Helambu, they have recently assumed a particular form for residents of the Gulphubanyang region. While Yolmo wa of Gulphubanyang hold many cultural and social affinities with those of northcentral Helambu, certain social and economic conditions presently exist in the former region that distinguish daily life from the major settlements found on the eastern slope of Helambu. In the villages on the original main ridge of Helambu, Clarke observes, the life of a community centers, geographically and politically, around the temple; "the temple is the distinctive and central feature of a Lama village."[43] All households who hold citizenship within a village participate in the corporate and religious life of the temple. Much of this participation includes the sponsorship of religious rites and donations of grain to the temple and to other households. These exchanges establish links among village households "not only in the temple itself but also in the everyday relationships within the community."[44] Ritual exchanges among temples, in turn, sustain ties with other villages.

In my travels through the original main ridge of Helambu in 1988, I found that the social dynamics Clarke reported a decade earlier were still prevalent. The temple remains the political center of each village and large collective rites take place throughout the year that identify the village as a unified polity. During a visit to the home of my field assistant, Karma, for instance, I observed the annual Lamaist rites performed during *lo gsar* ("losar"), the Tibetan New Year. On this occasion, lamas transferred spiritual "harms" into an effigy and then "threw" the effigy from the village confines. In the fall of 1988, I attended several festivals of *na rag* ("nara"), the second day of which members of other villages travel to the host village-temple to exchange hospitality and receive offerings of bread.[45] As the threat to the corporate system is one of fission, with households splitting off from the temple and villages breaking off into distinct factions, religious rites can be seen as an attempt to secure the integration of households within a village and villages within a community.

In Gulphubanyang, with its multitude of hamlets, the threat of fragmentation is ever-present. Yolmo wa of southwestern Helambu are tied, through kinship and property, to five villages that populate the mountain crest running north to south: Khutumsang, Dhupchughyang, Todhang, Chimi, and Chumdeli. The Lamaist lineages that founded each of these hamlets are offshoots of clans from villages in northern Helambu. The Yolmo presence in Todhang and Gulphubanyang, for instance, was established by Latu's father, Sangye Lama, who moved from a village in north-central Helambu to establish his own lineage (two other families control the temples in Dhupchughyang and Chumdeli). Sangye Lama, who lives for the most part in Kathmandu, continues to maintain a house in Todhang. Two of his sons built houses in Gulphubanyang, where they presently live, while the third, an architect, moved to Kathmandu and presently works in India.

The dispersal of Latu's family reflects some features of Yolmo society that have become prevalent in the Gulphubanyang region. When I returned to Gulphubanyang after witnessing the elaborate Lamaist rites in Karma's village, I asked Latu why such festivities did not take place in his own village. "We do it once in a while," he said, "but not too often. To hold such an event, you need a lot of people, and not enough of us live around here right now."

Latu's comment conveys something of the situation for the families of Meme, Pasang, and other residents of the Gulphubanyang region. The temple, the spiritual center of a community, is no longer its political center. The *dgon pa* ("gonpa") in the hillside Dhupchughyang, for instance, where

Photo 7. Tibetan New Year, Nigali, 1989.

most Lamaist rites take place, is isolated from the commercial exchanges that occur every day in Gulphubanyang. The rapid development of the latter village, a multiethnic community without a temple, has altered the character of the hamlets surrounding it: Yolmo villages are no longer "temple-villages" but rather are villages with, or without, temples. Large collective rites, which require the cooperation of a large number of people, are seldom performed. While Yolmo wa are at center stage economically and politically, in number they remain a minority to Tamang who live below. The ostensive political authority once wielded by lamas has been usurped by secular politicians, including educated Gurung and Tamang. In turn, many Yolmo families are now dispersed over an extensive geography: one brother might live in Inghir, another in Kathmandu, and yet another in India. Meme, for instance, has seven sons, five of whom work regularly in factories in India, and a daughter who lives in her husband's village two days' walk to the west.

The dispersal of families reflects a more pervasive fragmentation of village polities, for a shift has begun to occur from a corporate life centered around the temple to family-based household economies. The factors leading to this shift have been both social and economic. The tourist industry has brought additional sources of material wealth to select families along the trekking route running through Todhang, Gulphubanyang, and Khutumsang. Resettlements in Kathmandu have situated families within its market economy. The presence of Yolmo, Tamang, and Gurung households within the same bazaar has led to further dissolution of a corporate life, for Yolmo wa now relate to households and families that do not fit into the traditional corporate hierarchy. Patrilocal residence is more the ideal now than the norm, and married couples have begun to rent apartments in Kathmandu and houses in Gulphubanyang, and thus live away from the husband's father's village. The consequence of this situation is that wealth has lately been confined to select families rather than distributed throughout a village or a lineage. There are signs, in turn, that villagers are beginning to perceive nuclear family households as distinct from any temple-based corporate group, and the collective strength of extended families is waning.

The reorganization of Yolmo social structure in southwestern Helambu has led to typical conflicts among families within a village and individuals within a family. Often these conflicts, tied to the use of resources, coalesce around contrasting values of autonomy and interdependence. The cremation ceremony for one deceased woman, for example, was delayed because the two Lamaist lineages that were to perform the rites (one from the woman's natal village, the other from her husband's village) were involved in a protracted dispute over the use of grazing lands shared between them. In another instance, two stepbrothers followed different "lines" and built houses in different villages due to a dispute over the inheritance of land. Yet another pair of brothers preferred not to speak to each other when in the same social situation. In turn, families must now compete for shares of the revenue derived from the trekking industry (although the competition is not readily admitted to), and a pressing concern is whether a household's monetary profit from this and other enterprises should be shared with other households within a "family."

Yolmo collectivities, from body to household to village, assume a similar form: they possess a ranked hierarchy balanced by notions of equality, and fluid boundaries that mark the inclusion or exclusion of "inside" and "outside" forces. As a body is a unified whole unto itself, yet also interrelated with the other bodies that inhabit a house or village, contradictory values of autonomy and interdependence define its anatomy. The same tension applies to the physiology of a household, family, or village, and so continously patterns the evolution of Yolmo society. Throughout this evolution, the task for most villagers (particularly those of wealth and high status) has been to make body, household, family, and village work in a way that the members of those groups sustain social harmony, prevent conflict and fission, and contribute to the prosperity of all. Within the vicinity of Gulphubanyang, however, the dispersal of families and economic circumstances have accented the inherent potential for social entropy. My sense is that, with the proliferation in future years of market economies in this region, the smaller, more inclusive group of each set will begin to be privileged over the larger group: the household will take precedence over the family, the family over the village, and, to some extent, the individual over the household.

As the imagery of the body parallels the workings of Yolmo social groups, one can follow the history of Yolmo society in part by tracing (as we shall soon do) the physiology of a body such as Pasang's. The living mosaic of a Yolmo body, be it tending a fire or "shaking" with the divine presence of deities, constantly lends commentary on the basic forms and tensions marking Yolmo society. Through the everyday uses of the body— an offering of potatoes, the collection of firewood—villagers tacitly sense and reflect on the other corporate groupings found in Helambu and the relations among them. Villagers experience these events through sensory, visceral means; meaning results in the way a body momentarily stands, a hand grasps another, or ghosts "eat" at the flesh. These acts, in their constant reformation, give image to vital concerns, from the dialogue of brain and heartmind to the fragile borders of the body. To some extent, the physiology of Pasang's body, as a "natural symbol," legitimates the hierarchical structure of Yolmo society; the rule of head over heart secures the status of priests and men.[46] Yet her body also reflects dilemmas intrinsic to the social system, and so can be used as a creative force for critical reflection, if not change itself.

All this is to suggest that the full range of Yolmo life, from the sentience of bodies to the metaphysics of space, ties into unique grammars of experience. To gain a sense of how Pasang's body feels, how pain pierces her flesh, or how Meme "throws" ghosts, our own bodies must first come to terms with these grammars. And since the rudiments of Yolmo form are themselves the product of basic social concerns, from the contradictory values of autonomy and interdependence to the threat of fission, we must link the physiologies of taste and touch to the intricacies of Yolmo social life. The politics of experience that result from these key social concerns give rise, in turn, to local notions of grace, propriety, and social welfare. Indeed, the next chapter shows that values of this sort adhere to a pattern of social history, a history of forms shadowed by the threat of fission.

3. An Aesthetics of Experience

In late June 1988, Mingma Lama, a tall, thin Yolmo elder in his late sixties, suffered from weakness and frailty due to the loss of several life-forces. Mingma was born into a family of lamas and lived in the hamlet of Todhang to the south of Gulphubanyang. His wife died several years earlier, and he now lived with his son's family in a house that he, the father, built many years back. In meeting Mingma, I sensed he had been lively and energetic in his youth (as his son was then) but, despite a lasting smile, an aging body forced him to slow his pace in later years. His clothes drooped about his frame, especially since the last illness, and now formed a puddle of linen around his waist.

According to Mingma, ghosts "ate" five of his nine "life supports" (*srog*, "sok"), stealing them into "the land of the dead" (*shi yul*), and he risked losing the other four and thereby dying. In Helambu, *srog* stand for the supports of life (see Table 1). They live in the heart, constitute one's "breath," and imply a body's physical foundation or "backbone." *Srog shing*, which stems from the idea of a "life tree," equates with the spine: if crooked and frail, a person cannot walk. *Srog* also refer to the nine "beams" of the body found, for men, at the temples, eyes, spine, calves, and testicles: "If you're hit there," Latu warned of the latter location, "you're finished." If one or two *srog* are lost, others might easily follow, so it is imperative to retrieve them before the three main *srog*, the "roots," leave the body. "If you lose the *srog*," Meme taught, "you become weak and sick. You won't eat, your body becomes lazy, it melts. But only if you lose the three important *srog*, then you die."

Along with the loss of life supports, Mingma's "life span" (*tshe*) decayed "as parts of a biscuit crumble away" (as one man described the process in general). For Yolmo wa, the *tshe* or "life" denotes a person's remaining life energy. One has an optimum life span as determined by one's "fate" or karma (*las*, "le"). If a man's karma destines him to reach seventy years of age, he will attain that age if his "life" is complete. But if the life span "decays" (*nyams pa*), losing its brilliance "as a flashlight battery

TABLE 1.   Yolmo Life-Forces.

	rNam Shes	Bla	Tshe	Srog
Force	"Conscious-ness"; "soul"	"Spirit"	"Life"; "life span"	"Life Support"; physical foundation
Function	Awareness; consciousness	Vitality; energy; volition	Strength; fortitude	Physical support; strength
If Lost	Death (death causes departure from body)	Bla 'khyer zin (spirit loss); loss of vitality and volition	Tshe nyams pa (diminished life span); loss of strength and vigor	Srog dgu mi; loss of physical strength; bodily decay
Ritual Strategy	Transmigration of the soul through sbyang par ("purification paper") rites	Hooking, summoning the spirit (bla 'gug)	Enhancing the life (tshe grup)	Nine men of the srog (srog dgu mi)

weakens in time," he is prone to illness and even death before that time. If left untreated, *tshe nyams pa* causes the face to grow "dark" and the body to "dry up" and become thin, emaciated, and weak.

As the diminishment of Mingma's "life" made him physically weak and prone to an untimely death, it was essential to "raise" the lost life supports within his body and revitalize the diminished life span. Meme performed the requisite healing in early July and attempted to enhance the lost "life" and recover the nine *srog*, one by one, from the land of the dead (*shi yul*). A week after this all-night ceremony, which apparently succeeded, I called on Mingma at his home while he was caring for his grandchildren, and asked if he could talk about his illness.

"I'm just ill from old age, getting older, and afraid of dying," he said at first. He later told of having lost the life-forces. He had been sick for several weeks, with a loss of appetite, pain throughout his body, and difficulty in sleeping. On losing the life-forces, he dreamed of seeing dead persons, walking through a cremation ground, and descending downhill—all culturally recognized omens of illness.

"How does a person lose the life-forces, grandfather?" I asked.

"This can happen," Mingma spoke quietly, "when a man is frightened while walking at night, alone, on a road, in darkness."

Loss, darkness, and a downhill descent: in my estimation, the way in which Mingma evaluated his pain, the way in which he gave form and meaning to his malaise and experienced the healing process, was patterned by an implicit, politically driven "aesthetics" of everyday life. This chapter, and to some extent the core of this book, is an attempt to justify, theoretically and ethnographically, this last statement. I use the term "aesthetics" in a slightly irregular fashion, not to define any overt artistry or performative genres—art, music, poetry—but rather to grasp (and tie together) the tacit leitmotivs that shape cultural constructions of bodily and social interactions. I see such aesthetic forms—which include, for Yolmo wa, values of harmony, purity, and wholeness—as embodied through the visceral experience of cultural actors rather than articulated through concrete artistic or philosophic tenets. With the term "aesthetics of experience," then, I refer to the tacit cultural forms, values, and sensibilities—local ways of being and doing—that lend specific styles, configurations, and felt qualities to local experiences. As Yolmo aesthetics pattern how villagers make sense of the basic forms (body, household, village) that characterize their particular ways of living, so they shape the sensory grounds of experiences of suffering and the emotional terrain occasioned by those experiences. With Mingma's tale, intimations of bodily decay, spiritual erosion, and a deathly darkness characterize his descent into "soul loss."

Our focus on the cultural dimensions of aesthetic sensibilities complements the recent work of several anthropologists who consider the social "poetics" or "aesthetics" of social, ritual, and musical performances in a variety of cultural settings.[1] What I find most valuable in these approaches is that they link aesthetic performances to indigenous ideas about style, meaning, and personhood. Yet while such research attempts to show how social dynamics and ethnopsychological notions influence ritual and social performance, I wish to start from the other end of the spectrum, to indicate how local aesthetic principles, rooted in bodily experience and played out in social interactions, shape indigenous notions of person, emotion, and experience. Students of the aesthetic dimensions of healing (music, dance, drama) often talk of the need for their inquiries because the topic has been neglected in the past.[2] Yet a more significant contribution of this subdiscipline might be to show how ritual performance is grounded within, and governed by, a wider sphere of value and practice: the aesthetics of the everyday.[3]

Indeed, one reason I wish to examine the aesthetic dimensions of

Yolmo experiences is that current anthropologies of the self focus on certain issues at the expense of perhaps more relevant concerns. While there is a great deal of debate over whether conceptions of selfhood vary cross-culturally (perhaps sparked by worries over our own self-boundaries),[4] we pay little attention to the cultural philosophies of experience that shape human behavior. Mingma or Meme wouldn't bat an eye if told they were more "sociocentric" than "egocentric" (to use recent phrasings),[5] but they would express great concern if they felt their bodies were polluted, hearts clouded with emotions, or physiologies off-balance. This suggests that an anthropology of experience might profit from an analysis not only of the contours and boundaries of "selves" as they are culturally construed, but of the way in which social actors compose, manage, and evaluate their actions and those of others in everyday social contexts. Questions concerning the everyday use of bodies, and how these uses are evaluated, would then become more relevant than debates over the "true" locus of self-experience or whether "bounded" selves exist or not in any given society. Indeed, I believe that the ensuing shift in orientations would lead to a more comprehensive assessment of the social, moral, and political dimensions of cultural experience. In turn, a focus on the interactive dimensions of social discourse, in which people act in concert with others in the give-and-take of everyday life, can help us to further understand, on the one hand, the degree to which human experience is an "intersubjective" medium of shared psychophysiologic, social, and political processes,[6] and, on the other, the aesthetic underpinnings of these intersubjective processes.

In addition to the limited purview of many anthropological studies of selfhood, another ethnographic strategy has been to question the force and significance of aesthetic sensibilities in everyday life. Unni Wikan, for instance, criticizes Clifford Geertz's suggestion that, among Balinese, high aesthetics (notions of grace, composure, "stage fright") shape behavior.[7] While Wikan's point that everyday health concerns motivate behavior more than aesthetic concerns do is well taken, she largely fails to consider what, in turn, motivates these health concerns. Often, for Yolmo wa as well as Balinese, worries over one's health relate to culturally constituted aesthetics of personhood. Why do Balinese believe that the face, "withered" when marred by sadness, should be, as Wikan reports, "as smooth and clear as water"? Why do Yolmo wa imagine their bodies to fragment when weakened and souls to be lost if spooked? How do healers smooth wrinkled faces, cleanse tainted bodies, or revitalize waning souls? A phenomenology of embodied aesthetics might help to answer queries of this kind.

The phenomenology of these pages builds on the orientation of several literary critics and philosophers of art who argue that there exists no grand distinction between aesthetic and ordinary experience. "When we look at a picture," I. A. Richards exemplifies this pragmatic view, "or read a poem, or listen to music, we are not doing something quite unlike what we were doing on our way to the Gallery or when we dressed in the morning. The fashion in which the experience is caused in us is different, and as a rule the experience is more complex and, if we are successful, more unified. But our activity is not of a fundamentally different kind."[8] Richards goes on to outline the similiarities and differences characterizing aesthetic and ordinary experience. John Dewey, in turn, seeks to "restore continuity between the refined and intensified forms of experience that are works of art and the everyday events, doings, and sufferings that are universally recognized to constitute experience."[9] He concludes, in a book devoted to the task, that "artistic and aesthetic quality is implicit in every normal experience."[10] Dewey's position is that experience itself is founded on an organism's inter-action with an environment. As human interactions are based on a series of "doings and undoings," tensions and resolutions, so processes of aesthetic balance, harmony, and completion are, by nature, grounded in the rhythms of ordinary experience. The creation and perception of art forms are simply more perfected fulfillments of, and commentaries on, these experiences.

Since the development of these pragmatic approaches, philosophers of art have tended to debate the implications of the last statement: whether experiences of art differ fundamentally from the aesthetics of ordinary experience.[11] The idea of an aesthetics of the everyday, however, has been explored less systematically, particularly within anthropological circles. In this and later chapters, I therefore want to consider the aesthetic principles that shape and constrain how a Yolmo man or woman steps through a village, dresses in the morning, or loses his or her "spirit." The study is an imperative one, for it will greatly enhance our understanding of the every-day events, doings, and sufferings that seem to compose Yolmo experience. Such a study might also suggest how the stuff of ethics, narrative, emotion, and personhood ties into the aesthetics of everyday life. "Ethics and aes-thetics are one," Wittgenstein wrote in 1922;[12] the following pages suggest several reasons why this might be so.

One student of the aesthetics of experience, Joseph Kupfer, develops some of Dewey's ideas on art and education in his book *Experience as Art*.[13] Kupfer is interested in the "extrinsically valuable" aesthetic dimensions of everyday life, and how an appreciation of these dimensions can help to educate members of a society. The approach follows Dewey's understanding of the aesthetic qualities intrinsic to what he calls *"an* experience"—those memorable experiences that carry a sense of completion, significance, and coherence.[14] For Kupfer, some ways of going about sports, sex, and dying are more aesthetically fulfilling than others, for they convey balance, coherence, and moral value. Some actions, on the other hand, lack aesthetic quality. Sexual relationships that are defined by the dominance of one person over another lack an important aesthetic dimension: the balance between doing and taking in, activity and receptivity. In turn, Kupfer identifies a "perverse marriage" between the aesthetic and the violent in the modern West, in which violence is sought for its aesthetic qualities.[15]

While I find Kupfer's thesis that aesthetic qualities permeate everyday life to be a perceptive one, I have some trouble with his distinction between aesthetic and nonaesthetic experience, and the notion that some experiences carry more aesthetic weight than others. In my view, acts of violence and domination are no less fused with aesthetic value than are those of harmony and balance (though the acts might not be valued equally). The difference lies in the aesthetic (and political) sensibilities that lead to, define, and give significance to the acts. The point becomes highly significant when we speak of experiences of illness and misfortune. As I understand his position, Kupfer holds that an illness can be made into an aesthetic experience (as with the death of Tolstoy's Ivan Ilych), but this is often not the case. A person can suffer and die without grace, propriety, or moral significance. Yet I would contend that illness is always experienced and interpreted through a lens of aesthetic value; aesthetic sensibilities influence all moments of suffering, even if they lack coherence and completion.

This is not to say that pain is ever beautiful or aesthetically pleasing. Yet human beings do interpret, make sense of, and even transform pain through cultural sensibilities. A lot of misery is not pretty, but the criteria upon which judgments of ugliness are based are aesthetic ones. Pain, if it is to bear meaning, must be situated within a system of aesthetic value, a system that shapes the moral and emotional dimensions of the experience. In Helambu, the aesthetics of illness tend to reflect, in inverse form, the aesthetics of health and healing. Mingma's sense of loss and decline, I would argue, conforms to an aesthetic orientation that, in health, involves images of harmony, integration, and completion. In illness, however, the orientation figures body as fragmenting mosaic and spirit as waning vitality. And since these ways of suffering relate intrinsically to what it means to be a "good" and hence "healthy" person in Helambu, Mingma's method of aging draws on local understandings of "propriety"—moral perspectives, that is, forged by an aesthetics of the everyday.

Enduring political concerns color the ways in which Yolmo wa typically figure body and spirit. For Dewey, as with Kant, the aesthetics of experience arises out of the natural order of things. Following the work of Pierre Bourdieu, I want to question this reasoning. In *Art as Experience*, Dewey draws on "biological commonplaces" to explain "the roots of the aesthetic in experience"; he then traces the development of "common human activities," such as walking, feeling, and breathing, into matters of artistic value.[16] Biological commonplaces refer here to a live being's interaction with its environment, interactions that occasion the rhythms of order and disorder, loss and recovery, that characterize the experience of that being. Yet Dewey's perspective can not account for the diversity of aesthetic systems throughout the world, nor for the political underpinnings of these systems. In his recent book *Distinction*, for example, Bourdieu argues that common human activities among the French are less biologically than culturally constituted, set within a social system of classification, and tinged with political value.[17] For Bourdieu, "the seemingly most natural features of the body"—ways of walking or blowing one's nose, ways of eating or talking—govern a person's sense of what is tasteful, proper, and healthy.[18] And since different social classes are thought to have different tastes in foods, art, and leisure, these tastes engage a way of constructing and evaluating the social world so as to give the appearance of naturalness to social distinctions. These distinctions work, in turn, to legitimate the division of labor and the hierarchy of classes. "Taste, a class culture turned into nature, that is, *embodied*, helps to shape the class body."[19] The emphasis on the body as the "natural" vehicle for judgments of taste and value runs throughout Bourdieu's writings: "The ultimate values, as they are called, are never anything other than the primary, primitive dispositions of the body, 'visceral' tastes and distastes, in which the group's most vital interests are embedded."[20]

Reading Bourdieu, I find that, while his understanding of the political dimensions of bodily dispositions can be quite subtle, his theories linking physiologic processes to social aesthetics are generally more hypothetical than substantiated. Gregory Bateson, in contrast, offers a perspective that gets at the physiologic dimensions of embodied aesthetics but fails to articulate the political ones.[21] In outlining how "self-evident" paradigms of experience contribute to Balinese behavior, Bateson traces how the propensity of Balinese to enter into hypnotic trance derives from a particular kinesthetic socialization that draws on the body's capacity to engage in a circuit of "spinal reflexes."[22] Yet while Bateson demonstrates how cultural values can intersect with physiologic processes, he admittedly cannot explain why the "synthesis of gravity and spinal reflex" that he documents in Bali takes "the particular shape that is characteristic for Balinese culture."[23] Since Bourdieu's take on the politics of aesthetics would appear to be quite helpful in answering Bateson's quandary, a phenomenology of aesthetic experience might profit from an integration of the analytic grids of Bateson and Bourdieu, in which the strengths of each perspective would help to resolve the drawbacks of the other. The present chapter can be read as an initial attempt to develop such a bridge.

As social tastes and values come to life within the sensory experience of villagers, a phenomenology of Yolmo aesthetics must begin and end with the body. Yolmo bodies shape, and are shaped by, the patterned behaviors and commonsensical habits of everyday life. To understand an aesthetics of the everyday in Helambu, then, we must consider how Yolmo forms—from bodies to households and villages—function in everyday life. And since aesthetic (and hence moral and political) values emmanate from, and take root within, the body, we return to the realm of the sensory. Embodied aesthetics are a question of tact, of perception, of sensibility; these three acts originate in the visceral. Nietzsche wrote that the aesthetic is "applied physiology."[24] To what extent is this true in Helambu, and to what extent is Yolmo physiology applied aesthetics?

In an attempt to answer these questions, I sketch below several common dimensions of Yolmo aesthetics (harmony, control, integration, presence, and purity) as they relate to notions of illness, health, and "madness." In later chapters, I show how these somatic sensibilities combine to shape the felt quality, the Greek *aisthesis*, of feelings of grief, incidents of "soul loss," and shamanic healings. Through this analysis, I intend to make it clear that the most vital interests of Yolmo wa, particularly those who have the most to gain in maintaining the status quo (for example, men, lamas, those of wealth and high status) are similarly embedded in the primary dispositions of the body. The ways in which Mingma walks down a road, cares for his grandchildren, or grows old reflect the "ultimate values" of Yolmo society. These values account for how the various forms that populate Helambu—a village, a household, a body—cohere or fall apart, and I hold that the processes of integration and erosion that affect these forms are not entirely "natural" ones, but result from the exigencies of local social life.

As our concern is with the felt immediacies of cultural experience—

how villagers construe, sense, and experience their bodies in everyday life—the study requires an analytic approach distinct from current intellectualist, symbolist, or psychological paradigms. This is not to say that those paradigms lack value or that they should be dispensed with, but that their analytic grids fail to account for the complex of values, resonances, and sensibilities that an aesthetics of the everyday entails. In coming to understand the force and tenor of embodied aesthetics, we cannot simply map a society's system of beliefs, offer a thick description of symbolic actions, or ferret out the deep psychic meanings of cultural beliefs. We must attend to the surface imagery, felt qualities, and embodied values intrinsic to moments of illness and healing. Here the focus lies less on viewing bodies or social interactions as "texts" to be read or translated.[25] Rather, the focus is on the way in which a sip of tea, a conversation, or—the analogy continues—a work of art is "put together," and the constraints on form and style that underlie those compositions.

Whereas the idea of "meaning" most propels interpretive studies of suffering,[26] the notion of "value" is central to our present concerns. An aesthetics of experience does not tie solely into a system of beliefs, meaning, or logical criteria but refers to a schema of value, and therefore situates cultural experience within that schema.[27] Yet since these values are embodied and so appear self-evident, they go beyond the cognized sort common to intellectual reasoning. Anything embodied in accordance with an aesthetic is not neutral, but automatically entails a posture toward it, a "gut feeling," and so engages not just an intellectual approach to moments of pain or comfort, but a visceral, emotional, and moral stance.

To convey emotional resonances, the analysis moves from tangible image to felt quality. "Aesthetic value is like the wind," Iser tells us, "we know of its existence only through its effects."[28] To understand Yolmo aesthetics of the everyday, we must trace value as it crystallizes in concrete manifestations (an imagery of dreams, an old man's tale of aging) until the poetic force of these images begins to resonate within our own worlds. We must also comprehend the underlying philosophic tenets, aesthetic values, and moral constraints that go into the composition of any cultural interaction, from values of social harmony to moral ideals. For if, as A. L. Becker suggests, cultural assumptions on what makes a good "story" constrain the building of a plot,[29] then notions of what makes a good "person" frame experiences of body, family, and society. A phenomenology of embodied aesthetics seeks to understand what those notions are and how they are put into practice.

The Harmonium

The aesthetics of the everyday arise, for the most part, out of the exigencies of Yolmo social life. The task for most Yolmo wa (particularly those of wealth and high status) has been to make the basic groupings of local social life (household, family, village) function so that its members prevent conflict and fission.[30] An aesthetic of harmony and reciprocity similarly guided Mingma's actions when he cared for his grandchildren, sat down to talk with me, or felt pain, for a villager requires a sense of harmony, balance, and proportion if he or she is to remain healthy. Ideally, it appears, Yolmo wa experience their bodies as unified wholes. Despite the tension between inner and outer (and self and society), what lies within the body is typically seen, in health, as integrated, balanced, and harmonious.

First there is the geographic imagery: the body incorporates a spatial schema invoking a unified gestalt. Villagers often told me that a person's fingers, as well as the bones, present the five colored directions: east, south, west, north, and center. This unifying number also accounts for the five bodily substances and the five sensory "organs." The body itself rests in the "center" direction with the larger geographical context framing it; the house by definition lives in a neighborhood. And the "heartmind," emanating from the hub of the body, lends a centrality to experience, just as the "soul," or *rnam shes*, patterned throughout the body, bestows a sensory holism.

Ideas of photographic representation similarly reflect a gestalt of bodily integration. When I photographed Yolmo villagers, they often stressed the importance of encompassing the complete body in the frame, from capped head to bare feet, even if it meant the photographer standing back at some distance. This sensibility, where the whole person needs to be framed in the social order as much as the social order needs to be framed as a whole, is different from that found in the West, where a good "shot" often captures just the face—and sometimes only a portion of it. I once photographed Meme while he prepared for a healing in the dusk (see Photo 1). When I offered him a developed print a month later, he was disappointed, for one half of his face was covered in shadows. "It's ruined," he sighed.

Shamans dramatize much of the body's imputed unity when healing. As Meme taught, a *bombo* must imagine himself not only as encompassing the five directions and the five colors, but as at the center of the world as well. Indeed, he must envision his body as representing the cosmos. As I will later contend, images of balance, integration, and wholeness play a basic role in the transformative poetics of healing rites.

Yet while a Yolmo body aims to be a unified whole, it is a whole composed of distinct and finite parts. As noted above, villagers often image the human form as a hierarchical assemblage of disparate "organs" loosely bound together into a somatic whole. As with the Lamaist paintings that adorn temples, some Yolmo folk songs fashion the body in a slightly piecemeal fashion:

> On Pasang Bulti's head, he has a god's hat
> On Pasang Bulti's ears, he has gold earings
> On Pasang Bulti's neck, he has a turquoise
> On Pasang Bulti's chest, he has pearls
> On Pasang Bulti's waist, he has a gold buckle
> Pasang Bulti's pants are made from red cloth
> Pasang Bulti's shoes are cotton cloth boots
> On Pasang Bulti's feet, he has boot ties[31]

As the lyrics hint, Yolmo wa parcel their bodies into a segmented whole, a merger of head and feet distinct but bound together. In essence, Yolmo bodies model the corporate hierarchies of Yolmo households, families, and villages, and so assume the piecemeal form characteristic of these groups, with organs autonomous yet interdependent with one another.

If the body is a unified whole in health, it tends to fragment and decay in sickness. When afflicted by pathology, the body becomes incomplete, adulterated, off-balance, lacking. The imagery here is at times one of consumption: illness "eats" away at the body, tight shoes "eat" one's feet, adults threaten to "eat" off childrens' ears. To destroy a witch, one shaman explained, "One has to imagine cutting her up—heart, body, limbs—then throwing these pieces away in different directions." And if the "brain" (*klad pa*) is not "full" or its "inner parts" become "broken," a person can encounter "madness" (*smyon pa*, "nyonpa"). In turn, Yolmo wa often speak of the various forms of "soul loss" as tenacious processes of physical and spiritual decline. As with Mingma, the body can become weak, heavy, and tired; life-forces can become lost, diminished, and spoiled. Indeed, villagers are greatly troubled over the potential loss and deterioration of life-forces, for physical decrepitude occurs when a vitality such as the *srog* withers. There is the belief, for instance, that everyone, weak or strong, loses one of the *srog* each year. If a person does not recover the lost vitality, as Mingma was unable to do, ill health is imminent. While the above illnesses result from a corporeal loss or deterioration, others derive from the invasion of a foreign pathology: ghosts intrude the body's integrity, witches devour the flesh. In both instances, the body loses its integrity and ceases to be a unified whole, and the aesthetics of health give way to those defining illness.[32]

Yolmo dreams, which often bear divinatory knowledge, frequently reflect a similar imagery. Indeed, it is likely that the recollection of dreams offers a creative forum through which Yolmo sensibilities are continuously forged and reforged. Villagers speak often of what particular dreams presage. While dreams of tattered clothes and decrepit houses signify a lost life-force, images of full moons and mountain ascents commemorate its return. If a tree falls in a dream or many men are seen cutting wood, a close relative will die: if an old tree, someone old; if a sapling, someone young. If an upper tooth falls out, a relative will die, while the loss of a lower tooth foretells the imminent death of a sibling or parent. A setting sun signs the death of the dreamer's mother; a waning moon, his father. A landslide or a burning, dilapidated house also foretells a death in the family. The intimations of bodily decay and spiritual erosion that mark the body in illness thus haunt the dreams prefiguring these same ailments. Health, conversely, is announced through images of completion, purity, or ascendency: new houses, clothes, or hats; the rise of the sun, the waxing of the moon, or a bright, clear light; the consumption of "sweet" white foods such as milk; snow falling on the body; and ascending into the Himalayas. Notions of wholeness and integration, in sum, seem to impinge on Yolmo experiences of the body. An aesthetic of loss and fragmentation marks imageries of illness.

Balance

As the bearers of organic mosaics, villagers often stress the importance of intracorporeal communication and coordination. The "heartmind" (*sems*) and "brain" (*klad pa*) need to coordinate their actions in order for a person to think, remember, and move bodily parts. For this psychic ballet to proceed unencumbered, the two organs need to "tell" one another what's "on their minds," as one villager put it. In turn, different bodily parts need to work in harmony for the body to function properly. Whereas feet "fall asleep" in Boston, they become "mute" (*'on pa*) in Helambu, failing to communicate with the heartmind or the rest of the body. "Fainting" occurs when the soul-like "consciousness" (*rnam shes*) becomes inactive, ceasing to inform the heartmind of its sensory perceptions. Alcohol debilitates physical coordination by polluting the entire body "like a drug injection," prohibiting the brain, heartmind, and motor organs from working efficiently. The aesthetics of Mingma's body thus parallel—and so seemingly embody—social mores, for while members of a household, family, or village need to work in harmony, coordinating and communicating their actions, so should a body's interlocking organs. A fear of fission marks a person's physiology as much as it does the politics of the village in which that person lives.

Yolmo wa such as Pasang and Mingma generally strive, in accord with the need for social and somatic coordination, to retain balance in their bodies and lives. This concern probably derives from Tibetan medical theories, themselves rooted in the Ayurvedic tradition of South Asia (and in part, I believe, from pre-Buddhist indigenous beliefs).[33] In the classical "science of long life," the primary cause of illness is the upsetting of the balance of the three humors—wind, bile, phlegm—or a blockage of their actions.[34] Insanity, for instance, is an unsettled condition of the mind (consciousness, perception, memory) derived from humoral upset.[35] The disequilibrium can result from any physical, psychological, social, or cosmic conflicts, such as the "pursuit of a lifestyle which runs contrary to the inherent disposition of the afflicted person and his spiritual destiny."[36] To secure proper health, then, a person must maintain humoral balance not only within his or her body but "in accord with the forces of the natural environment and the psychological life of the individual."[37] Curing here strives toward the harmonic "restoration of serenity of mind" so as to recreate a "dynamic state of equilibrium or homeostasis."[38]

Largely unaware of this history, Yolmo villagers attend to the aesthetic of balanced harmony in their daily lives. Stress or an excess of emotions can lead to illness, especially "madness" (*smyon pa*, "nyonpa"). I once asked Karma if he thought excessive sorrow (*sdug*, "dhuk") could make one ill. "If you have too much of any [emotion]," he replied, "you might go mad. If you have too much of grief, sorrow, or happiness, people might say, 'Hey, you're about to go crazy.' In any case, you should not exceed any limits of anything . . . then you'll go crazy."

The balance applies to work habits as well. One woman, troubled over the marathon letter-writing sessions I occasionally engaged in while shut up within my cabin, warned that if a person thinks too much, the brain is bound to become "ruined"—similar to the "eating" of the brain caused by daily annoyances (such as children playing noisily). Another person suggested that illness may occur if the equilibrium between the body's "heaven" and "hell" (good and bad thoughts) becomes offset, causing—to use his coinage—"umuch-tumuch." Spirit loss, in turn, causes a disequilibrium of the heartmind. "With the loss of your spirit [*bla*]," Meme told me, "your heartmind is inconstant [*talpul talpul*]. No balance. The *sems* cannot decide on things." And just as "consciousness becomes disturbed" in Ayurvedic theory "when the inner winds circulate in ways and places they shouldn't,"[39] so Yolmo organs must be in their proper places. Fainting can also occur, Meme explained, when one's consciousness (*rnam shes*) "is not in its right place, moving around like a madman throughout the body." A villager typically seeks balance and proportion, then, within the interrelated realms of body, behavior, and social relations.

Control

Since Yolmo experiences balance precariously between autonomy and social conformity, equilibrium must be maintained not only within the body but within a person's social relations. The fragile groupings of Yolmo society make harmonious relations between and within different groups of crucial importance. This leads the residents of Helambu to characterize social and political relations by the degree of accord (or disaccord) between two parties. Latu, for instance, explained that he was not going to attend a wedding in a village to the northeast of Helambu because his and the groom's families did not agree. "We don't mix well," he said while holding his two index fingers at cross angles. An aesthetic of social assonance thus often defines social ties and motivates demands for personal propriety. To keep the social peace, villagers usually strive to achieve a smooth personal facade when interacting with others. For instance, when Yolmo wa are frustrated with others, they often try to retain a calm demeanor to hide their anger. I once told Karma of the times when I expressed anger in Helambu. "We don't have that here," he said. "We don't show it. If you're very angry you might just break out and fight. So you won't show your anger until suddenly it explodes."

Yolmo wa have, like other citizens of Nepal, a penchant for making plans to do things without intending to show up. For Karma, they agree to such terms merely to appease their friends: "They just want to be agreeable;

they don't think of the consequences [of later causing disappointment or anger]." It is better, that is, to agree rather than to disagree when talking with another, even though any mutual accord reached may be impermanent or superficial. Immediate surface harmony usually takes precedence over any "inner" antagonism between two parties, and fights occasionally occur when the surface harmony can no longer be maintained.

An aesthetic of smooth surfaces also relates to local ideas of guilt and shame, for villagers are troubled more over issues of shame—of being socially condemned, of feeling "shy" (*ngo*, "no")—than with notions of private guilt.[40] Indeed, as Karma pointed out, there is no word for "guilt" in the Yolmo language, and moral ideals seem to reflect social relationships more than introspective concerns. "People are just worried about what others will think," he explained. The result: villagers tailor many behaviors in response to how they might be regarded by others.

As it is essential to control one's personal desires in deference to the social welfare, Yolmo wa stress the need for self-restraint. In fact, Yolmo psychophysiology seems founded on these concerns. A person needs to inhibit personal desires falling against the social grain, and the brain censors the heartmind's whims. Deliriums of illness, in turn, can trigger a pathologic lack of self-control. "You cannot control the heartmind when you're unhealthy," Latu told me. "If you have a very high fever, you won't even know where you are. You might be speaking out words from your heartmind without even knowing." When the body is thrown off-balance, feelings of desire and anger, no longer bottled within the heartmind, override self-control. "Alcohol," a villager explained, "tells us to do the opposite of what we should do. It increases the emotion. A person becomes angry, wants to hit people. The brain cannot control the heartmind any longer. The person does whatever he wants to do, says whatever he wants to say, without the brain's control." The dangers of delirium and inebriation, in other words, are that a person can no longer contain or "hold" volatile emotions within the heart. The subsequent tensions between subjective passions and collective mores threaten the delicate harmony that needs to exist within and between bodies, households, and villages.

Presence

Along with struggling to control subjective desires, Yolmo wa often strive for perceptual control of their behavioral environment. Villagers, perhaps aware of the dangers of mountain living (one man died when he slipped into a ravine one foggy morning), seem, from my perspective, to continuously attend to what's going on around them. Context is all-important to Yolmo wa, and illness can strike when this familiarity is lacking. A young girl wishes to be photographed in front of her home (rather than with the backdrop of snow-white summits that the ethnographer preferred), ghosts prey on the distracted, and life-forces are lost when a person is alone, becomes frightened, or loses his or her footing. Dreams of encountering strangers or wandering in foreign lands often presage illness, a fact that underscores Yolmo fears of unfamiliar places. *Behos* (n.) or "unconsciousness," finally, may occur on hearing startling news: as Karma said of fainting in general, the heartmind thinks "what to do" and the person, "unable to do anything," faints.

We can counterpose the ever-present needs for solid perceptual footings to those of Balinese, who, according to Bateson and Mead, occasionally drift off into detached moments of "awayness" and thus remain imperceptive to the world around them.[41] In contrast, Yolmo wa exude an ambience of "hereness": a person attends to the flux of life around her, chats with others, smokes a cigarette, shoos fluttery chickens.

Kinesthetic attentiveness is a necessary ingredient for health, for it is best not to dwell on what memories recall or what the future promises. I was told on several occasions that if the heartmind lingers too long in the past or in a different land (such as when a person languishes over the absence of loved ones), its owner may fall ill due to its prolonged absence from the body. It is therefore dangerous to speak of those who "have no need for names" (the dead) for their memories invoke an incurable longing for the past. "If you think about the dead person," Meme advised, "then your heartmind will go with him. In general, you don't want to think too much about the past, for the *sems* will stay there, and you will become sick." It is best, then, to keep thoughts focused on the here and now, with the living rather than the dead.

A Yolmo wa should separate reality from imagination (and present from past); he or she must also avoid undue tension between what the heartmind desires and what the body can possibly achieve—as regulated by the brain. "What the *sems* thinks," Meme noted, "and the brain orders to do—like building a home—but you cannot do, then you will become affected, you might fall ill." The danger of unfulfilled desires combines with the heartmind's imaginative excursions outside the body. "If you think of some place," one farmer imagined, "then your heartmind goes there. If

Photo 8. Presence.

your body can't go there, as in planning to go on a pilgrimage, you will become sick, for your *sems* remains at this place after thinking about it. . . . If your heartmind goes to many places [thinks a lot], then it affects the brain, for it cannot decide what to do or what to focus on." And so a villager must "keep the heartmind clear" by prohibiting it from dwelling on times, places, or possibilities that cannot be realized. What the body requires for health is a mindful presence in its immediate environment, free of lingering distractions.

Purity

The body, like the heartmind, should be kept "clean." As with other Himalayan peoples, Yolmo wa typically strive to keep their forms free of "pollution" or *sgrib* ("tip"). In Helambu, *sgrib* falls "like a shadow" on a person's form, causing discomfort by adhering to the surfaces of the body. Pollution is felt to be an external blemish, manifested in skin rashes and wounds, which causes the afflicted to feel slow-witted and fatigued.[42] The local logic relates to the way in which villagers give spatial form to the link between body and soul: as the defilement derives from material contaminations external to the person, it primarily affects the surfaces of the body. But as a dirty container soils its holdings, so a body's impurities can taint one's spiritual life.

The concern for purity seeps through many of the domains of Yolmo social life. As pollution often leads to misfortune, a person will not take food touched by another, nor eat with the (feces-cleansing) left hand. Women are considered impure when menstruating. On leaving a cremation, villagers "cleanse" their bodies with incense and water. Childbirth, like death, brings pollution, and the place of birth is defiled until purifed by a lama. For fear of pollution, shamans should not enter a house where a person has died or a child recently born. Unless a bombo is pure, deities will not enter his body to divine: "The gods won't accept us," Meme advised. Nor will they accept an impure sacrificial animal. In short, much thought is put into keeping the body free of spiritual pollutants, for fear that its owner will suffer harm if tainted by them. Consequently, feelings of fatigue or weariness can spark concerns that the body has been soiled. These concerns tie into notions of social status and relational selves, for "pollution" can be transferred from one person (usually of lower status) to another (usually of higher status).

Karma

And yet an even more pervasive force than *sgrip* affects Yolmo experience, for as the lay of a land shapes a river's path, so one's "karma" (*las*, "le"; "work" or "action") determines the course of a person's life. The idea that a person's behavior determines, and is determined by, future and past behaviors descends from the theological tenets of Tibetan Buddhism. In Helambu, as in other parts of South Asia, the concept of karma involves a cosmic theory of causation, an ideology of unequal suffering, an "as you sow, so shall you reap" moral philosophy.[43] Karma's teleological principle determines the "fruits" of human action, from the nature of a person's rebirth in a future life to the length of his or her "life-span" (*tshe*) in the present. For Yolmo wa, the stress is on the determinative. "Humans cannot change the *tshe*," Meme said, "we can only mend it [restore its proper length]."

Yolmo wa consider a person's karma to be inscribed on a mirror lodged within the skull. "Everything," one villager affirmed, "is written on the forehead. What will happen to you, when you will become ill, when you will die." This means that death as well as life is fated. The mirror reflects the coming of *Yama Rāj* (n.), the god of the dead, who decides when a person is to die. "*Yama Rāj* is like a forester," Latu once said, "who puts signs on trees, saying when they will be cut. We have our fates marked out for us by *Yama Rāj* on our backs and foreheads."

The logic of karma fits into the "order" (*chos*, "cho") of the universe, a "customary way" on which religious action is based. *Chos* is a Tibetan word that can be alternatively glossed as the "doctrine," "law," or, more commonly, the "dharma" of the Tibetan universe.[44] Yet Buddhist dharma refers less to a concrete cosmology than to a metaphysical system. By its very nature, the system determines the proper order of the universe and so defines which actions are correct and proper. As Clarke writes of *chos* in Helambu, "It has a sense of 'morality' or 'correctness,' but it is not just the religious order in the sense that religion has today in the West: it is *the* proper order which stands behind all aspects of nature and culture, behind all possible worlds. If there is a landslide, if there is a storm, if one is sick, if a building collapses, if trade is bad, the answer is always *chos*."[45]

A villager's actions intrinsically relate to the proper order, but either in a positive or negative way (improper actions, for instance, counter the proper order of the universe). The cumulative effect of these actions then determines a person's "merit" (*bsod nams*). And since personal "merit" itself ties into the teleological determinism of *chos*, "merit" defines the nature of a person's future actions, welfare, and status. Villagers thus often try to act in a way that increases their amount of merit, with acts of "virtue (*dge ba*, "gewa") increasing and those of "vice" (*sdig pa*, "dikpa") decreasing this amount.[46] The accumulation of merit advances one's moral worth, which can be cashed in for a better life: a high store of merit at the end of this and previous lifetimes contributes to a higher status (and so further prosperity and health) in future lifetimes.

While Yolmo wa acknowledge that karma determines the vicissitudes of life (from falling off a cliff to becoming a drunkard), they simultaneously fear the whimsical attacks of malevolent shades. Whereas the priestly lamas often hold that illnesses are determined by a person's karma, shamans rarely speak of a cosmic determination of personal action. For them and most villagers, illnesses typically derive from more worldly, capricious concerns—innocently urinating on the home of a serpent-deity (*klu*), bumping into a ghost at a crossroads, becoming the prey of an envious witch. Aware of the lama's philosophy, villagers live the shaman's creed.[47] Fate sculpts the contours of a person's life, but the shadowy details of this work leave room for chance. For the most part, villagers approach these uncertainties with apprehension.

Overall, the notion of karma contributes to the dominant ethical principles of most Yolmo wa. The flip side of the Karmic law—that whatever a person does, good or bad, comes round again—provides a strong motivating force for behavior. Many good deeds are conducted because the actor believes that he or she will reap its rewards in a later life. "It's all your karma," villagers say, "the works you do now are the things that decide your future." Meme, for instance, said he performed the strenuous work of healing to assure himself of "a good place in heaven." And so along with determining a person's future actions, local notions of "merit" often shape behavior in subtler ways as well. Indeed, as Clarke observes, they also legitimate the hegemony of lama landlords over tenet farmers: the latter group, if they are to increase their merit and so improve their impoverished position, must act according to Buddhist precepts and support the temples of their landlords.[48]

Much goes into the crafting of Yolmo ways of being. We have seen here that, just as Yolmo experiences are bound by karma's guiding hand, so implicit aesthetic principles apparently shape not only how villagers interpret their experiences but also how they live and lend value to them. Ideally, the body is a distinct whole, a center of energy and awareness, a sacred harmonium suggesting a unified gestalt. But as this is a unity built of distinct parts, diverse bodily functions, such as the brain and heartmind, need to work in accord with one another, communicating and coordinating their actions. The stress on physiological balance holds true for psychological notions as well, for a villager must attain an emotional equilibrium in his life. As harmony must reign in social relations, a person must "hold" private desires within the heart, lest they spark social conflicts. Perceptual control over one's behavioral environment must also be continuously worked for, with a state of presence being the desired goal. The body should be kept as pure as the heartmind should be "clean," for pollution can soil the skin and cloud the mind. And karma, which shapes behavior through its teleological determinism, provides the impetus for moral action.

The various qualities of Yolmo experience, abstracted above, appear to pattern the felt sense that someone like Mingma has of his body in moments of illness and health. Qualities of integration, balance, and fortitude tend to define Yolmo bodies in health; a sense of fragmentation, imbalance, and weariness mark them in illness. When Yolmo sensibilities of health are fulfilled, when the various parts of a body are in harmony with themselves and the world at large, a person exudes a vitality and fortitude that, in themselves, define local experiences of health. If decrepitude and decline characterize the body in sickness, strength and integrity tend to mark it in health. When well, the body is often said to be "light," "clean," and "straight." If the heartmind is "big" and the "life-span" is "as complete as the full moon," a person cannot be "touched" by illness. Healthy villagers typically dream of sunrises, sporting new clothes, and climbing high into the Himalayas to drink its untainted snow. "We can do almost anything then!" Latu claimed.

Methods of Madness

And yet there are moments when the balance is thrown off, when life-forces wane, when the heartmind weakens. The body becomes frail, prone to attack. Its inner mechanics cease to work well together; psychological functions become "mixed" and thrown off course. A person becomes sickly, disheartened, and confused. Tattered clothes and decrepit houses cloud one's dreams. Body and soul no longer signal health.

Yolmo "madness" (*smyon pa*, "nyonpa") is one such moment—and one worth examining. By listening to what villagers say of this affliction, how they explain its genesis, interpret its manifestations, and suffer its consequences, we may grasp the underlying values that largely create, in illness as in health, local experiences of body and soul. Alongside the self's looking glass (the cultural ideals of person and behavior) stands a second, more opaque mirror: the image of the mad. Holding this prism up to the first, we spark a dark alchemy: a cultural discourse on what it means to be mad, to be sane, and hence to be Yolmo.

Yolmo sensibilities become a bit clearer if we consider common views of causes and manifestations of "madness" in Helambu. Villagers claim that *smyon pa* results from either psychological malfunctioning or the assault of supernatural forces. If the brain is not "full," if it is retarded or if its "inner part" becomes "broken," it cannot work properly. The afflicted cannot comprehend life around him, for "there is no sense in the mind" and the brain "wanders" erratically and jumps from thought to thought.

As noted above, excessive emotional stress, such as grief or pain, can cause a pathologic imbalance in a person's heartmind. "If a man becomes anxious [*sdug sngal*, "dhukngal"] or feels great sorrow [*sdug*]," said one woman, "he may go mad, roaming about." Mental confusion can also trigger madness: during my apprenticeship, Meme repeatedly warned that if an initiate studies under two gurus he will go mad because the two "learnings" (n. *bidyā*) do not "mix." Imbalances also disturb the inner workings of the body: usually all components stay in the "right place," but sometimes organs become "mixed." One man went further: "Everything thinks, 'What to do, where to go,' with no particular decision, then things become mixed, and madness comes."

Witches, deities, demons, or the "forest shaman" can also cause *smyon pa*. Madness accompanies shamanic experiences throughout the world,[49] and among Yolmo wa the *ri bombo* may strike one with madness. When this "forest shaman" kidnaps an adolescent to teach him shamanism, the boy might go mad if he is impure or if the instruction ends unfinished (as when villagers try to rescue him from the forest). The initiate is then torn between the sacred and the profane: "He cannot be a proper man, he cannot be a proper shaman." The *ri bombo* assaults lay citizens at times, inducing madness, paralysis, or causing his victim to go deaf, dumb, or "shake like a shaman" (epilepsy?). I attended the healing of one woman, Sumjok, who was attacked by the *ri bombo* after a painful miscarriage; Sumjok appeared withdrawn, morose, tense—a striking image of the forest shaman's power to inflict distress.

As with its etiology of imbalances, and impurities, and the erratic assaults of supernatural forces, many of *smyon pa*'s effects on body and mind inversely reflect cultural ideals of personhood. When the cultural units of self-identity fall apart (as they do with madness), its pieces shatter into patterns no less recognizable, for the aesthetic sensibilities that structure cultural experience also teach a person how to go crazy. In Helambu, images of madness, conveyed through villagers' explanations, tacitly address the values and ideals of Yolmo experience, precisely because they assume a form inversely reflective of them. It is as if Yolmo wa were advising, to paraphrase Devereux on ethnic disorders, "Don't go crazy, but, if you do, you must behave as follows . . ."[50]

According to Yolmo wa, the stress on kinesthetic presence dissolves, for the mad cease to attend to the reality around them. "*Smyon pa* people see and hear things that we cannot see. Sometimes they sing songs, sometimes they cry, laugh." A person afflicted with *smyon pa* becomes senseless of his actions; he cannot "contain" his thoughts or dreams. Roaming the forest or uninhabited lands—asking "where to go, what to do"—he walks "thoughtlessly, without purpose."

As with drunkenness, motor coordination falters; the body's sense of balance stumbles. "When healthy, a person walks straight, but when *smyon pa* comes, he doesn't know the straight way and might walk crooked and fall down."

"Madness" comes and goes, disrupting one's life, causing erratic behavior patterns. "Suddenly it attacks [n. *chhopnu* 'covers'], suddenly he clearly remembers, suddenly it leaves [n. *chornu* 'separates']. It causes this line [pattern]."

The brain loses control of the heartmind, and thoughts, no longer censored, sound out. "He speaks without care, saying whatever comes to mind."

Self-restraint breaks down, prohibitions are ignored, proper human behavior effaced. "He just likes to wander about, not wanting to stay in the house. He doesn't like to work." "He catches everything near and around him. He tries to eat everything, even if it's not food." "He'll enter someone's home, grab their food, spit it out."

Emotions usually kept within the heartmind reveal themselves inappropriately to others: "Some walk all day crying, showing their sorrow."

The mad discard the garments defining their social identity: "He tears off his clothes, walks naked."

The social ambience that pervades so much of Yolmo life perishes, for the mad shun human relations. They are said to wander alone in forests while their heartminds linger in foreign lands. "Some do not speak with anybody. Sometimes they walk 'straight' [not talking to anyone]."

The loss of presence, mental balance, and motor coordination; the lack of restraint; the shunning of social relations and proper human conduct; the destruction, in sum, of the relational self—these are Yolmo methods of madness, elicited and formed by the aesthetic values that impinge on Yolmo experience. There is an economy of morals here, a "technology" of the self as Foucault uses the term: a set of "rules, duties, and prohibitions . . . which permit individuals to effect by their own means or with the help of others a certain number of operations on their own bodies and souls, thoughts, conduct, and way of being, so as to transform themselves in order to attain a certain state of happiness, purity, wisdom, perfection, or immortality."[51] An aesthetics of experience sets cultural norms for conduct and so regulates the ideal proprieties on which villagers base, judge, and transform personal actions. The values bodied forth by the aesthetic mesh with (and secure) the vital political concerns of Lamas, and the aesthetic values according to which villagers compose bodily experience compare to those according to which they compose social relations.

The idea that methods of madness reflect core cultural values is not an original one.[52] But I want to stress that cultural values and perspectives on mental illness both accord with an aesthetics of the mundane. Since life's pathologies define the nature of Yolmo health as much as its harmonies do, images of illness tend to reflect the tacit aesthetic sensibilities—and so ethical principles—that guide Yolmo behavior. These varied sensibilities contribute to the artistry of everyday experience among Yolmo villagers. Together, they provide the aesthetic means through which a woman dresses in the morning, a child runs through a village, or an elder squats low to the ground to smoke a cigarette.

"Just Ill From Old Age"

The sensibilities also situate more than a few instances of pain within a lament of loss and decline. When I visited Mingma at his home a week after his healing, he led me to a wooden bench on the edge of a clearing alongside his house, where his grandchildren were playing. He took off his coat, folded it, placed it on the bench, then sat down on it. I took my place next to him, and his grandson ran over and climbed up onto his lap.

Mingma was caring for the child and the child's elder sister while their parents sowed millet in a sloping field to the east of the house. The monsoon rains had temporarily abated and sunlight broke through the cloud cover and lit up patches of the muddy ground. He spoke in low, quiet tones, pausing often, eyes still.

"I'm just ill from old age, getting older, and afraid of dying."

Any discussion of Yolmo sensibilities (the push for harmony, integration, control, purity, or presence) inevitably pales in the presence of Mingma's own speech and gestures. Yet aren't these same sensibilities, dull in the abstract, responsible for much of the power of Mingma's few words?

As I see it, Mingma's loss of strength and vitality embodied a culture-specific interpretation of human aging, an interpretation infused with cultural ideals and societal values.[53] While some societies portray illness through vegetative imagery (the body "decays," "withers," but subsequently "rejuvenates"),[54] and others draw on metaphors of the body as factory, machine, or metropolis (physiologies "break down" but "get fixed" if in need of "repair"),[55] Yolmo wa often speak of illness as a tenacious process of physical and spiritual entropy. In Helambu, the "age of darkness," the present Buddhist epoch, is marked by moral deterioration (*nyams pa*); Yolmo bodies are troubled by similar dissolutions. Spiritual (and hence physical) affliction often relates to a deterioration of vital life-forces. The image of the moon highlights the process: life-forms wax and wane through the reincarnations of life.

Mingma's body seemed to erode like a waning moon. The loss accorded with Yolmo aesthetic values, embodied sensibilities that spoke of dispersal, fragmentation, and decline. The *srog*, which were the backbone of Mingma's strength and support, were lost, one by one, to the land of the dead. He lost sleep, suffered pains, lacked an appetite and a sense of presence. He dreamed of corpses, cremation grounds, and downhill descents. He had been walking at night, alone, on a road, in darkness. As with the misfortunes of other villagers, this malaise came with the lingering sense that it was a natural, even fated, process. "*Jiwan esta chha*" they say in the Nepalese hills, "Life is like this."

As Mingma's story suggests, the aesthetic sensibilities of a people condition the sensory form that personal malaise takes. With Mingma, they positioned his pain within a cadence of loss. Local political concerns pattern the tenor of such a cadence. The threats of social fission, reviewed above, have led to high values placed on harmony and integration. These values apparently contribute to the felt qualities of bodily experience. Good health, by its very nature, entails a sense of balance, harmony, wholeness, purity, and presence. Illness takes form through images of dismemberment, impurity, decay, and loss—an absence of form.

Mingma's losses, it thus appears, reflected some of the basic concerns of his society. And since the concerns seemed natural, so did the losses. To some extent, Mingma's lament engaged a culturally valued way to grow old. In Helambu, there are proper, "sensible" ways to age, to lose vitality, to feel pain (ways, that is, which accord with bodily dispositions and cultural ways of being). Intrinsic to these ways of suffering are aesthetic sensibilities that tell what imageries of illness (a cremation pyre, a waning life-force) are all about. Values of harmony and integration provide the configurations through which experiences take form and lend a sense of moral significance to those experiences when communicated to others. Mingma's aging body, with its waning vitality, might have conveyed for him and his neighbors a culturally patterned sense of loss and decay. If so, the idiom of communication was one of value and image; the visions of dead men and downhill descents, given the aesthetic system within which they took place, said what ailed him through a patterning of images.

Life-forces are lost, Mingma tells us, "when a man is frightened while walking at night, alone, on a road, in darkness." The meaning of a solitary jaunt lies in the poetic force it embodies, the associations it evokes—the threat to one's balance, self-control, and sense of presence. These associations, if they are significant ones, correspond to tacit forms of experience and the themes and tensions occasioned by those forms. It is this formal resonance, this consummation of aesthetic forms, that can make a tale such as Mingma's a particularly telling and engaging one for its listeners. The aesthetic sensibilities that influence Yolmo experience can lead to the sense that it is only natural that Mingma's body and spirit erode as they do. But this erosion, precisely because it recalls the tensions, fears, and concerns intrinsic to many Yolmo forms, can evoke a ghostly presence that touches the lives of those who learn of it in its concrete manifestation: an old man, sitting on a bench, grandson in lap.

Embodied aesthetics pattern the ghostly presences of cultural experience. Because of this, the way in which we should go about understanding their force and tenor is less like interpreting a text[56] or unraveling a symbolic code[57] than it is like appraising a series of art works—the artistry of human forms—to apprehend and experience their style, tone, texture, and overall mood or spirit. The ways Mingma wields his body or engages with others in everyday life is more a matter of "composition" than of belief, symbol, or deep logical "structure." Any study of these compositions must come to terms with their meanings, but it must also assess the ways in which cultural sensibilities assert particular values to those meanings and how, in turn, values register, as felt qualities, in the everyday.

The fact that the compositions take shape through images calls for a novel form of ethnography. It becomes less important to map the semiotic lineage or intellectual heritage of specific imageries than it is to evoke their presence in concrete manifestations (a weathered house, a waning moon) so that the reader can sense and evaluate their force and significance. We must also consider how human experiences are variably composed within a cultural setting, and the moral, philosophic, and political "building blocks" of these compositions. What are the culturally honed values, forms, and constraints that go into the making or unmaking of a "healthy" person? In an attempt to answer this question, we have searched out some of the living metaphors (broken bones and bodies), ghostly imageries (darkness, degeneracy, deadly descents), and patterned similarities (hierarchical societies and ordered physiologies) that make up the bodies and households of Mingma and his neighbors. In subsequent chapters, we consider how Yolmo sensibilities relate to feelings of pain, senses of spiritlessness, and a calling of lost souls.

4. Pain Clings to the Body

> With head placed on a pillow,
> puddles an ocean of tears
> sorrow falls to the daughter,
> whichever way she turns
>
> Whichever way she turns,
> pain clings to the body
> Oh precious one have pity,
> pain clings to the body

Padma Lama, a prestigious, heavyset "priest" from the village of Dhup-chughyang, helped to perform the anniversary funeral rites for a Todhang woman who died the previous May. He danced and drank a bit at the close of the ceremonies, walked at night with his wife and neighbors up to their homes, slept in his wood-framed bed, and died, for unknown reasons, sometime during the night. Latu and other lamas cremated the body the next morning, then performed a series of funeral rites at Padma's home, which culminated in the *sbyang par* ("changpar") rites conducted in the aging temple in Dhupchugang within forty-nine days of the death.[1] On the third and final evening of these rites, a procession of lamas, trumpet-bearing musicians, and mourners slowly walked from the temple, climbed down a hillside path lined with green stalks of corn, and entered into Padma's home to receive an effigy (*tshab*, "sob") of his body made of his clothes, a funerary "crown," and a white cloth (and the glasses he wore in life) for the face. The lamas accepted a ceremonial tea as they sat beside the effigy. They then carried the effigy, protected by an open black umbrella and led by family members carrying foodstuffs and a long, white *lam bstan* ("lamten") banner "showing the road" to heaven, out of the house, back through the cornfield, around a prayer flag, and into the temple to consummate the transmigration of Padma's soul into the heavens "above."

As the lamas walked to the house to receive the effigy, the mood, as with other moments of the funeral, was somber, expectant, reserved. Faces were tense, rigid, but open signs of sorrow were few. A teenage boy

Photo 9. "Showing the road."

announced a different scene as we waited outside Padma's house for the lamas to return to the temple: "Now they bring the dead man out and the people cry," he said, moments before the effigy and banner began to snake out of the house and mourners began to cry while singing a sorrowful dirge and Padma's younger brother, running about to photograph the departure, wailed in loud, painful sobs between snapshots.

What was in this climactic moment that produced a display of sorrow otherwise unexpressed during Padma's funeral (a display that repeated itself with every funeral I attended)? How did the ceremony at this point—effigy, trumpets, and spiritual dirge—trigger openly expressed grief among mourners, signaling that then (and only then) was the time for tears? For villagers, the sight of Padma's effigy being taken from his home affirmed the final departure of his "memory" from the world of the living. As Nyima said of the funeral that she herself declined to attend, "As it was the last day of giving food, the last day of the gathering of relatives, and especially as it was the last departure of the dead person, people's hearts ached [*sems pa tsher ka*]. The memory of the person was leaving, and so their hearts hurt [*sems*

Photo 10. Funeral in Todhang, 1988.

pa sdug po]." Note that, for Nyima, funeral participants did not mourn
Padma's departure so much as his tangible memory, as if an effigy and a
long, white banner were the iconic keys to memory's existence—and memory, like the deceased himself, perished with the dissolution of these images.

Emotional experience, like memory, works through images. Just as the
names of the dead induce their ghostly memory (and thus "should not
be spoken"), so a stream of images—an effigy, funeral dirge, the lamas'
march—effected a world of grief. The mourners' tears during the effigy's
transport were triggered by cultural cues bound within banners and music
that spoke of longing and separation, and thus *sdug* or "sorrow."

After I witnessed several of these events, I asked Karma why he
thought his neighbors felt the way they did during the effigy's transport
from home to temple. Aware of my desire to relate image to experience, he
brought to mind the cremation process, when villagers carry the corpse to a
hilltop to burn it, and the sentiments of grief spontaneously invoked by that
journey. "It may simply be social background [conditioning]," he suggested, "but they are not pretending. It just happens simultaneously. Even

when they are taking the body to the cremation ground, and they see the ground, they have some different reaction. If you have to describe it, it's a kind of illusion that makes them do that. Everything is like that. Because their relation binds them to whoever is dead, binds them in a kind of love."

For Karma, the sight of the cremation ground triggers feelings of longing and binding love among the bereaved. The sentiment is a common one in Helambu, where a death is thought to negate the "bonds" between loved ones, and funerals help the bereaved to realize their losses. Once the lamas carried Padma's effigy within the temple, they orchestrated a series of rites. Family members offered foods to Padma, whose "soul" (*rnam shes*) rested within the effigy, but they did so with arms crossed at the wrists to signify the inverted exchange of living to dead. They performed protestations to absolve him of any "vices" committed while he was alive. His brother, wife, and son then spoke to Padma, telling him that he was dead and that, since he could no longer remain with loved ones, he should not "contain" them within his heart.

"You are now apart from us," they pleaded, "you mustn't love us anymore. Just eat these things and go!"

Earlier the lamas divined that Padma's soul "clung" to his daughter's at death. They therefore "cut" the two souls apart in exorcistic fashion: a black string was tied from the daughter's to the effigy's left hand, and a white string linked the two right hands. When the black string was severed, the daughter fled from the room, taking the white string with her. Finally, the head lama transferred Padma's "soul" onto a sheet of rice paper enscribed with a human figure and with words marking his name, sex, and other biographical information. The lama annulled the sins of Padma by setting fire to this "purification paper" (*shyang par*, "changpar"): Padma's soul escaped into the land "above" in the form (it is said) of a white letter "A" while the effigy was dismantled into a pile of loose clothes.

The *shyang par* rites, as they are collectively called in Helambu and in Tibet, can be read as dissolving Padma's relational self. Similar transactions, wherein the living sever their social ties with the dead, are common to funeral rites throughout the world.[2] In Helambu, Yolmo society is based on relations within and among several corporate groups (household, family, village), such that villagers experience selfhood in terms of these relations. The strength of this "relational" self is most evident when it becomes most problematic—in death. No longer alive, Padma had to be separated from the living. The funeral rites achieved (symbolically, at least) this separation. The absolution of "sins" and "debts," the separation of the dead from the

Photo 11. Effigy of the deceased, Todhang, 1988.

Photo 12. Burning the "purification paper."

living (inverted exchange, declaration of death, cutting of familial bonds), and the re-creation and disintegration of Padma's identity (incineration of identifying paper, dismantling of cloth effigy) marked a transformation of his social identity, divesting him of the rooted relatedness that characterizes, in life but not in death, Yolmo experience.

Yet letting go for villagers involves more than a few ritual sleights of hand: the dismemberment of Padma's identity was not achieved without evoking sentiments of grief and pain among the bereaved. These sentiments were most evident when family members talked to the deceased, tearfully explaining that he must leave, and during the lamas' procession that led to this scene, with its dirge of remembrance. Anthropologists have often noted that funerary rites "recreate the elementary structure of the society of the living, a society temporarily threatened in the breach of death," as Holmberg eloquently writes of Tamang mortuary feasts.[3] With Yolmo wa, however, death threatens not only the integration of the society but also the welfare of particular members of that society. A death severs the "bonds" of love between family members, spawns feelings of loss and longing among the bereaved, and thus calls for ritual measures to attend to that pain.

∗   ∗   ∗

One way in which villagers collectively come to terms with loss is to sing of it, and I want to consider the power of Yolmo funerary poetry to create feelings of longing, love, and comfort, and so evoke and alleviate personal distress. The scene, again, is the conclusion of the funeral ceremonies. While the *sbyang par* rites take place inside the temple, with the deceased's soul being sent "above," a second group of lamas and mourners gather in an open clearing to participate in the final religious rite of *mani*. Here, lamas chant from Tibetan religious texts as a community of women chorus the Buddhist prayer *om mani padme hum*. After sunset, while the *sbyang par* rites wind down, the seated chanting turns into dance as the lamas, followed by the women, walk in a circle in time to the graceful lead of the cymbal-bearing senior lama. Soon a bonfire is built, and around this fire two groups of men and women dance, each group constituting a chain of interlinking arms that forms a complete, revolving circle. First the singers chant a formal series of religious *mani* hymns that aid the deceased's soul in its journey "above," and then, toward dawn, they sing of "pain" and "sorrow."

Villagers sing "songs of pain" (*tsher glu*, "tsherlu") alone or in a group—a boy herding cattle in the forest, a band of women traveling to a distant funeral. I have heard a young girl sing of "pain in the heart" (*sems pa tsher ka*) while collecting kindling in the forest, and an adolescent whistle a sad tune while navigating a mountain path. During ceremonial occasions, such as funerals or the Tibetan New Year (*lo gsar*, "losar"), same-sex groups exchange verses, often in time to intricate dances. As the men and women sing group duets at funerals, they exchange *tsher glu* couplets: as the men complete the first line of one couplet (1a, as below), the women begin theirs (2a); then the men finish the second line (1b), and the women complete their couplet (2b)—only to be followed by a new couplet started by the men (3a), and so on in a gradually quickening tempo (4a, 3b, 4b, 5a . . .)—such that sets of couplets are interwoven like the fingers of two intertwining hands:

	MEN	WOMEN
1a	There is nothing but heart-ache, we are never happy	
2a		Amongst the *pama balu*, [flies] the *kesan dolma* bird

Photo 13. Funeral dance steps.

1b Father is nothing but remem-
    bered,
    he is never forgotten

2b   Do not mind your sorrow,
                                    the *balu* flowers may bloom

3a Let us not feel heartaches,
    let us not sing songs of pain

4a   Do not mind your aching
                                    heart,
                                    do not mind your weary body

3b The year our father passed
    away,
    we had to sing songs of pain

4b   Even if you feel sorrow now,
                                    once you may be happy

5a As we feel thirsty,
    we reach the side of a river

6a   On one rhododendron,
                                    flower buds are blooming

5b   When remembering father,
      we reach a forested summit
6b   Like the blossoming flower,
                                          may your hearts also bloom

    I wish to examine closely this late night song to suggest how its lyrics might help in the passage from grief to comfort. For, whereas the final journey of the effigy moves men and women to tears, this and other songs transcend feelings of pain to invoke an atmosphere of community and celebration. Yet to grasp the transformative poetics of the song, we must develop an understanding of emotionality in Helambu, from the complexities of "heartaches" and "sorrows" to the social nature of distress and the local ethos of emotional restraint and avoidance. As I see it, these motifs form within the song an interwoven world of image, affect, and experience; the meaning and efficacy of the song is tied to the set of contextual relations from which each couplet draws.[4] The song works by alluding to distant realms of experience—other songs, ghostly memories, the pains and tensions of Yolmo life. "Words with a sideward's glance," the Russian critic Mikhail Bakhtin wrote, gaze out at other words and other contexts.[5]

    I first stumbled on Yolmo "songs of pain" six months into my field stay, in early October, when, while trekking through the central ridge of Helambu, I stayed overnight in a lodge run by a Yolmo family. After I told them why I was living in Helambu, a son pulled out a pamphlet containing several Yolmo songs printed in Nepali script. The book was penned several years back by an amateur Swiss missionary who lived in Helambu long enough to learn the local language and compose an anthology of folk songs. Along with "drinking," "flirting," and religious songs were several *tsher glu* or "songs of pain," including the one above. That evening, I was able to translate just a few words with my hosts' assistance, but the lyrics that I did understand struck me with their beauty and poignancy. Couplets such as "There is nothing but heartache, we are never happy" revealed much of what I intuitively sensed of the Yolmo ethos but was unable to pin down in talking with the villagers. Though the Lama people, like other Sherpa groups, present a singularly jovial disposition to outsiders, in time one senses a mix of tension beneath the surface smiles.[6] Along with these "inner" tensions, many of the songs spoke of *tsher ka*, a heartfelt "pain" or "affliction" not much discussed in everyday discourse, though often present like a shadow. Hoping, then, that these songs could open a window into aspects of Yolmo life that villagers were unwilling or unable to discuss otherwise (I was curious as to how "heartaches" matched the depressive languor marking "soul loss"), I asked to borrow the songbook, hoping to translate it with Karma's help.

Soon I was back in Gulphubanyang, roaming the countryside with pain-songs in my pockets, reciting to willing ears the couplets I had transcribed and asking my audience what this poetry was about. I asked them to tell me what *tsher ka* meant, what it felt like when it pained their hearts. They responded as best they could, in words I cite below. As I hoped, the songs were distanced enough from the front lines of local feelings to provide a safe forum for the discussion of Yolmo distress. Villagers sang to me further songs of separation, offering variations on the couplets I had already collected and a running exegesis of their meaning. Young girls giggled their way through the compositions they knew; Mingma came surreptitiously to my cabin and chanted beautifully of *tsher ka* into my tape recorder.

How I was able to neglect such an important dimension of Yolmo life for so long related, in part, to my single-minded interest in shamanic practices. Although I often heard villagers sing while they foraged for wood, trekked between villages, or danced at funerals, I thought it necessary to first learn the subtleties of the shaman's craft. But more significantly, what I was unable to see was what villagers were reluctant to show me. Yolmo wa hesitate to reveal the more private aspects of their lives, such as personal histories and feelings, especially when confronted by an attentive outsider. Thus while villagers were willing to discuss their songs with me, they refrained from talking of the pain felt in their own lives. Adolescent girls who sang couplets told me only that they were about "pain in the heart"; Mingma sang of *tsher ka* only after shutting my cabin door lest anyone hear him.

Mingma's cautious approach to the songs was typical. For villagers, a few words could evoke painful memories, and personal encounters with *tsher ka* were often best left alone. Indeed, the common notion that "heartaches" and "sorrows" were not simply semantic categories to be discoursed on but deeply felt experiences that were often feared and avoided because they could "cling" to the body, has led me to question the orientation of many recent anthropological studies of emotions. Above all, these studies treat ritual laments and personal expressions of grief as rhetorical strategies tied to the politics of social life rather than as reflections of personal or communal experience.[7] The contributors to a recent symposium entitled "Language and the Politics of Emotion," edited by Lutz and Abu-Lughod, make some of the strongest claims along these theoretical lines. To demonstrate how emotions are used, socially and politically, within a society, they consider emotion as "discourse" rather than as felt experience.[8] The theoretical stance of these scholars, influenced in part by post-structuralist thinkers like Foucault and Bourdieu, holds that we must not mistake discourses on sentiment for bodily experience.[9] Since the "sincerity" of talk on emotions is always in question, investigations into personal experiences of distress are unsound.[10] In turn, a focus on emotion as discourse is necessary in order to pry emotion loose from psychobiology and "the false attribution of the project of psychologizing to others."[11] As a concern for meaning is predominantly a Western one, the "more interesting" tack is to focus on "practice rather than meaning"—a shift from what is "said" in discourse (its "putative referents") to "what discourse is, what it does, and what forms it."[12]

No doubt these orientations offer an invaluable attempt to break through the "prison house of language" created by structuralism and certain strands of semiotics ("where everything but the words themselves are excluded from the field of attention and analysis").[13] They also help us to better understand the social and political contexts in which all emotional experience and expression seems embedded. But it strikes me that the above approaches discuss everything save what poetic discourses themselves seem to speak about: most commonly, profound experiences of grief, sadness, and pain. Abu-Lughod, for instance, argues that a love song recorded by a Bedouin youth—

> My warnings are to the old man
> who imprisons the freedom of youths
> who's forgotten a thing called love
> affection, desire, and burning flames . . .

—embodies a "discourse of defiance" by young men against the political authority and economic control of their fathers and uncles.[14] What is lost in the analysis, however, is the sense of longing and despair also evident in the song. As with other studies, many of the potential resonances of the lyrics, for both poet and audience, are overlooked. Whether this general tendency to neglect the experiential force of plaintive poetry results from quandaries over the sincerity of emotional expressions, a sense of anxiety occasioned by the subject matter, or the professional interests that dominate current anthropological research,[15] I cannot say. But it seems to me that unless we develop a way of talking about the relationship between cultural forms and emotional distress we will continue to skirt what seems to lie at the heart of poetic expressions of grief, sadness, and despair: namely, experiences of grief, sadness, and pain. Since any reference to emotions implies, by definition, something "felt," and since any rhetorician must convince her audience that she is, in fact, feeling the pain or anger to which she refers, we need to take into account the play, however hypothetical, between language and feeling.[16]

For these reasons I offer an approach to Yolmo "songs of pain" distinct from those advocated by the above scholars. Using the funerary song above (printed in uppercase letters) as a basis from which to explore other songs (in lowercase), I want to consider how Yolmo wa talk of *tsher ka*, how they lend music and meaning to it, and how they try to "cut" it from their bodies. I argue, by way of demonstration, that the import and efficacy of the song cannot be fully appreciated without grasping the linguistic echoes that it weaves together. In so doing, I seek not to divorce "meaning" from "practice," but rather to study the two in tandem, mapping the nature of meaning in practice and the social practice of meaning. This is not to overlook the fact that discourses on emotions are distinct from lived experience. Rather, it is to suggest that the relationship between language and experience must be a central focus of study if we are to better understand how cultural discourses on suffering relate to visceral experiences of distress and healing. The songs, often conventional, seldom communicate sentiments of pain in a direct, indexical fashion; they do seem to refer, however, to the felt immediacies common to local experiences of "sorrow" and "heartache".[17] It is these communal experiences, the contexts from which they arise, and how they might be transformed that most concern us here.

*   *   *

Commencing the song with slow, shuffling dance steps and a deep, deliberate harmony, the men begin:

THERE IS NOTHING BUT HEARTACHE,
WE ARE NEVER HAPPY

The opening lyrics, the start of a series of rhyming couplets, follow the theme and structure of many "songs of pain." Each line of a couplet divides into two halves, with each half possessing three words of two syllables each.[18] When sung, the phrase "*ui canchhi*" ("is it not, youngest daughter?") rounds off the first three words of each line, while "*le ro se ro*" ("friends one and all") completes the second three. The couplet above, for instance, sounds as:

sems pa tsher ka min pa, ui canchhi	heart/pain/nothing but
me tsher nam yang mi 'dug le ro se ro	unpained/never/not

The poetic form is identical to other song genres, such as "drinking" and "flirting" songs, with differences in tone, tempo, and context distinguishing the emotional tenors that need to be sustained by the songs. In Helambu, distinct melodies signal precise domains of experience: a lama's chants involve a steady, lyrical exposition of syllables, a shaman's repertoire includes a range of frantic beats, and "songs of pain" engage a somber cadence of voice. Couplets of the latter songs typically begin with a clear and singular statement, move through the melody charted by the dyadic words, then fall with *le ro se ro* into an abrubt and resonant silence. A doleful, spirited tone accompanies the best of performances: when Mingma sang into my tape recorder, he chose a soft and delicate melody which, at the end of each couplet, bottomed out into silence.

Slow, sonorous, lugubrious, the opening words "call the context"[19] of the present song—that there is nothing but *tsher ka*. "What is *tsher ka*?" is thus the first question we must ask, as I did several villagers.

"It's so unpleasant," warned Pemba, recently separated from her natal village by marriage. "When you have to go to a new place—that kind of feeling."

Meme, who lost two wives to early deaths, stared uncomfortably into the hearth's fire, "*Tsher ka*, my friend, means the heart is not well."

"With *tsher ka*, there is great pain in the heart," recalled one woman as she offered me a cup of tea.

"*Tsher ka*," an elderly man, marking the anniversary of his wife's death, simply affirmed, "is not good."

"It is like the Nepali *viraha* [longing in separation], it is *udas* [unhappiness], but also *susti* [slowness, lethargy]," Latu's brother Dawa explained, trying to get a handle on *tsher ka*'s semantics.

Tibetan-English dictionaries tell us that *tsher ka* means "sorrow, grief, pain, affliction," while *sems tsher* suggests "fatigue, weariness, and disgust" in the "heartmind."[20] But those are just words, glosses that neither touch on the richness of the sentiment nor address its specific Yolmo qualities.

Tsher ka is distinct from the "sorrow" spawned directly by the death of others. That is *sdug* ("dhuk"), villagers say, a Tibetan term that derives from the pivotal Buddhist notion of *dukkha*, the "suffering" that is the common lot of sentient beings. Whereas the original Pali term *dukkha* includes connotations of "imperfection," "impermanence," and "emptiness" (literally, a life "out of joint"),[21] for Yolmo wa *sdug* refers more to incidents of grief, misery, and bodily pain. *Sdug* typically smacks of a visceral burden that *tsher ka* does not. In opposition to the corporeal "warmth," "comfort," or "happiness" of *skyid po* ("kipu"), *sdug* cuts at the heart and wounds the body, and so includes domains of pain outside of mourning: a hard day's toil in the fields causes "sorrow" as does the loss of one's father. "When one is sick," one man told me, "or has wounds on the foot, people will say, 'Oh *sems pa sdug po*' [the heart hurts]." A body stricken with *sdug* is a weary, overburdened body; a *sems* filled with *sdug* is a heartmind in sorrow. *Tsher ka*, when not associated with the *sems*, can also refer to bodily pains or aches, and the word occasionally refers to a "piercing" pain felt in the back and shoulders (such as Pasang complained of). But while the pain of *sdug* is largely visceral, weighty, and diffuse, that of *tsher ka* is sharp, piercing, and heartfelt.

Tsher ka is also distinct from "worry" or "anxiety." That is *sems khral* ("semghal"). "When your mother and father die, and you don't know what to do," said one young man on his way to collect wood to burn at his mother's anniversary funeral (*nebar*), "that is *sems khral langs zin*." Worry "arises" within the heartminds of the parentless.

Nor is *tsher ka* the sadness that is found in the West. Whereas sadness among Americans connotes feelings of rejection, personal failure, and a lack of control,[22] *tsher ka* speaks more of isolation, a depressive melancholy, an unwelcome pensiveness, and an inability to communicate trials of the heart to others. And there is something finite with *tsher ka* that distinguishes it from the vaguer components of Western sadness. Personal loss, failures and frustrations, grievances and disappointments—all this can be the stuff of America's sadness but not of *tsher ka*.[23]

For *tsher ka* is the pain of separation. Such pain afflicts the heart when the body "cuts" from the company of others ("When," said a young man, "one is separated from one's father"), and one grieves the loss of intimacy affected by such partings. Villagers say that *tsher ka* compares to the Hindu *viraha*, the "longing in separation" in the absence of the beloved, and typically strikes the "heartmind" when a daughter leaves her parents' hearth in marriage, a son ventures alone to India or Kathmandu for employment, or children mourn the death of parents.[24] "If one day your friends all come to your room," the newlywed Pemba explained, "and the next day you're there alone, the heart aches [*sems pa tsher ka*]." For villagers, the relation is simple: isolation equates with *tsher ka*, and this pain induces further distress. As one couplet puts it,

> When the sun shone we were not pained,
> when the sun was lost *tsher ka* fell
> When friends gathered we were not pained,
> when we parted *tsher ka* came

The ironies of *tsher ka* mark the funeral song as well. The men's somber declaration, accented by the use of three negatives ("heart-ache-nothing but, unpained-never-not"), suggests an ethos of despair to be reproved by the women, to which they respond:

AMONGST THE *PAMA BALU*,
[FLIES] THE *KESAN DOLMA* BIRD

Pa ma ba lu nang la,
bya yi ke san sgrol ma

The *pa ma ba lu* tree is as colorful as the *ke san sgrol ma* bird is beautiful. In Helambu, birds represent motion, a freedom of spirit, an escape from the heaviness of the human body and the weariness of Himalayan travel. In Yolmo poetry, birds often reveal the stark ironies of human misfortunes; dwelling in the *pa ma ba lu* tree, the *ke san sgrol ma* flutters in the shadow of another song:

> Above a dead tree,
> no birds circle
> around a daughter feeling *tsher ka*,
> neither friends nor family come

One senses here, and in the couplet above, that *tsher ka* is deeply tied to feelings of isolation and abandonment. Indeed, to villagers, *tsher ka* is a sentiment of and response to loss. But this distress is not simply a loss of friends and intimacy, but a loss of context, a loss of identity. When I asked Mingma what happens when one's heart is filled with *tsher ka*, he responded with a wistful smile, "You ask yourself, 'Who am I?'"

As the definitions suggest, *tsher ka* cannot be divorced from the social contexts in which it occurs. To understand the pain involved, we must consider how much of Yolmo identity relates to others. Yolmo society presently consists of corporate groups (household, family, village) that relate to one another through networks of kin, status hierarchies, and reciprocal exchanges of resources and hospitality. It is precisely because Yolmo experience is founded on a rich network of kindred ties that ruptures in these relationships (such as are symbolized in the funerary *shyang par* rites) are distressing. When a part of the corporate family breaks off, there is heartache. Without the familiar social context of everyday life to guide them, villagers are at a loss to say who they are. To be without family is to amputate much of a person's self-identity. *Tsher ka* is an intersubjective force as much as it is a subjective one, for it is engaged, mediated, and resolved through shifts in one's social context.

Tsher ka cuts at the very heart of Yolmo identity, for perhaps the greatest fear among these people is of being alone. Happiness (*skyid po*, "kipu") is being with others, and villagers almost always strive for this togetherness, whether eating, working, or traveling. Solitude does not comfort as it can in the West. Children can become terrified when they encounter strangers or lose sight of their caretakers, spirits are lost when one ventures alone into the night or forest, and "heartaches" harm those unfortunate enough to be separated from friends and family.

Fears of abandonment do not stop with the cessation of life, for the afterlife can be seen as a terrifying odyssey into solitude. Yolmo wa fear death, Karma and others expressed, primarily because it "cuts" the deceased from loved ones. And if a person does not receive a proper funeral, he or she is destined to haunt the earth as a ghostly *shi'dre*, homeless and destitute. A villager consequently fears being deprived of family, for when she dies there will be no one to assure that her body is properly cremated; this fear often keeps young women from leaving their families when faced with marriage.

But perhaps the most telling image of Yolmo loneliness is the plight of the recent dead. Villagers claim that when a person dies he is unaware that he no longer owns a body. The "soul" (*rnam shes*), devoid of its corporeal abode, wanders through village and pasture, casting no shadows, leaving no footprints, and returns home each day at dusk to eat with family. But since the dead lack corporeal form, the family fails to see or hear him. "What's wrong?" he might ask, as Latu once imagined Padma's plight: "My family doesn't talk with me. They don't give me food. They say 'Come and eat' and partition the food, but they don't serve me. When I talk, they don't respond." Horrified by such negligence, the dead person leaves in despair and slowly learns that he no longer remains with the living.

Separations from family, through death or travel, thus deprive villagers of the familiar context so important to them. Daughters, uprooted from parents and friends, find themselves in an abyssal "nowhere":

My father, my father,
why has your life been shortened
father when your life was shortened,
your daughter found herself to be nowhere

—while sons seek counsel from surrogate fathers:

To me who has no father,
head lama,
please offer me guidance

to me who has no father,
wise official,
please offer me counsel

For Yolmo wa, the loss of family and intimacy profoundly disrupts one's personal life. *Tsher ka* leads one to pine away and languish over the broken bonds of intimacy. The thoughts invoked by *tsher ka*'s descent on the heart (recollections of home life, remembrances of lost lives) invite distraction and discontent. "With *tsher ka*," Karma said, contrasting it with the more visceral pain of *sdug*, "you become more pensive, you start thinking about yourself: 'If I weren't here, what would I be doing.' You think what other members of your family may be doing."

The questions asked of others' lives soon reflect back on a person's own, for in *tsher ka* one begins to probe the components of personal identity. When separations disrupt the context supporting one's identity, they throw the identity itself into question. Similar to Mingma's doubts ("Who am I?"), another man conceded that, with *tsher ka*, "You ask what lies within your heart." While introspection of this kind can be valued in the West, in Helambu it is unwelcome, even feared. Such brooding triggers further melancholy; an excessive amount can cause madness.

Discomfort of this kind can make the mind unsettled and restless, clouded and confused. Soon the heartmind cannot focus on a single subject and wanders through the landscape of one's thoughts. "When you go to a new place, you feel *tsher ka*, you don't know anyone, your heartmind keeps wandering, going hither and thither," a farmer said with a sweep of his arm over the expanse of hills before us.

The distracted wanderings of the heart often induce a restlessness of the body, for an unsettled *sems* makes a person unwilling to stay put. "*Tsher ka*," one woman told me in the mist of the monsoon, "is when you don't feel like staying in your house any longer, and wish to wander about, such as in the forest." With *tsher ka*, a villager becomes restless, jittery, anxious.

The restlessness of *tsher ka* makes work difficult. The most common definition of *tsher ka* offered by villagers was that it meant "feeling lazy" in the sense of not wanting to work or move constructively about: the anxious pensiveness of *tsher ka* causes a lethargy of body and spirit. "With *tsher ka*, you don't feel like working," one woman explained. "You sit down to work, but find you're not up to it." I asked Karma what the body felt like with *tsher ka*. "If you're not feeling well," he said, "if you're feeling lousy, as with *tsher ka*, then you don't have any energy in your body."

With *tsher ka*, finally, a person sees life through melancholy eyes. "When you have *tsher ka*," one man explained, "and think about a topic, it makes you sad. . . . It is like this: you might be thinking it's funny, but when you have *tsher ka*, you might be weeping."

Yolmo "heartaches" reinforce, and are reinforced by, the Buddhist sense of "suffering" that patterns many Himalayan cultures. Although it is often problematic to trace, in a straightforward fashion, the folk religions of Himalayan societies back to their parent institutions (the so-called Great Traditions of India and Tibet),[25] it seems clear, in this case, that Yolmo attitudes toward suffering derive from the basic tenets of Buddhist religion, including the Buddha's Four Noble Truths.[26] The first of these truths, that "life is suffering [*dukkha*]," infuses Yolmo perspectives on life with a particular ethos. Philosophically, Yolmo conceive of mortal existence as a "wandering" or "passing through" (*samsara*) of successive lives, an unending cycle of birth, misery, and death as determined by the karmic law. The basic way to transcend worldly misery, the lamas say, is by performing acts of merit. Yet it may be that the awareness of the reality of suffering in the Helambu valley helps villagers to get on with their lives as much as any devotion to religion does. Similar to the Sri Lankan Buddhist theology of "hopelessness, suffering and sorrow" that (as Obeyesekere observes) makes meaningful those affective states considered "depressive" in the West,[27] "songs of pain" might enable Yolmo wa to come to terms with their losses.

In turn, the Buddhist philosophy of "suffering" may be a direct response to sentiments of sorrow spawned by psychosocial structures common to many South Asian cultures: relational selves make incidents of loss and separation particularly disruptive, and thus they need a moral code. The consequence of this particular theology of suffering for Yolmo wa is that they appear particularly sensitive to moments of pain, grief, and sorrow. Understandings of suffering appear "hypercognized," to use Levy's terms; there is a wealth of idioms, metaphors, and images to convey states of pain and sorrow.[28] At the same time, villagers are reluctant to use such phrasings, for they recall well-known but typically feared and painful experiences.

As Yolmo "heartaches" are products of the unique form of social corporateness that defines Yolmo lives, these core sensations characterize Yolmo concerns much like a shadow delineates the object it silhouettes: through absence. With shadows, there is absence of light; with *tsher ka*, there is an absence of the quintessential features of Yolmo identity—companionship, intimacy, presence, context, relationality, emotional stability. In parting from "home," cutting from family members, a person loses this identity, the felt sense of who he or she is. *Tsher ka*, in its ideal form, is the feeling of loss tied to partings: an isolation, a loss of intimacy, context, and identity—and a pining melancholy, tormented self-reflexivity, and anxious lethargy of body and spirit engaged by that loss. Yet the experiential contours of *tsher ka* are often less clearly defined when the sentiment crops up within the messiness of everyday life, especially when a villager dies. With bereavement comes a murky blend of "heartache" and "sorrow" in a diffuse medley of pain.

The funeral song intones this medley, evoking sentiments commonly evinced by loss. Following the women, the men round off their first couplet:

FATHER IS NOTHING BUT REMEMBERED,
HE IS NEVER FORGOTTEN

yap chen dran pa min pa,
ma dran nam yang mi 'dug

"Father" parallels the first line of the couplet, which reads as

heart/ache/nothing but,   unpained/never/not
father/remembered/nothing but,   forgotten/never/not

and suggests that pain is to remembrance as happiness is to forgetting. The song thus involves a lament for one's father, a song of mourning in remembrance. And yet the lack of pronouns (no "I", "you," or "we") signals that it is everyone's father. The lyrics bespeak a commonality of experience; grief is shared by all.

To understand the lyric's import, we must inquire into the nature of Yolmo memory, of the lingering ties to absent fathers and friends. As villagers do not find comfort in *tsher ka* or in the loneliness, pensiveness, or melancholy associated with it, many have developed habitual methods to deal with the onset of these sentiments. In most situations, the antidote for "heartache" is company with friends and family. Villagers often expressed that *tsher ka* comes for "one moment only"; "Then you're with friends and you're happy." The best way to escape from *tsher ka*, then, is to be with others, to laugh and to sing. When I asked Pemba how to get rid of *tsher ka*, she responded, "Oh, just be with friends for a while in a pleasant [n. *mito* "sweet"] atmosphere with pleasant talk, and it will go away in just one moment."

Tsher ka and friendship thus are polar forces. In fact, we could define *tsher ka* as a lack of companionship and emotional intimacy: "When friends gather we are not pained, when we part *tsher ka* comes." As the force of *tsher ka* inversely depends on the strength of social ties, friendships are highly valued on an emotional level in Yolmo society (beyond any sociopolitical considerations).

> The blossoming flowers of summer,
> if only they could last through winter
> we friends who have gathered together,
> if only we could last through life

Friends here is *nyenjen*, denoting both kin relations, such as an uncle or cousin, and non-kin associates, such as one's neighbors.

Why are friendships so valued? For the companionship they offer, a communality that drowns out the anxiety, loneliness, and pensiveness that otherwise disturbs moments of solitude; for the role they play in sustaining personal identity, for Yolmo identity is, by definition, composed of social bonds; and for the intimacy they provide, for friends enable a person to slip past the harsh cultural limits to what he or she can know of another.

The last point relates to a common way of knowing in Helambu:

Beneath the mounds of snow,
soil or rock, we cannot know
Kin from beyond the mountains,
friends or foes, we cannot know

In this mountaineous "screened place," where a villager feels called upon to ask in song what lies beneath a pile of snow, over the next hill, or within a neighbor's heart, we find an epistemology bearing on surface appearances, inner realities, and hidden motives.[29] The limitations inherent to Yolmo knowing begin with one's neighbors, for it is considered difficult to know what another person is thinking or feeling. As a body or house hides its contents from the eyes of others, subjective realities are considered largely unknown to the outside world.

Villagers perform an unacknowledged routine during funerals that demarcates a similar epistemic space. When the funeral party carried Padma's effigy from his home to the Lamaist temple to perform the transmigration of the soul, men entered inside the stone structure while women, reluctant to enter, rushed to the windows to glimpse and comment upon the ritual drama within. It is this idea of peering through dark windows—unable to enter but groping for a view—that defines Yolmo ways of knowing, be they of funerals, social relations, or the human heart.[30]

The aesthetic value of smooth surfaces underscores Yolmo limits to knowledge. Yolmo society, based on a set of fragile, interlocking corporate groups, requires harmony and equilibrium in the realm of social relations. Most often, villagers strive to maintain this eqilibrium by controlling the expression of personal desires. They therefore hesitate to let others know what they are feeling. In turn, the ever-present threat of fission and social rivalries occasions the fear that if others know too much, they might take advantage of this knowledge (through witchcraft, business affairs, etc.). These two factors lead villagers to pursue a culture of privacy, revealing little of their inner worlds to others. I once asked Karma how difficult it was to know another's heartmind in Helambu. "It is difficult to do that in our society," he said. "They hide things, they close things, they're not very open—like when you offer food to someone and he refuses it, you're not sure if he really wants it or not. They also feel it very hard to express things."

Since villagers keep private much of their feelings, it is understood that they often just tap into surface knowledge concerning each other. While a person develops empirical knowledge of a friend by observing his actions and expressions through time, this is at best a shaky science: a villager never really knows what is in another's heartmind by merely interpreting her behavior. "If I were a god," Latu once said, "I could get inside your heartmind. But since I'm not, how can I know what lies within your heart?" Karma once said something that pertains to Yolmo capacities for empathy. "It's just the apparent thing they're knowing," he explained, "not the real thing. If a person is feeling sad, unhappy, and someone comes to comfort him, he'll just consider that they don't know what he truly feels. They've come to say, 'It's nothing,' and he'll say back, 'You don't know what's inside me' . . . One doesn't know the true intentions." Yolmo wa are therefore reluctant to infer another's state of mind or body. As I soon learned, questions pertaining to the thoughts of a third party are often met by the response, "How can one know what is in another's heartmind?"

Because of this limitation, language becomes the prime medium through which friends bridge empathy and understanding. "One can know about another's feelings only if he tells about it." But even here villagers tread cautiously, for while two individuals may agree in conversation, such accord may be lacking within their hearts. "Our tongues are the same," Latu's brother Dawa told me, "but not our hearts. Only with words do you show yourself, in words you agree, but there is not necessarily agreement in the *sems*." Karma put it this way, "I might be agreeing with a friend, suggesting things, but in the heartmind, I'm asking, '*Ci yin pa, ci yin pa?* [What is there?].'"

The social epistemology that doubts the motives of another fosters a climate of ambiguity and suspicion. Since a villager cannot see beneath the surface of a neighbor's facade, he or she wonders what qualities, good or bad, lie within. Two folk songs intuit this idea:

You are a *bum pa* [ritual vase] of gold,
how is the sacred water within?
We are a *bum pa* of clear crystal,
we are visible within and without!

The sons are diamond and pearl,
they are crystal clear
the daughters are coral and turquoise,
what is within?

While hearts of crystal, diamond, and pearl are transparent, those of solid gold, coral, and turquoise foster suspicion. The playfulness of these lyrics, where visibility evokes honesty, matches the veiled seriousness of others, where opacity breeds distrust. A sentiment similar to the poem above was sung to me by several teenage girls:

> White cow of the East,
> how is your milk
> so-called friend,
> how is your *sems*?

Just as cow's milk cannot be tasted unless released from its udder, so an acquaintance's nature cannot be judged if hidden within the heart. Much of Yolmo relations thus range from suspicion to intimacy. Friendships take root when villagers are neither wary of deceit nor threatened with the loss of personal privacy. Yolmo society, divided into "inside" and "outside" people, breeds both communality and caution.

As it is difficult to know what lies beneath a neighbor's facade, villagers value the ability to penetrate such barriers. Friendships, while respecting the dignity of personal privacy, hint at such intimacy:

> For a rectangular house,
> windows are more beautiful than doors
> for a rectangular house,
> windows are more beautiful than doors
> for friends behind these windows,
> bones are finer than flesh

As transparent windows are more beautiful than impenetrable doors, "bones," because they constitute a friend's inner being, are valued more than exterior "flesh." In declaring the beauty of corporeal interiors, the song praises friends for revealing what lies beneath the social facade. The metaphor simultaneously reaffirms, however, that the facade exists: a house holds walls as well as windows, and it is better to respect the inner space than to trespass through doorways. Yolmo friendships, like other attachments, balance precariously between intimacy and mistrust.[31]

With the onset of *tsher ka*, however, villagers struggle with recollections of absent friends and family who are distanced either by space, time, or death.

Save for feeling *tsher ka*,
there is no moment otherwise
save for remembering friends and family,
there is no moment otherwise

As *tsher ka* equals the remembrance of lost loves, villagers often sing of memory in their songs of separation. Memories, an essential component of *tsher ka*, haunt Yolmo wa like ghosts, tormenting their owners with the images they bequeath.

One mountain crossed, no soreness [*tsher ka*]
two mountains crossed, no soreness
[but] when crossing the third mountain,
I remembered father and mother clearly

The song recounts a journey away from one's homeland, such as a bride would take in marriage. Only after crossing the third mountain does the poet recall her lost parents, an elusive vision that accompanies the corporeal "soreness" of *tsher ka* (as Karma translated the word here). Similarly, when I asked one woman why *tsher ka* fails to separate from the daughter's body in the song of grief that begins this chapter, she said, "It's because the girl cannot forget her father, she keeps remembering him."

Yolmo fears of the visceral force of memories explain their reluctance to permit the heartmind to travel back into the past, for one may fall ill due to its prolonged absence from the body. This threat underscores Yolmo trepidations over wandering too far from home, and explains a bride's soreness in remembering her absent parents.

The trouble with memories is that they invoke desires that cannot be quenched—

The water from a rocky hill,
we cannot drink if thirsty
father, our father,
we cannot meet if remembered

—and images that cannot be realized:

When I slept at night,
I saw my brother as if he were real

> when I woke in the morning,
> I realized it was a dream

sang a Yolmo girl in a tape-recorded "letter" to her brother in Kathmandu.
Memories, in short, fail to provide the soul with the sustenance it
requires (tangible companionship, intimacy, a sense of home), while re-
minding the emotionally impoverished that they lack these nutrients.

> In our true homeland,
> we find what we wish to eat
> but in remembering our family,
> we take no nourishment from this food

Thoughts of memory thus inform the verses of the funerary song. To
sing that "father is never forgotten," as the men do, carries a note of anguish
and ambivalence. We should not and cannot forget the departed, the lyrics
suggest, but we all might be better off if we could.
To this quandary the women respond:

DO NOT MIND YOUR SORROW,

sems pa sdug po ma byas

"Sorrow" here is the *sdug* of *sems*, the ache of grief, the cutting pain of
loss; it is the body's visceral counterpoint to the heartmind's "pain." And
so, literally, "do not attend to," "pay no heed to," or simply "ignore" this
sorrow. The mandate hints at a key Yolmo sensibility: just as it is dangerous
to journey into the past, so it is best not to dwell on present thoughts.

> Better not to think,
> if I think my heart aches
> to work with one's thoughts,
> it doesn't help anything

For when villagers do think, there is, at times, nothing but pain:

> Observing the hues of the forest,
> the *fayu* flowers bloom
> observing the spectrum of my thoughts,
> tears fall to the eyes

Yolmo wa generally try to avoid introspective moments, either by avoiding the circumstances that may lead to such situations, denying their relevance, or refusing to dwell on them. Since *tsher ka* afflicts the "heartmind" when it is at rest, villagers try to keep body and heartmind occupied. And as introspection is known to foster melancholy, some tend to shun it. When Karma told me that with *tsher ka*, Yolmo wa ponder over family members far away, I asked if they try to avoid such thoughts. "It's hard not to be pensive when you feel *tsher ka*," he replied, "for that is one of its features. Some people say, 'Hey, don't think about that.' Because if you can stop being pensive, it may help."

"How does a person stop from feeling *tsher ka*?"

"Some people might not want to be disturbed, talk with others, they might want to go off alone. Others might try to do something else, other things, to try to forget whatever caused this *tsher ka*."

It is my impression that villagers often pursue the latter course of action—staying busy, chatting with companions, keeping the heartmind focused on the here and now—in the hopes of escaping from *tsher ka*'s grasp. Rather than confront the terms of heartache in everyday life, villagers tend to evade them in order to feel better.[32] They also create buffers to protect themselves from potentially distressful situations.[33] In turn, as Yolmo wa try to keep the social peace, they usually refrain from expressing troubling thoughts to others. Outside of maintaining a pleasant, jovial facade—the surface congeniality of everyday life—a person generally tries to "hold" her heart, not letting on that she feels grief, anger, or heartache.

I once asked Karma why several "songs of pain" speak of the necessity of hiding one's heartache from others. "It's just a cultural thing, like feeling shy [*ngo*]," he said. "Someone might feel you're being fussy about stuff. So you hide it. You don't want to show others. If your heart aches, you'll only confide in your very close relatives. If you're angry, you pretend you're not angry." In fact, most villagers consider the ability to "hold" one's emotions to be more refined among adults than children and among men than women, for the former are "stronger" than the latter.

Anger, in particular, is rarely expressed openly in Yolmo society, for it can greatly disrupt the smooth flow of social life. As Karma's words, noted above ("We don't show it . . ."), hint, Yolmo wa strongly value the opportunity to express personal distress, such as anger, lest it "suddenly explode." One man confided, "If you have all this anger or grief inside you, you tell these things to the very near, close friends. They say, 'If I'm angry with you, and I don't show it, I might show my anger at someone else. The next person that comes along, I might shout at, beat up.'"

The idea that unvented anger builds until it suddenly explodes suggests a "hydraulic" theory of emotional expression common to several Western and non-Western philosophies of the self.[34] Among Yolmo wa, the value of "cleaning" the heartmind of distress is culturally agreed on. "Lice fill my hair," rues the singer of one *tsher glu*,

> but I've no mother to extract them
> thoughts fill my heart,
> but I've no mother to explain them to

Just as mothers are appreciatively known to pluck lice from a child's scalp, so their ability to listen to the heart's grievances is highly valued. Separated from family, the singer bemoans a head infested with lice and a heart full of worries. As Latu put it, "The song says, 'If there are no friends and family, then much remains within the *sems*. So when painful thoughts come, to whom can we speak?' Just as a man needs to clean his hair and clothes, so he needs to be able to clean the heartmind."

"But why, elder brother," I asked, "is it good to be able to talk about what is in the heartmind with others?"

"If you're having an argument, fighting with others, but cannot really do what you want," Latu explained with boxing gestures, "you can usually talk with your family about it later. But if you cannot tell about this to others . . ."

"I see."

"—Just as you need to clean your hair and clothes, so you need to be able to clean the heartmind. As with clothes, usually your wife or mother does this cleaning. But if these persons are absent, then you have to do this by yourself, or the clothes stay dirty."

In Helambu, intimacy is usually found and expressed within the relatively closed circle of the family—with "inside" rather than "outside" people. Hence, despite the social value of hiding feelings from the gaze of others, Yolmo wa consider it important to clean the heart free of pollutants by "talking" them out at home. The Buddhist aesthetic of purity contributes to this idea: the heart needs to be cleansed of such thoughts, as if they were dirty or harmful, just as ghosts need to be "thrown" and pollution "cut" from the body. Otherwise, sentiments can tear at the heart or explode onto the social scene.

Yet despite the acknowledged need to express anger, grief, and heartache to others, this does not come easily for Yolmo wa. A culturally constituted paradox defines Yolmo experience: whereas a person needs to "cleanse" the heart free of troublesome thoughts, it is often difficult to do so, even with one's intimates. Due to the cultural constraints on communication, villagers find it distressful to convey their distress to others, and so lament the limits of empathy:

When a forest catches fire,
everyone sees it
[but] when one's heart catches fire,
only one's own self [*rang*] knows

Several times I asked villagers if, as the couplet suggests, they thought it true that one cannot share sorrows with others. They often responded, "Yes, it is like this," and looked sheepishly away. One man stated what for him was the obvious: when a person is worried inside, he cannot tell his thoughts to anyone. "Because it is in our heartmind, which no one can see, nobody will know of it." As Karma put it, "It's like there's no one to share your sorrow. Even if you're feeling sad, but others won't be feeling sad for you. Even if they know it, they can't say it."

With *tsher ka*, the difficulties in communicating distress are twofold, for an essential component of such pain is the inability to express one's plight to others precisely because the intimates with whom one is most able to share thoughts are absent. A vicious circle is thus created, and a sufferer of *tsher ka* is left without an open vehicle to express distress. Villagers told me that, within the karmic wheel of life, the greatest torment of animals—chickens, dogs, buffaloes—is that, deprived of a language, they cannot communicate the pains of their existence, particularly those burdens enacted on them by their human custodians. Yolmo wa, lacking an open vehicle to communicate distress, often resemble these creatures.

If we stay our hearts will ache,
if we go our little feet will hurt
the sorrow of little feet hurting,
to whom can we tell?

The funeral song seems to propose an answer to this couplet's lingering query: "Do not mind your sorrow" it advises. Do the words speak to an ethos of avoidance? Perhaps, but here I believe that the sentiment, while building on a similar experiential form, implies the beginning of a cathartic transformation—by letting go of sorrow to ultimately "cast" out one's grief.

But why should we try to forget our sorrow? For, the women suggest:

THE *BALU* FLOWERS MAY BLOOM

ba lu me toy shar to

—tying the couplet's conclusion to its opening line via the *ba lu* image and positing a further significance for this rhododendron tree. In Nepal, flowers connote health, vitality, and even life itself.[35] Here, rhododendron flowers "might bloom," or *shar to*, which describes the opening of May flowers and the expansiveness of the rising sun, suggesting an image of potential beauty, health, and completeness, if not renewal proper.

To whom are the women speaking? The words imply a command, an imperative, and, hence, a "you." I take this "you" to be the men or, more precisely, the role assumed by them in the song: that of those racked by grief. The song thus embodies a dialogue of the heart for both singers and audience; the men's and women's couplets, engendering sexual reciprocity, alternately debate the dialectic of corporeal "sorrow" and "comfort."

To understand the implications of this dialogue, we need to map out the cultural and gendered aspects of Yolmo expressions of pain. Whereas the sorrow of little feet hurting often goes unannounced in everyday life, songs of pain apparently offer a poetic medium to express sensations that, otherwise, villagers cannot readily articulate.[36] The poems, in recounting *tsher ka*, focus on an arena of Yolmo life that is rarely touched on through other means: that of subjective experience. The cultural limits to empathy permit cigarettes, not weary hearts, to be shared among friends. But through song, Yolmo wa sing of the otherwise silent toils of little feet hurting. While Yolmo mores pose harsh limits to direct social communication, an indirect discourse exists through which empathy can be achieved.

Yet while the most disturbing and personal of experiences lie at the heart of songs, lyrics enable singers to distance themselves from the immediacies of pain. Like the Yolmo language in general, the songs lack pronouns and specific agents of action. "We," "I," or "you" are implied but not stated. But whereas in everyday conversations the context of speech often indicates to which party a verb refers (making pronouns unnecessary), the context of a song's lyrics typically remains unmarked. The couplet of little feet hurting, for instance, sounds as:

sdod na sems pa tsher ka,
'thon na rkang chung na tsha
rkang chung na gi gi 'dug,
su shi gang la bshad byung

If staying-heart-ache,
if leaving-little feet-hurt
little feet-pain-hurting,
to whom-can-to tell?

While the anguish of little feet is revealed, their owner is cloaked in impersonality: *whose* feet is left unstated. And since couplets are relatively standardized, the personal locus of any pain alluded to in the songs can be denied. "It's just a song," singers can say (as they have to me), "it means nothing." But the point is well taken; wounds are exposed and hearts are cleansed. Similar to the Delta blues, pain is affirmed with anonymity and the poet can still claim that she has "held" her heart.

Despite this impersonality, villagers occasionally note the messages potentially veiled within the songs. One afternoon Latu carefully listened to a series of *tsher glu* that I had collected in Kathmandu, including the song noted in the beginning of this chapter ("with head placed on a pillow . . ."). The third couplet of this song sounded as:

My father, my father,
why has your life been shortened
father when your life was shortened,
your daughter found herself to be nowhere

After hearing these lines, Latu asked if Karma's sister, one of many singers with whom I worked, taught me this song. When I asked why he would think this, he said, "Because her father died last year, and maybe her heart still hurts [*sems pa sdug po*]." Though Karma's sister was not the singer of this song, Latu's readiness to link it to her grief tells us much.

Although the songs may be impersonal, this is where their greatest efficacy seems to lie. While dirges do not identify particular individuals as their protagonists, they address themselves to all who hear. Without an explicit "I," listeners can assume a "we." The sentiments evoked in the songs convey a commonality of experience. Through shared discourse, support is fostered, bonds strengthened, feelings made communal.

The potential of *tsher glu* to communicate personal distress, foster empathy, and create an emotional *communitas* is suggested in the songs sung by the "unfortunate daughters" who typically must leave their natal village in marriage. The social position of Yolmo women derives, in part, from the frequent requirements of patrilocal residence, requirements that occasion one of the key structural tensions of this society: women often must inhabit an intermediate space between home and a "foreign land," neither "going" nor "staying."[37] An archetypal "heartache" ensues from this tension. Brides must leave their families to live in a unfamiliar village (often at a considerable distance from their natal village) where they are deprived of the intimacy they once shared. As Yolmo women tell it, moving to the groom's household is one of the most traumatic moments of their lives, a lasting moment often marred by pain in separation. Indeed, many informants conceded that *tsher ka* falls to the daughter more than the son because she must undertake this journey.

> For richly sprouting *sdong po* plants,[38]
> measures of length and shortness are unequal
> for the children of one family,
> shares of pleasure and sorrow are unequal
>
> Between a rosary's beads and ornaments,
> pain [*tsher ka*] falls on the ornaments[39]
> between a son and daughter,
> pain falls on the daughter

I asked one woman if she thought it true that daughters suffer more pain than their brothers. "Of course," she said, "because she must leave her family and go to a new place when she gets married." A young woman, betrothed against her will to a boy she perhaps has not seen before, is fated to become a "daughter without good fortune" (*bsod sde med pa'i bu mo*), landing on the doorsteps of unfamiliar others.

With this parting from home can come feelings of despair, neglect, and anger—sentiments that a Yolmo woman finds difficult to express to intimates, let alone strangers. I would suggest that Yolmo songs of pain construct a bond of empathy and communality among women. They also provide a medium to express these feelings, a moral testimony embodying a strategy of "social reciprocity" wherein declarations of *tsher ka* are "not simply a sign of despair and defeat but an active form of appeal, implicitly or explicitly expressed, for payment of an incurred loss."[40] The songs enable Yolmo women to bear witness to their pain and indirectly reproach those who inflict it.[41]

For instance, daughters sing of the apprehension they feel in moving to a foreign land—a fear of strangers and treacherous journeys.

> If we walk in the fields of summer,
> we fear we might slip
> when a daughter parts for a foreign land,
> she fears gossip might fall upon her

And they speak of the isolation that comes with moving to a husband's village, the solitude one suffers when divorced from family.

> A *kalde* dwelling *jolmo*,[42]
> arrives in the valley below
> when the valley becomes too hot,
> no one calls it to return above

The aura of abandonment, separation, and neglect embedded in these lines (a direct result of core social tensions in Helambu) borders on anger. In expressing the hardships of marriage, women hint at the resentment and sense of betrayal that they suffer.

> For a flask full of wine,
> don't give your daughters to others
> But if you must give us away,
> don't send us beyond the mountain

> Our mother and father had told us:
> "do not enter the foreign lands"
> but due to the fate of their daughter,
> she arrived at the door of others

Notice that the daughter does not reside securely within the groom's household, but stands on his doorstep, as if she were more unfamiliar guest than intimate family. Indeed, she is not with family but with *mi*, literally, "people" but with the connotation of "others" (as with *mi yul* "foreign lands" and *mi kha*, the harmful gossip of "human talk").

At times, women express the anger they feel in being forced to leave their natal homes while deprived of family wealth—

Of her father's inheritance,
a daughter receives nothing
a necklace of turquoise and coral,
to have even a small one

—and the security that her natal home could offer her but instead denies:

The pillars beneath the house,
we daughters build ourselves
But beneath the roof we build,
we have no chance to live

A symbol of integrity and identity, a house denotes the domestic security of the household. Ironically, though daughters "build" such structures through the toil of their early years, they end up on foreign doorsteps. The second line *bu mo nga rung gzheng song*, reads literally as, "daughter(s)/ (myself)ourselves/build"—and so stresses a communal "we" and an acknowledgment of shared sorrow.

In all, through poetry Yolmo wa express sentiments of sorrow, heartache, and anger that linger in their bodies but cannot be "thrown." A daughter-in-law, separated from family and deprived of a full voice in ordinary discourse, can rarely speak of the pain in her heart, let alone vent the anger she might feel toward those considered responsible for her estrangement. But through verse, she can do so. Testimonies of despair, *tsher glu*, also involve pleas for compassion.

Father when your life was shortened,
tears fell upon my eyes
Oh friends have pity,
tears have fallen upon my eyes

Yet while *tsher glu* poignantly convey (and, at times, overcome) difficulties in communicating personal distress, they also help to create the limits to empathy. When a Yolmo woman laments the anonymity of little feet hurting, she seems to confirm the problem as much as she decries it. Though music reveals the fires of our hearts, the songs say, our pain will remain hidden, save in times of poetry.

Hence both the possibilities and limits of social communication are culturally constituted. While social norms permit Yolmo wa to articulate distress through (and often only through) poetry, limits to knowledge and empathy are in effect elsewhere—primarily because the fragile social interdependence defining Yolmo social life encourages an aesthetic of restraint. By validating cultural limits to emotional knowledge yet also providing loopholes to these empathic constraints, language becomes prison house and emancipator.

The songs, then, are a tutelage on emotions, informing singer and audience of the nature of Yolmo experience—how to feel, how to express feelings, and the constraints on (and political force of) such expression.[43] "The songs about pain in our hearts are the first we learn," one woman told me. How true, for villagers often learn of *tsher ka* through songs long before they confront it in life. Young boys bewail the death of parents in song before they suffer such losses; young girls lament a daughter's misery in marriage before they themselves marry. Through song, Yolmo children learn of *tsher ka*, the constraints it will place on their lives, and how to bear it properly. The songs also give semantic shape to an imminent, ill-formed malaise. Indeed, oral poetry is one of the main idioms through which Yolmo articulate emotional experience: Yolmo sensibilities present a "black box" approach to subjective interiors, with personal distress seldom discussed in everyday life; songs of pain, to adopt Geertz's terms, are as much a model for, as a model of, lived experience.[44]

An ideology of affect thus courses through Yolmo sensibilities, local ideas of agency, and the lyrics of *tsher glu*. Often, this ideology relates to gender, for Yolmo society inculcates a sexual division of feeling. The differing dispositions of women and men stem from the social status of the two sexes, with the former subservient to the latter. While "strong-hearted" men are thought to be secure from emotional distress, women, children, and the elderly possess "weak" hearts that make them vulnerable. The lack of an Adam's apple disables women from keeping secrets within. Devoid of restraint, women find it difficult to "hold" their hearts; lacking a "strong heart," their bodies often succumb to distress. Women are devalued—in everyday discourse, for their weak-hearted frailty, and in song, for their opaque mysteriousness. "The sons are diamond and pearl," one *tsher glu* teases,

they are crystal clear
the daughters are coral and turquoise,
what is within?

Just as domestic practices often map sexual hierarchies within individual bodies,[45] so poetry reaffirms local notions of gender. Of the many models of Yolmo experience versed by the songs, one outlines the differing emotional dispositions of men and women.

It is within the context of differing emotional dispositions that men and women exchange images of heartaches and sorrows, memories and flowers. The funeral song gives voice to emotional distress, but, in so doing, also shapes the gendered nature of such experience. As the women dance in the aftermath of their own lyrics ("Do not mind your sorrow . . ."), the men begin another couplet with an ever quickening tempo:

LET US NOT FEEL HEARTACHES,
LET US NOT SING SONGS OF PAIN

sems pa tsher ni ma yong,
tsher glu len ni ma yong

Ma yong means "let it not come." The men, following the women's lead, voice a hesitant resolution, neither to sing of *tsher ka* nor to permit its presence to fill their hearts (note how the experience of pain immediately begets the singing of it, as if one implied the other). We therefore move from the fatalistic opening ("There is always heartache") to a will to escape *tsher ka*. But here, in contrast to daily life, one escapes "pain" by confronting it; the men acknowledge their grief to alleviate it.

The women buttress this idea with the start of a new couplet:

DO NOT MIND YOUR ACHING HEART,
DO NOT MIND YOUR WEARY BODY

sems pa tsher tsher ma byas,
lus po sdug sdug ma byas

The *ma byas* ("manje") structure links the women's third couplet to their second, as the second was rooted to the first through the arboreal image. The "sorrow" of the preceding couplet presently divides into two idioms of pain: the "sorrow" of the body (*lus po sdug*) fleshes out the "heartache" of the *sems* (*sems pa tsher ka*). *Lus po sdug*, specifically, is an "overburdened" or "tormented" body (such as the physical discomfort felt at the end of a long day's toil), a burden that reveals how distress can be experienced on a physical plane among Yolmo wa.

The dialogue between the body's sorrow and the heartmind's pain relates to a specific tension inherent in Yolmo experience. To wit, a strong mind-body duality permeates Yolmo culture, a duality founded on the Buddhist distinction between the "residence and its residents"—the corporeal abode (*lus*, "li") and its "heartmind" (*sems*) and reincarnating "soul" (*rnam shes*).[46]

> My body grows older and older,
> [but] my *sems* feels younger and younger
> one only gets older,
> growing younger cannot be

When asked if these lyrics meant that body and heartmind don't get along, Latu said, "Yes, it's just like a house with people living inside. The house may get old, so the people wish to move to a new one." Yolmo wa, like Tibetans, often see the body as being distinct from, and occasionally at odds with, its spiritual holdings. As one Tibetan sage instructs, "The *sems* must not grow fond of the body, the body must not grow fond of the *sems*. Guard the liberty of body and *sems*, so that each can rest in itself."[47]

The mind-body duality broaches, among others, the realm of feeling. A primary tension exists between the longings of the heart and the limits of the body—between that which the *sems* desires and that which its abode can allow. In the couplet above (as with other *tsher glu*), an implicit "but" linking the first line to the second marks a specific irony of human experience. Here, the body can never "grow" younger, though the heart moves into a second childhood as the years unfold. While a person inevitably wishes to move into a new home when the old one decays, only through death can the soul end its lease on the body.

The homesickness found with *tsher ka* amplifies the tendency of body and heartmind not to "get along," for the *sems*'s fleet-footed desires to return home are blunted by the body's inability to transcend the limits of hills and valleys. For Yolmo wa, body is of "flesh and bone" while soul is like "air"—

> This body of flesh and bone,
> I'll stick in the cremation grounds
> this soul like air,
> I'll leave in the land of *bar do*[48]

—and the airy freedom of spirit is weighed down by the heaviness of the body.

> My body rests in a foreign land,
> yet my thoughts dwell in my own
> as my thoughts wander,
> if only my body could roam

Without a body to anchor them, Yolmo souls are destined to wander about "like a feather tossed about by the wind."[49] With a body, they are doomed to a life of unreachable desire—the "if only" of pure incorporeality.

> Like the clouds above, moving, moving,
> if only I could go
> the land of birth and family,
> if I go now I can reach

As above, "if only" suggests that home will not be reached; the heartmind will linger in "pain" as long it is burdened with a body.

The body tempers desire. Life's burdens, meanwhile, snub out individual passions.

> When the fire is aflame,
> the sparks fly
> when one's head sticks out,
> the golden yoke is afixed

"When one's head sticks out" indicates a moment of personal maturity: as a person's head emerges from the womb at birth, so he or she achieves individuality in adolescence. Yet while a fire's sparks range freely, the "yoke" of family responsibility and social commitment soon restrains youthful passion.

With this maturity comes experience, and so, despair:

Long ago in the womb of mother,
better if I had not been born
even if one's head sticks out,
despair has already come

As Latu made sense of this couplet, a child possesses neither knowledge nor experience while in its mother's womb; there is pure innocence. But with birth and later development, life, with all its concerns, doubts, and tainted wisdom, brings "anxiety" or *sems khral*. When I asked my companion to explain this term, he groped for words. "It's, you know, like night cold thoughts"—the winter worries that beset sleepless nights.

The elderly, above all, are known to think such thoughts, for though their hearts grow younger through time, they mourn the loss of physical strength and agility. For Karma, one becomes more "perceptive" (sensitive) in old age "because the elderly have the feeling that maybe, 'We're becoming older, we can't do anything.' It's a feeling of desperation"—the despair, no less, of mortal body over mind. Perhaps Mingma had this despair in mind when he told that he was "ill from old age, getting older, and afraid of dying."[50]

Yolmo songs of separation thus pattern a basic dialectic between desire and corporeality, comfort and actuality. But whereas Westerners locate desire within the body, Yolmo wa situate it most within the heartmind. In Helambu, the body is an obstacle and affront to personal desire; the "reality principle" emanates not from the heartmind but from the body. Because the body denies the *sems*'s fancies, something always seems amiss for Yolmo poets—some wish unfulfilled, some pain unsoothed—and the heart seems perpetually to long for another land.

In tea, tea leaves are discarded,
in *chang* beer, sediment remains
within our own land,
my heart still lingers

While the body, stuck in a foreign land, remains detached from home, the heart, wishing to be home, lingers in the land from whence it came. As with unquenchable memories and intangible dreams (fathers remembered but dead, brothers imagined but absent), desire latches onto the body like a leech, draining it of any settled peace of *sems*.

At times I wish to go,
at others I wish to stay
the desire to go sticks to the body,
when I stay I feel restless

The couplet illuminates a culturally defined tension between rest and travel; "Going nor staying, neither can be," another version concludes. As with many *tsher glu*, the tension comments on specific burdens of Yolmo life. Elsewhere, the implicit "buts" linking couplets together mark specific ironies ("One only gets older, growing younger cannot be"), dilemmas ("Thoughts fill my heart, but I've no mother to explain them to"), and schisms (body and mind at odds, self and family apart). Art has been said to serve a "corrective" function, bringing into awareness alternative ways of being and seeing.[51] But the ironies, double binds, and paradoxes teased out by Yolmo *tsher glu* appear to involve less "the imaginary correction of deficient realities," as Iser identifies one of literature's functions, than a cultural critique.[52] The fault lines of everyday experience, the limits to human empathy, and the quandaries of desire reverberate through various songs, touching the sore spots of Yolmo experience, their linkage to bodily distress, and the causal roots of "heartache" and "sorrow."

The songs, in sum, comment on, attend to, and lend moral meaning to the sentiments revealed. It remains to be seen, however, whether Yolmo wa articulate their wounds to soothe them, to bemoan them, or to transcend them. If the latter, how might a funeral dirge take steps toward such transcendence?

Songs of affliction, the men recalled, we are not to sing. And yet:

THE YEAR OUR FATHER PASSED AWAY,
WE HAD TO SING SONGS OF PAIN

a ba shor kyi lo la,
tsher glu len gyi byung gsong

"We had" here means "we had occasion to" or "we were forced to." And so the words can be read as: "The death of our father caused us to feel *tsher ka*, and thus the need to sing of it." Although it does not benefit us to feel *tsher ka*, the losses we suffer in life make such pain inevitable.

On what occasion are the words sung? They are sung at a funeral, of course, marking sentiments of loss in the wake of a death, such as Padma's.

But the song also recalls other deaths (as suggested by the recurrent "we" of both past and present) and the "heartache" spawned by these memories. The space rendered by the singers is communal, a moment betwixt and between ordinary experience. Within this liminal moment, the singers achieve a heightened awareness of what threatens (and silences) them in their everyday lives (loss, mortality, isolation). The epiphany in poetry scrambles to parry the threat. While death is the murkiest of realms, denying the presence of language, it invites, precisely because of its opacity, the most poetic of words. The lyrics above, as a form of art, form a moment of grief.

Yet they also work to transform that grief. "We had to sing songs of pain" implies both the ritual duty and the psychological need to voice one's distress in the wake of death. Yolmo wa maintain that funerals are needed to prevent the deceased from becoming ghosts, condemned to wander the earth and haunt the living. The truth in this notion seems to exist on at least one level, for funerals help the bereaved to engage in the "work of mourning" necessary, as Freud found, to transcend feelings of grief subsequent to a loss.[53] Indeed, it is likely that if the bereaved did not participate in the lengthy series of funeral rites performed by Yolmo wa (each of the first seven weeks after a death, and one year later), sentiments of grief would fail to fully separate from their bodies. Although villagers often experience profound distress at the loss of a kinsman or neighbor, they usually seem reluctant to grieve due to the cultural constraints on emotional distress: wishing to keep their hearts free of pain, Yolmo wa attempt to avoid thinking of, or expressing, sentiments of loss. Funerals, forcing the issue, prompt the bereaved to submit to the mourning process: while the ceremonies (including the singing of *tsher glu*) promise intense emotionality and thus discomfort, there exist strong social pressures to participate in them. The fulfillment of social obligations thus often compels mourners to confront their grief.

One of the tasks of the present song, then, is to help those who sing its emotional cadences to work through feelings of grief. Yet grief, to be transcended, first needs to be evoked, and the song gives voice to sentiments that might not otherwise be expressed in tea shops or back rooms. The logic of efficacy here speaks to a local link between language and experience. In Helambu, words often possess the power to evoke experiences: a shaman's mantras create a magical reality by mimetically portraying it; the names of the dead should not be spoken lest they invoke their presence; and the singing of *tsher ka* seems to be deeply caught up with one's experience of it. Hence a cadence of loss needs to be sung in order to evoke, then assuage, one's grief. Yet if scenes of separation prompt feelings of pain, where do images of balance and comfort take us?

"Do not mind your saddened heart, do not mind your weary body," the women sing, as if in response to Nyima's dilemma. For:

EVEN IF YOU FEEL SORROW NOW,
ONCE YOU MAY BE HAPPY

da lta sdug po myong na,
thengs gcig skyid po myong do

The women's optimism balances the men's sorrow. Paradoxically, the emotionally "weak" teach the men how to buck up, perhaps because women are more familiar with personal loss. "Happy" here is *skyid po*: comfort, warmth, and pleasure, in contrast to the pained discomfort of *sdug*. The couplet thus adds to the litany of balanced tensions culled by the song: body and heartmind, "sorrow" and "heartache," absence and presence, men and women, pain and comfort. The potential reconcilement of these "discordant qualities," to use Coleridge's words, fulfills key Yolmo sensibilities (the need for harmony, balance, and completion) and so contributes to the aesthetic experience engaged by the poetry.[54] Each duality is suspended in a state of dynamic equilibrium in which the discord between body and soul, life and death, are, if not resolved, then of a whole. The circle danced by the singers admits the need for balance.

Another contribution to the aesthetic experience is the narrative kinetics engaged by the song. *Thengs gcig* ("lenchi") means "one time," "once again," or "at some later time." *Once* you may be happy: not will be, but may be, as the *balu* flowers may bloom. And so we witness a progression from the past ("the year our father passed away") to the present ("now") and on to the future—moving from despair to comfort.

And on to:

AS WE FEEL THIRSTY,
WE REACH THE SIDE OF A RIVER

kha yi skom pa'i sgang la,
chang bu bo la sleb song

The line conjures the ghost of another song, a hallowed reminder of the anguish of memory:

The water from a rocky hill,
we cannot drink if thirsty
father, our father,
we cannot meet if remembered

As water from a rocky hill cannot be tasted if inaccessible, father, though remembered, cannot be "met" if no longer of this world.

But here we find a different denouement: the thirst is quenched, the water can be drunk. "The moment thirst fills our mouth, we have already arrived [*sleb song*, "lepsong"] at a river." But can such magic work for the presence of fathers?

Before this is answered, the women begin their final couplet:

ON ONE RHODODENDRON,
FLOWER BUDS ARE BLOOMING

Tan gu tung bu gcig la,
me toy bum bo shar song

The singularity of the "one" (*gcig*, "chi") stands out in a language that has little appetite for modifiers and thus accents how this couplet links up with its predecessor. From the *pama balu* to the rhododendron, the women carry the flower motif. But here we glimpse winter's unfolding into spring, the first budding of trees and the flowering of May. In Helambu, the brilliant colors of the rhododendron flowers, red or white, receive praise for their striking beauty. But what does this have to do with those in grief, for those pained by the thirst of memory?

WHEN REMEMBERING FATHER,

yab chen dran pa'i sgang la

the men sing. Will this follow the same fate as the song above, "we cannot meet if remembered"? No, not here:

WE REACH A FORESTED SUMMIT

ri yul che la sleb song

The second line of the couplet adopts the structure of the first: "when remembering father," literally, "we arrive at the top of a forested land." And so to outwit the ironic impossibility affirmed by another song (" . . . we cannot *meet* if remembered"), we can satiate memory's cravings as much as we can quench our thirst. But note that the thirst is not quenched on a physical plane (fathers do not return, save as shades of memory). Instead, it is fulfilled spiritually: when remembering father, long since dead, we ascend to spiritual heights matched only by the purity and divine grace of mountain summits. Through poetry, the irony is transcended, the tension effaced. Like the germination of flowers, songs of *tsher ka*, though painful, can transform.

The women celebrate:

LIKE THE BLOSSOMING FLOWER,
MAY YOUR HEARTS ALSO BLOOM

me toy shar kyi le mu,
pu jong sems pa shar to

The song ends with an open simile: the human heart is likened to a blossoming flower, telling us something of poetry's capacity to transcend—to mold the pain of grief into beauty. The blossom anticipates a harvest to come. "May" suggests a hope, if not an affirmation for change, but also a plea, for it is inconclusive and ephemeral. Spring, evolved to summer, will chill to winter once again. "The blossoming flowers of summer, if only they could last through winter."

*   *   *

The night cold song holds six couplets, thirty-six words, seventy-two syllables: a poetic economy comparable to the haiku of Japan. Within this binary body of word and image, a chain of signifiers moves the listener from the slow, dolorous despair of the opening statement to the vivid hope and beauty of the closing theme. The transformative power of the poetry can only be suggested; overtly, "It's just a song." But in this spiraling dance from grief to consolation, and so a lessening of grief, we stumble on the path of healing. The work of mourning has been engaged.

It is true that we shall find no direct evidence that songs of pain alleviate grief (though Yolmo funerals as a whole clearly do so). Yet their poetic form models how such a transformation might occur. Yolmo "heart-aches" entail a sense of loss, abandonment, and separation. These events are occasioned by pitfalls specific to Yolmo social life: the separation of family members, the patrilocal travels of women, the death of children and elders. Since the pitfalls are common ones, sentiments of *tsher ka* imply a core emotional pattern, a "plot" that narrates a loss, a separation, a sense of abandonment; the consequences of these events (weary bodies, pained hearts); and then a struggle to avoid, escape, or transcend those burdens.[55] The pattern of experience accords with other sufferings. Earlier we learned that threats of loss, dispersal, and fragmentation disturb the physiology of Yolmo bodies, households, and villages. *Tsher ka* is the visceral correlative of these images. Its dark presence speaks of broken bodies, lost birds, and downhill descents.

The funeral song works with *tsher ka*'s plotted sensibility to effect change. The lyrics retell a common story—a world of pain, a father remembered, a call to ignore the pain, and an attempt to "cut" it from the body. The singers, by giving image to grief, create a moment in which the bereaved realize some of the basic forms and tensions of their existence. My sense is that the epiphany can be a powerful one for Yolmo wa, not only because the moment is revelatory but because the world revealed by it accords with basic bodily dispositions and so seems apt and valid and of the natural order of things. "What he encounters is his own story," Gadamer says of a spectator to a Greek tragedy.[56] The same might be said of a villager dancing a song of separation. The singers move themselves and their audience through the successive stages of a burden that they usually do not wish to confront in their everyday lives. The song's ghostly rhythms, in telling a tale of grief, evoke the experiential contours of loss and, in so doing, summon the imaginative forces needed to soothe that grief. Toward that end, the messages hidden within the recesses and echoes of the poem are as significant as its discursive strategies.

Those messages often hold to the level of the body. Feet grow weary, hearts blossom, desire "sticks" to the body. The songs evoke and recall the most visceral of experiences, as if one of their key functions is to engage the body, to alter human sentience. The likelihood that Yolmo bodies are the true authors for, and audiences of, the songs implies a great deal. Recent ethnographies claim that emotions should be treated as "discourses," more sentiment than feeling, less visceral than cerebral.[57] But the evidence from Padma's funeral and Yolmo songs of separation force us to rethink the body-as-text conceit. The couplets voice a handful of words, but those words speak of "heartaches" and "sorrows" as supremely felt experiences that the participants of a funeral seem most ready to avoid. Such experiences are not in any way "psychological" ones, as modern English defines the term—that is, as belonging more to the mind than the body. Rather, they consist of gut feelings that rain from head to foot.

Still, when I listen to the songs, I come away with the sense that Yolmo experience is profoundly locked into the larger social context influencing it. Yolmo sentience is itself deeply cultural. Feelings of *tsher ka*, spawned by losses, partings, and constraints on emotional expression, reveal a web of somatic, social, and political fields and forces. Any study of suffering in Helambu must therefore appreciate how Yolmo history and a person's distress inform one another. But to reduce the songs to rhetorical strategies only, to a politics detached from the heart, would do justice neither to those who sing them nor to the burdens that they bear. We often come to know others by listening to what they say (or sing) of their experiences. While this makes an assessment of those experiences profoundly difficult (is it just words or truly an expression of lived experience?), it would be a mistake to say it is only talk. Pain lives in the flesh as well as in words, though we may never see it that way.

5. Soul Loss

"Another man died last night," Nyima said as I stepped up to her home late one rainy morning.

"Yes sister," I said. "I saw the lamas descend from the temple and arrive here last night."

She was leaning against her storefront doorway, trying to shield a cigarette from the wind so she could light it. Her hands were shaking.

"Did you drink tea?" she asked with quick, high-pitched breaths.

"Yes. I drank."

Raindrops snapped against the tin roof and the road beneath us was muddy and slick.

"Another man died last night," she whispered.

She lit another cigarette before realizing that the lit end of another hung over the edge of the store counter.

She stared out into the rain for several seconds, then whispered the Buddhist prayer, "*om mani padme hum.*"

Her eyes were damp and I thought she was going to cry.

She turned from me, whispered the prayer again, then walked, alone, into her house.

The evening before this conversation (which occurred on the four-teenth of June, the start of the rainy season), Urgyen, an elderly man from the village of Todhang, died after several days of intense fever. Nyima, who lived in Todhang before marrying Latu, had called Urgyen "uncle" since she was a child; they belonged to the same "family." Upon his death, the younger men from Todhang rushed through Gulphubanyang on their way north to call the head lama to perform the cremation rites. They stopped by Nyima's home first to alert Latu of the death and to take the Lamaist drum, horn, and cremation instruments in his possession back to Todhang. Late that night, flashlights tracked the lamas' descent on the northern hillside as the priests hurried south to the home of the deceased. Early the next morning they cremated his body.

This was the second death in as many weeks for the community of Gulphubanyang. Padma, the lama from the village of Dhupchughyang, died in his sleep fifteen days before. In the days following Padma's death, villagers prepared for his funeral, which was to take place in early July. Now they readied themselves for a second series of Buddhist rites.

In the weeks following Urgyen's death, Nyima lost her *bla* or "spirit." Though she appeared distressed during this time, sitting by her storefront with a pained and weary expression on her face, I only learned of the illness on the thirtieth of June, when she told me that a Tamang shaman performed a small ceremony the night before to "call" the lost vitality back into Nyima's body.

Nyima had been sick a fortnight, having lost her spirit upon falling down while crossing a stream on her way to the temple to attend one of the weekly funeral rites for Padma. Her spirit had fallen into the hands of a "forest *shi 'dre*," a particularly dangerous shade, and she suffered from a fever, swollen glands in the neck, a headache, and a heavy body. She dreamed of going to a stream, approaching a water mill, meeting police officers, reaching a new, unfamiliar place, and feeling afraid. She did not want to walk, eat, or work.

"I do not wish to go anywhere lately," she said. "I only want to rest."

The morning after the healing rite, Nyima expressed confidence that the shaman had recovered her spirit, for she felt a jolt of "electricity" through her body when it returned.

"Today," she said, "I feel a little better."

Several days later, on the eve of Padma's fifth week *dge ba* ("gewa") funeral, Nyima still appeared to be distressed—worse, even, than prior to the healing. On the day before the funeral, I found her sitting by herself, glancing toward the ground, observing the life of the village but not participating in it.

"How does your body feel today, sister?" I asked.

"It's okay," she said.

"Then, will you be going to the funeral?"

"Yes."

Nyima (and Latu) did not climb the hill to Padma's house the next day. That evening, while most villagers (including myself) attended Padma's funeral, a Yolmo shaman from Todhang came to Nyima's home and performed the much larger *srog dgu mi* ("sok ghumi") rite in a second attempt to recover her waning vitality. The second healing combined soul-calling with exorcism to separate the nine *srog* or "life supports" from the clutches of an afflicting ghost: in a rite reminiscent of the "cutting of souls" performed during some funerals (wherein the *rnam shes* of the deceased is ritually separated from a close family member), the shaman "cut" the ghost from Nyima's body and rescued her life-forces from the land of the dead.

Two days after the healing, Nyima said the rite was successful. She felt well since the healing, claiming that the shaman recovered the life-forces from the haunts of deadly ghosts. "Afterwards, my body felt light, I wanted to eat again, and I could walk." Her main symptoms of spiritlessness (insomnia, heavy body, lack of volition, ominous dreams) were "lost." In the weeks following the healing, my observations matched her assessment, for she appeared to be much better than in the days preceding the second healing. She was full of energy and eager to talk.

*   *   *

I want to explore the ways in which Yolmo aesthetic sensibilities influence how and why villagers such as Nyima lose their life-forces, what the losses feel like, and why this form of illness prevails around Gulphubanyang. There are many ways to approach the issue of "soul loss." The literature on *susto*, an oft-studied form of "fright"-induced spiritlessness common to many Latin American societies, offers several paradigms. Freudian-minded researchers argue that *susto* is a symptomatic expression of psychic conflict and its resultant stress.[1] Rubel, O'Nell, and Collado-Ardon suggest that *susto* in Oaxaca, Mexico, arises out of stressful social situations in which the sufferer cannot live up to his or her social role.[2] And Bolton finds a positive and significant correlation between Peruvian *susto* and hypoglycemia.[3]

In my estimation, these models, though valuable in their own right, are limited. They fail to consider how forms and sensibilities specific to a society shape not only the conception but the experience and expression of illness. Nor do they develop adequate theories to account for the effectiveness of traditional healing as understood by patients themselves. At the same time, "ethnopsychological" studies of cultural experience, which do focus on patients' experiences, tend not to go beyond indigenous accounts. I find these approaches to be problematic as well, for a society's explicit psychology does not simply entail "reflections on" or "of" subjective experience;[4] it embodies an ideology that can be at odds with personal desire. Sherry Ortner points out that American anthropologists have typically looked at "the ways in which society and culture shape personality, consciousness, ways of seeing and feeling."[5] Yet much remains to be learned about how cultural ways of seeing and feeling tie into experiences of personal distress—how, for instance, social constraints on knowledge and empathy contribute to the nature and frequency of culturally recognized forms of suffering, or how healing rites attend to these complaints.[6] If culture is like a city, with a maze of narrow streets, haphazard alleys, and old and new houses (as Geertz, adopting Wittgenstein's trope for language, suggests), then anthropology's task is only first "to work up some rough sort of map of it."[7] We must also grasp how a culture's various dead ends, blind alleys, and makeshift detours either aid or hinder the lives of those who live within. To do so, we must ultimately step outside the city and view it, with the savvy of a local, from a distant hill.

Hoping, then, to blend a phenomenology of Yolmo experiences with some cross-cultural perspectives, I examine the play between aesthetic sensibilities and emotional distress, particularly the social forces that shape, make sense of, and occasionally exacerbate Yolmo feelings of loss. My thesis is that Yolmo philosophies of experience, and local ways of being, profoundly relate to the felt "sensibilities" of spiritlessness in Helambu; an understanding of these dynamics (and the tensions that they can spark) might help us to understand how Yolmo wa lose, and potentially regain, a sense of vitality.

The first steps in many ethnographies of suffering are to assess the social bases and cultural meanings of specific illnesses.[8] The present approach follows these leads. Yet for Yolmo wa, what Nyima's spiritlessness most means for herself and others is what it feels like: a heavy body, a wilting spirit, dark dreams. It therefore becomes crucial to understand not only the semantic but the sensory folds of Yolmo spiritlessness. In my mind, this suggests a need to complement a meaning-centered approach with a sensory-centered one. The goal of the former is to map the semantic networks within which specific idioms of distress ("heart-distress" in Iran, "heartache" in Nepal) are embedded.[9] The task of the latter would be to grasp and convey the sensibilities engaged by specific illnesses—what Nyima's body feels like as she sits on a porch, eyes down, hair unkempt.

Yet how can we begin to evaluate the weight of Nyima's body? Richard Shweder contends that we can begin to understand dysphoric experiences of this sort by reflecting on what we ourselves feel when we lose our souls: "When your soul leaves your body you feel empty. . . ."[10] Yet while Shweder's phenomenology seems to get at something basic about human feelings of emptiness, his universalism only takes us so far: what Nyima feels when she loses her spirit, and the cultural values underlying this loss, appear to be quite different from an American's sense of depression. And so rather than try to understand Yolmo dispiritedness by asking what such a loss might feel like to us, we first need to comprehend the local sensibilities that pattern the causes, import, and sensory grounds of specific incidents of malaise. Only by grasping the force, import, and felt presence of Nyima's discomfort can we begin to sense the heaviness of her body. The work of the previous chapters helps us here.

*   *   *

The notion of life-forces that can be lost is common to many Tibeto-Burman peoples, from the priests of Lhasa to the folk healers of Cambodia.[11] In each valley, however, the function of the life-forces, and the connotations of their loss, vary. "Soul loss" in Helambu takes several forms, from a loss of "spirit" (*bla*) and life-supports (*srog*) to the diminishment of one's "life span" (*tshe*) (see Table 1, Chapter 3). For Yolmo wa, the *bla* implies the vital essence of a living person, a spiritual support on which other psychological functions (volition, motivation, energy) rest.[12] *Bla* (pronounced "la," with the "b" a silent Tibetan prefix) bestows energy to the body and volition to the mind. It is a spiritual essence that provides the volitional impetus to engage in life—the "spirit" to get out of bed, eat, and walk up a hill to talk with family. Like a person's *rnam shes*, the *bla* can depart from the body; unlike the "soul," its loss causes not death, but illness. Represented in one's shadow, a healthy *bla* gives energy, vitality, and volition; when this shadow fades, a person falls into a lethargic slumber, wanting neither to eat, work, talk, nor sleep.

A loss of spirit (*bla 'khyer zin*, "la kelzin"; literally, "the spirit has already been taken away") is distinct from the diminishment of a "life span" (*tshe nyams pa*). While sitting with me one rainy afternoon, Nyima gestured toward a gaunt but spritely old man bearing a heavy bundle of grass on his back. "He can carry a load that big and he's eighty years old!" When I suggested that he must have a healthy "spirit," she corrected me, explaining that it would be the *tshe*, not the *bla*, that would be "big." As I then learned, *tshe* refers to the ability to perform such endeavors (to be able to carry grass), and *bla* involves the volition to act (to want to carry the grass). In turn, while the "life span" is thought to diminish slowly like the waning of the moon, the *bla* typically leaves the body when a person is startled: a quick fall, birds rustling in a dark forest, or a nervous, solitary walk near a cremation ground can spook the spirit from the body. "When we go into the forest," Meme explained, "or into the night, alone, and something scares us, we can lose our spirit."

"Spirit loss" often relates to the frail sense of "presence" that marks Yolmo consciousness: "If you are concentrating, thinking of only one thing," Karma told me, "and someone frightens you, you become scared, and lose the *bla*." Another common cause of *bla* loss, particularly among children, results from falling down, either along a path or while crossing a stream or river. Spirits are also lost when one is alone. "If you are alone," Latu told me, "in the forest or by a stream or at night, then the *bla* can easily be lost." The ensuing fright startles the spirit, which vacates the body to wander, unbenownst to its owner, "hither and thither," near forest, stream, or cremation grounds. Once parted from the body, the *bla* can fall into the hands of a ghost or witch and thus be carried into the land of the dead.

The loss of the *bla* can be an insidious process, without the afflicted knowing, for several days, that his or her spirit has been lost. Often dreams foretell of the imminent loss of vitality. An airplane, bus, horse, or motor traveling through a child's dreams forewarns that the *bla* has flown from the body. The dispirited may also envision themselves sleeping face down, wandering through a forest, roaming the cremation grounds, descending into a valley, or encountering a stream that proves difficult to cross or return upon.

When a person loses the *bla*, he or she loses the will and spirit to act in life. As Latu put it, "A healthy *bla*'s function is to give energy and vitality. If the *bla* is present in the body you can do anything; if lost, you cannot." "*Sems pa ma yong*," said Dawa: "No passion comes." "When the *bla* is lost," a farmer recalled, "a man falls asleep, feels tired, sleepy, lazy. He cannot get up quickly, can eat just a little, and wants only to stay at home." In turn, a person feels tired and restless, but "sleepiness" rarely enters the heartmind. The pulse slows and becomes irregular "like a watch that is not ticking properly." "Dullness" (*tumtum*) wells within the heartmind, dimming the afflicted's thoughts, memory, and sense of alertness. "The *sems* is not constant [*talpul talpul*]," Meme characterized the heartminds of the spiritless. "There's no equilibrium, no balance. The heartmind cannot decide on things, it keeps changing thoughts."

Along with those typical symptoms, sufferers of *bla 'khyer zin* occasionally report bodily pains not directly tied to cultural notions of the illness. The discomfort is usually linked to the assault of a ghost preying on its victim, for a weakened vitality makes a person prone to further illnesses. "Spirit loss does not cause pain," Nyima said in reference to the fever, headache, and swollen neck that she suffered, "ghosts do."

The discussion above outlines the sensory range of Yolmo spiritlessness. Yet while bouts of "spirit loss" bear common features, each incident presents a slightly different form and etiology, from Nyima's anxiety to Mingma's frailty, such that a precise and singular symptomology fades. We therefore need to review, one by one, distinct incidents of of the ailment, a method that contributes to the eclectic, mosaiclike pattern of this chapter.

*   *   *

Nyima stumbled while crossing a stream on the way to Padma's funeral; the ensuing fright led to the loss of her spirit. Yet my sense is that Nyima fell ill not solely because of any fright, but because she suffered a complex of emotional/bodily distress that was intensified by an inability to deal with that distress. Several stressful events preceded Nyima's malaise: three villagers close to her died (her uncles Urgyen and Padma and a twelve-year old "niece" who died of a sudden fever; see Table 2). I would suggest that these losses led to her illness. Nyima appeared deeply distressed by the losses she suffered and by the cultural ramifications of that distress; both her "sorrow" (*sdug*) in the wake of death and the high cultural value placed on avoiding sorrow contributed, it appears, to her feelings of malaise.

Nyima's behavior on the morning of Urgyen's cremation seemed to reflect her turmoil and offer insight into her subsequent spiritlessness. Shaky, nervous, slightly evasive, highly but not openly emotional, she acted in a manner tacitly patterned by Yolmo aesthetic sensibilities. These sensibilities shape and constrain personal experience. With Nyima, they directly contributed to the force of her grief. While Yolmo wa greatly value friendship and close social bonds, they also lament the loss of friendships and loved ones, suggesting that the importance of kinship relates to an acute sensitivity to loss. Unfortunately, there are presently many occasions for familial separations in Yolmo society: parents die, daughters leave home in marriage, and sons and husbands seek employment in foreign lands. For villagers, the loss of friendship or intimate ties, by way of separation or death, brings pronounced distress, for such ties largely form the content and tenor of Yolmo experience. A death disrupts the emotional balance of the entire community and throws into question notions of personal and communal identity.[13]

TABLE 2.   Chronologies: Nyima and Mingma.

Date	Event	Nyima	Mingma
5/24	Nyima's niece dies		
5/29	Padma dies		
6/13	Urgyen dies		
6/14	Urgyen's cremation	Distress observed	
Late June		Loss of spirit	Loss of spirit
6/29		First healing: calling of spirit (unsuccessful)	
7/1			Healing: *srog dgu mi* rite (successful)
7/4	Padma's *dge ba* funeral	Second healing: *srog dgu mi* rite (successful)	
7/9			Interview
7/20	Urgyen's *shyang par* funeral		
9/14		Interview	
12/10	Padma's final funeral	Falls ill; recovers within a week	
2/14	Departure from field		

In Helambu, the manifest, culturally prescribed reaction to death is one of restrained mourning, but more private feelings of loss often haunt the bereaved. These felt immediacies, which range from bodily pains to dreams of the deceased, are compounded by cultural constraints on the expression and interpretation of distress. Although villagers perceive all forms of distress to be highly troublesome, the high value placed on corporate solidarity leads to powerful social constraints against openly or excessively expressing troublesome feelings. Villagers thus value the ability to "hold" one's heartmind—to "hide" one's thoughts within the body and not let on, when faced with grief, pain, or anger, that one is hurting. Compared to "the rhetoric of complaint" found in the Mediterranean, where a man copes with suffering by openly expressing his plight to others,[14] Yolmo wa evince a "rhetoric" of silence, holding that they must hide their sorrows. The aesthetic value of smooth surfaces occasions this disposition.

Nyima exemplified the rhetoric of silence. Her anxiety on the morning of Urgyen's death suggests she felt greatly distressed over this loss, particularly so since it followed the deaths of two villagers close to her. Despite her pain, Nyima struggled to contain it, to "hold" her heart and maintain an outwardly stoic face. She tried to "hide" her heart in front of me and, we may infer, most others. She asked if I had taken tea, busied herself with cigarettes, and retreated into her house.

But even within the privacy of her home, I suspect Nyima struggled with distress and confusion. Just as Yolmo wa disapprove of the social expression of personal turmoil, so they learn to shun it privately. A villager realizes, through visceral, tactile means, that it is an entirely sensible strategy to avoid emotional distress and so keep the heartmind "clear." The Buddhist aesthetic of purity leads to the maxim that it is "better not to think" of worrisome sentiments, for they can only bring pain.

All this added to Nyima's anxiety. Presumably, Urgyen's death troubled Nyima. Yet so did her feelings of *sdug*. Her sorrow, which burdened her body as much as her heartmind, was unwanted, painful, and frightening; she wanted to evade it. She was torn between the need to "cleanse" her body of painful pollutants and a reluctance to directly confront her distress.

Nyima's distress, intensified by two contradictory values, could apply, in varying intensity and duration, to many villagers after a close death. Yet only Nyima lost her "spirit" after Urgyen's death. Nyima's husband Latu, for instance, learned of the death just as Nyima did, but at no time did he complain of illness. In turn, Latu's younger brother Dawa told me on the day of Urgyen's cremation that he was feverish and that his right hand "hurt," yet he did not experience the lingering malaise that Nyima felt. Why do some suffer from spirit loss after a death but not others?

I would contend that Nyima's spiritlessness was due to a failure in the "work of mourning," a failure precipitated by tensions embedded in the Yolmo spectrum of values. In 1917, Freud proposed that the difference between mourning and melancholy rests on an individual's ability to "work through" one's grief.[15] Anthropologists have subsequently argued that elaborate mourning rituals in many cultures reduce the risks of depression and maladaptive grief by facilitating the expression and transformation of fears, anxieties, and emotional tensions.[16] Rosenblatt, Walsh, and Jackson, for instance, found that members of societies that perform final funeral ceremonies months or years after the actual death lack prolonged expressions of grief.[17] Members of societies that lack final funerals, on the other hand, exhibit prolonged expressions of grief, suggesting that final rites help resolve lingering distress. These ideas are supported by Keyes's account of Mrs K., a Thai woman who suffered depression subsequent to her mother's death.[18] Keyes found that the death of Mrs. K's mother, who was central to her life, produced a marked loss of self-esteem, which contributed to a depressed mood.[19] Yet in my opinion, Mrs. K's melancholy could also be read as a failure in the work of mourning, for she was unable to participate in mourning rites on her mother's behalf.

The lengthy series of funerary rites performed by Yolmo wa (each of the first seven weeks after a death, and one year later) might similarly help the bereaved to soothe the cutting pain of loss. While these ceremonies promise intense emotionality, there exist strong social pressures to attend to them. As suggested in the preceding chapter, the ritual content of funerals often helps participants to alleviate and transcend sentiments of grief ("Do not mind your aching heart, do not mind your weary body"). A strategy of successive funerals would be of particular importance to Yolmo wa, for, with the dominant ethos being one of emotional avoidance and restraint, a series of funerals would prompt the bereaved to submit to the mourning process. Clinical research, meanwhile, suggests that the unwillingness or inability to undergo "grief work" may lead to a morbid or "pathological" grief reaction bearing a symptomology similar to that of depression.[20] As Lindemann writes, "One of the big obstacles of this work seems to be the fact that many patients try to avoid the intense distress connected with the grief experience and to avoid the expression of emotion necessary for it."[21] Subsequent research has proven that, while this kind of pathology does not occur as frequently as Lindemann reported, the principle holds true.[22]

The observation seems to hold true for Nyima as well. While other villagers attended Urgyen's "wake" and subsequent funerary rites to mourn his death, Nyima avoided them. As far as I know, she did not visit Urgyen's home after he died nor did she attend the culminating funeral ceremonies for Padma.

"I don't like going to funerals," Nyima said on the eve of Padma's funeral. "They make me feel sad. I don't like all the crying, the time when people cry."

"Why is that so, sister?," I asked.

"Because I am an old woman now. The songs we sing make our hearts hurt [*sems pa sdug po*]."

I took Nyima's words to imply a cultural belief that, as a woman (or man) ages, the more she ponders and fears death. By skipping the funeral, Nyima sought to avoid the *sdug* promised by the songs. Indeed, her reluctance to attend to her sorrow, reinforced by Yolmo sensibilities, might have related to the loss of her spirit. If it is necessary, as Freud proposed, for an individual to work through one's grief subsequent to a loss (with the meaning, import, and sensory range of "grief" and "loss" being culturally defined), then cultural dynamics can either facilitate or impede this process. Gorer, for instance, suggests that the fear and denial of death entrenched in British and American societies hinders the normal mourning process, making sentiments of grief problematic for its bearers.[23]

Similar themes haunt the residents of Helambu, though the "grief" they know of is of a very visceral sort. With Nyima, an ethos of emotional avoidance and restraint exacerbated her distress, trapping her between the desire to "cleanse" her body of its weariness and the reluctance or inability to attend to that sorrow. The funerals might have been effective in themselves in assuaging feelings of loss (as they apparently were for Latu, Dawa, and others), the culminating "songs of pain" might have offered final passage from sorrow to consolation, but Nyima avoided the rites because of the intense emotionality promised. Unable to deal with her sorrow, she was unable to cut it from her body. She attributed the ensuing feelings of malaise to a loss of "spirit."

*   *   *

Yet if emotional distress lies at the root of spirit loss, where does the etiology of "fright" come from? I believe it runs parallel to the symptomology and repercussions of fright in childhood. Childhood patterns of spirit loss differ from what adults experience of this illness. While there is one "illness" category ("spirit loss"), there are at least two "diseases." Adult experiences of *bla 'khyer zin* include a diffuse spectrum of distress ranging from lack of volition to bodily fatigue; "spirit loss" among children involves a more specific dynamic and etiology.

Children are known to lose their spirits more readily than adults do. As Karma explained, "Most *bla* loss occurs with children, because they're more prone to frightening events. They scare easier and automatically show their fear. Maybe they're not conscious of it, but they show it, and the *bla* goes." Perhaps due to these indications, it is easier to divine when children suffer spirit loss. As Nyima once said, "It is difficult to know when adults have *bla 'khyer zin* but we can easily tell when our children do." Spirit loss among children bears a precise behavioral patterning: the child becomes silent, withdrawn, numb.

"Fright" plays a major role in causing these symptoms. In fact, I believe that sudden frights do, indeed, spark spirit loss among children. Spirit loss occurs when a child is "shocked," to use the phenomenologist Schutz's terms, by a sudden disturbance in "the reality" of his or her "everyday life."[24] As the Yolmo universe is founded on social relations, a child's world is precariously built out of close social ties, a well-defined environmental context, and a tacit dependence on this context in order to function healthily in everyday life. If this context is breached or threatened, the shock frightens a child's spirit from the body.

But what does it mean to say that a child lacks a "spirit"? When a Yolmo boy loses the *bla*, he becomes detached, reticent, out of it. He declines to speak, even when prodded to do so, and no longer participates in the activities that formerly engaged him: eating, playing, and socializing. In turn, the desire for "presence" is lost, for spiritless children cease to carefully attend to the immediate reality about them. This combination of symptoms suggests that the "spirit" actually lost is a child's urge to attend to and interact with his or her environment. One six-year-old boy, for instance, arrived at a local festival with his mother. Silent, lethargic, and distinctly expressionless, he clung to his mother's legs and refused to eat.

"He fell down yesterday," his mother said. "Maybe his spirit is lost."

Mingma's timid three-year-old grandchild, meanwhile, reportedly lost his spirit on the eve of a funeral. The infant was not in the mood to play, was easily upset, and refused to leave his parents' arms.

"Something frightened him earlier," his father said. "He must have lost his spirit."

What struck me most about these instances of spirit loss was the withdrawn, retractive demeanor of their young sufferers. It was as if the spirit had not, in fact, escaped from the body, but had retreated within, to hide within its protective shell. Notice how local rudiments of form tacitly frame the event: the image is of a frightened child withdrawing into the safety of his home, bolting the door shut, and peeking through closed windows to view the seemingly tempestuous activities of the world outside.

The act of retreating into the body relates to a distinct behavioral pattern found among Yolmo children when faced with frightening situations. As I spoke one night with a young woman who was preparing a dinner for her family, we began to compare funeral practices in Nepal and America. At one point, I asked how she would feel if her mother were to die. Her eight-year-old brother Babu listened to our conversation as he snacked on boiled potatoes. After several minutes, I noticed he was acting in an uncommon fashion: he sat motionless, without eating, speaking, or interacting. He held a blank, emotionless face, save for wide eyes that gazed out on us. I tried to joke with him, as we were playing moments before, but he continued to sit and stare blankly.

"Is something wrong?" I nodded toward the boy.

"Oh, he does that whenever someone is talking about dying, or any other time when he gets scared," his sister said.

Minutes after we moved to another topic, Babu began to interact with us once again.

Babu's retreat resembled the behavioral pattern intrinsic to children's experiences of spirit loss. When children are very anxious, they seem to withdraw, tortoiselike, into their body. Frightened by what they have encountered in the outside world, they decline to participate in it. To use the metaphor of the house, they apparently shut the doors and windows of their body and passively watch the outside world from the corner of a window, refusing to come out again until they know it is safe to do so.[25]

Distinct but similar patterns are evident when Yolmo children experience anger or pain. On another occasion, I visited Babu's home late in the morning. His mother was trying to get him to eat before going off to school, but he silently stomped about the house in an apparent attempt to avoid interacting with his parents and older siblings yet still make his presence felt.

"He doesn't wish to eat?" I asked.

"No," his mother said. "He's angry at us and will not eat or talk."

A child's reticence to engage with others also occurs when he or she suffers pain. One morning I encountered Norbu, a classmate of Babu, along the path to Meme's home as he and his sister were on their way to the schoolhouse. Norbu lay on the side of the road with his face to the ground as his elder sister attempted to attend to him. She told me that he had fallen and scratched his face against a rock. I tried to turn Norbu toward me so that I could see his face, but he buried his tearstained face in the ground again.

"He won't let me look at him either," his sister said.

The inclination to withdraw from one's environment, remain silent, and cease to interact with others characterizes spirit loss among Yolmo children. In all cases of the malady that I observed among Yolmo children, the symptomology was similar: children became very passive and ceased to talk, move their bodies, or make facial expressions. They stopped engaging with their environments. In my estimation, this behavioral pattern is structured by local sensibilities of body and person. As Yolmo experiences are founded on interactions between a body and its outer environment, children greatly extend themselves into their immediate environment in normal circumstances: they rarely keep to themselves, constantly interact with others, and derive much of their identity from these interactions. At times of stress, children feel the need to sever ties and retract, as a defensive measure, into the inner realm of the body. Spirit loss is the name applied to this tortoiselike retreat into the body. The ways children act (or fail to act) lead villagers to believe that a child's spirit quits the body, but it may be that the "spirit" (as a metaphor for the interactive self) remains hidden within the confines of the corporeal abode.

*   *   *

Yeshi, a young, recently married woman, lost her spirit in late spring. Meme told me of this illness when I visited his home one evening, and I accompanied him to a healing performed on her behalf. At dusk we climbed down a hillside trail until we came to an isolated, single-chamber household, where Yeshi lived with her husband Tenzin, their two young children, and Kusang, her widowed father-in-law. In the several visits I paid to the unprosperous home, the atmosphere within struck me as tense, constrained, and troubled. It was the same the night of her healing. Compared with other ceremonies I attended, the participants remained quiet and somber. Few neighbors came. While Kusang watched the proceedings from his bed and Tenzin cooked the evening's meal, Yeshi stared into the fire and nursed her youngest child. Reticent, aloof, spiritless, she sat benumbed as Meme searched the lands of death for her spirit.

"What is wrong with our sister?" I asked shortly after arriving at the one-room house, suspecting it was improper to address Yeshi directly.

"She lost her *bla*," Tenzin caught my eye for a moment, then turned to the hearth to prepare a pot of rice.

"What does she feel?" I asked.

Silence. The glare of the fire.

"She has felt dizzy, and a piercing pain [*tsher ka*] hurts along the neck, the arms, the back. She often feels like vomiting."

"How long has she felt like this?"

"About six months now."

"How do you know a lack of spirit has caused these pains?"

"We just know. It has happened before."

"Then tell me, elder brother, how did she lose her spirit?"
"That is something we don't yet know."

I never spoke directly to Yeshi, though from what I observed of her life in the months prior to and after the healing, she appeared (to me) to be uncommonly lifeless. She displayed slow motor movements, lack of affect, and a general apathy toward her surroundings. At the festivals, funerals, and healings where our paths crossed, I found her to be quiet and reserved—weary, perhaps, of her recent marriage, a child clinging to her knee, and another sucking on her breast. Most of all, I was struck by the aura of spiritlessness that engulfed her: she expressed little, be it of joy or sorrow.

Yeshi's malaise can be better understood if set within the context of her life at this time. Along with the heartache potentially found in parting from family, a Yolmo bride must come to terms with the heavy work load and conditions encountered in a husband's household. By all accounts, these conditions are less severe than those faced by Hindu women in Nepal and India, but the tasks are still trying ones.[26] As a newlywed, Yeshi could retreat to her natal home for long periods of time if dissatisfied with or frightened by her marriage. But after giving birth, she is tied to her new home. Most Yolmo women claim and appear to be content with marriage after several years, but they often recall the first years in their husbands' homes as the most difficult of their lives.

Yeshi appeared to be facing such difficulties—even more so, perhaps, than other young Yolmo women. Her natal village lay a significant distance from Tenzin's, making it difficult to visit her family frequently. As her mother-in-law died years before, she was the only woman in an impoverished household, and so cut off from the kind of intimacy often built between mother- and daughter-in-law once the latter bears children. Neither Tenzin nor Kusang acted particularly warmly toward her, speaking to her in cold, commanding terms. In sum, Yeshi appeared to be under significant stress, had few outlets to express her grievances, and perhaps saw no conceivable way to transcend them.

The loss of Yeshi's spirit may have resulted from these burdens. Like Nyima, she was caught in a no-win situation in which she forsaw no way out of her dilemma. But while Nyima's spiritlessness was brought on by loss and the vicious circle of distress induced by contradictory values, Yeshi lost her spirit due to an untenable living situation and the perceived inability to escape that situation. In a different cultural context, Yeshi might have had recourse to a social role or strategy that would have offered her an escape from her distress (such as becoming a religious adept).[27] But as a young Yolmo bride, she had no meaningful options available to her, nor legitimate means to communicate her distress, and so fell ill.[28] She lost her spirit—the will to act, speak, or eat. Lacking hope and power, she could no longer cope with the frustrations in her environment and simply gave up. Her family found her to be ill, though it was questionable whether the sick role offered relief.

The last point breaches the limits of current thinking on "somatization." Somatization refers to "the presentation of personal and social distress in an idiom of physical complaints and a coping style of medical help seeking."[29] In this view, a somatizing body re-presents psychological distress, with physical ailments serving as "metaphors" of a more basic psychic pathology.[30] As Shweder writes, "frayed nerves, tired blood, splitting heads and broken hearts can be thought of as the metonymic metaphors of suffering."[31] Kleinman advocates this position, taking somatization to include "a coping style of medical help seeking."[32] Here physical pain is, by definition, a strategy toward coping with distress.

The notion that pain embodies a poetics of expression (and so a coping strategy) ignores the fact that Yolmo spiritlessness may not, at times, be an expression of distress, but simply a response to it. I find it difficult to envision Yeshi as a "poet in search of metaphors adequate to express [her] predicament," as Kirmayer suggests of somatizing sufferers.[33] Yeshi hurts, but not in order to communicate her despair or to resist her plight. Her silence and apathy betray less a "coping strategy" than an inability to cope. She receives few gains for being sick, the sick role brings more pressure than relief, and healing ceremonies offer only limited remedies for her distress. Without denying the significance and prevalence of "somatoform" disorders in Helambu and elsewhere, her spiritlessness reminds us that there are times when pain is simply pain.

It is for these reasons that I wish to steer away from the concept of "somatization" and instead advance the idea of somatic sensibilities. By "sensibility" I mean a lasting mood or disposition patterned within the workings of a body. A sensibility is occasioned by the specific (and often shifting) concerns marking a person's world. It denotes a particular way of being and so shapes how a person feels and engages with that world. This engagement takes root within a body that, in Helambu, is the primary means of giving form and meaning to experience. As Yolmo experience works more by way of sensation than symbol, a sensibility constitutes the sensory grounds of a person's experience (wherein the distinction between body and mind does not apply), and so pulses through a body's blood, fingertips, and dreams. States of grief and sorrow, we have seen, are not simply restricted to Yolmo heartminds; they trouble entire bodies. The same with spiritlessness, which must be seen as something an entire body experiences.[34] And yet a sensibility does not take form only when a body is distressed: it suggests how well the corporeal mosaic is put together at a given moment and so characterizes a villager's reality in illness and in health, in pain and in comfort.

Realities of this sort are grounded in Yolmo aesthetic values. The sensibility of a healthy person includes a sense of presence, harmony, and bounded integration. The sensibility of an ill person lacks one or several of these qualities. Physiologies can become lacking, off-balanced, or assaulted by ghosts. Each of these possibilities equates with a certain mood or disposition that tends to reflect (but does not necessarily "represent") the pressing concerns of the afflicted. Yeshi, for instance, holds her body one evening in a slouch, eyes down, face vacant, hair unkempt. Pain pierces through her neck, arms, and back; her pulse beats slowly. Her body, in having taken this sullen form, is not necessarily trying to "express," "communicate," or "recall" something to herself or others; it simply comes to incarnate, through its everyday uses in her husband's household, a certain disposition, a somatic sensibility that, by its very nature, reflects the particular concerns, comforts, and tensions of her life. Yeshi feels a sense of loss, a lack of presence, and a waning vitality; these feelings fall within a spectrum of aesthetic value.

The sensibilities of Yeshi or Nyima do not, in themselves, denote precise symbols, idioms, or metaphors that convey to these or other villagers precise meanings. A sensibility does not represent a more basic distress; it is the visceral presence of that distress. A sensibility engages a felt quality, a general mood or disposition, that, for the most part, remains tacit within a person's flesh, dreams, and actions. Until villagers apply a semantic category (such as spirit loss) to a sensibility, it is more the visceral sense of a way of being, a whispered melody lingering in fingertips and gestures, than a concrete expression of that way of being. A sensibility is therefore more visceral experience than intellectual category, more the sentience of health than a detached interpretation of a condition. Nyima's body grows heavy, Dawa's right hand hurts. Yolmo aesthetics of the everyday fashion the sensory grounds of spiritlessness. The seemingly natural need for presence, restraint, harmony, and repletion influence what the body feels like when a woman feels a loss, when pain clings to a bride, or when an old man grows older.

*   *   *

Mingma suffered from the loss of several life-forces (the *srog* and *tshe*) the same time Nyima did, after the death of Urgyen. Urgyen's house was a few steps from Mingma's and, from what I understood, the two had been close friends since childhood. I was alerted to Mingma's illness after being called by Meme to attend a healing ceremony on Mingma's behalf, which took place in his home on the last evening of June. I learned, on arriving at Mingma's home, that he suffered from the loss of several life-forces. Consequently, Meme was summoned to "call" the lost life-forces back into his body. As with Nyima, the elaborate *srog dgu mi* ("sok gumi") rite was performed to rescue Mingma's lost *srog* from the land of the dead and to enhance his diminished "life span" (*tshe*).

Mingma did not appear to be gravely ill before or during the healing, but he suffered, at least, from a severe cold and lung congestion. Thin, quiet, reserved, he rested on his bed alone or with his young granddaughter when he was not required to participate in the rites. After the healing concluded early in the morning, the participants of the healing went to sleep to the sound of his coughing and congested breathing.

When I spoke with Mingma the following week, he said Meme divined that a ghost "ate" five of his nine *srog*. He lost the "life-supports" one by one, and the threat of the other four being lost (and hence of dying) was imminent. "The bombo told me," he added, "I had the same illness as the man who died [Urgyen]."

Upon listening to Mingma's tale, I was struck by the fact that, as with Nyima, the loss of life-forces occurred after the death of a close friend, a loss that itself followed the passing of another friend (Padma) several weeks earlier. These losses were of particular significance for Mingma, for he too was approaching death, an event that he was apparently apprehensive about. He dreamed of death, but unlike Nyima, who dreamed of ghosts and haunted memories of death, his dreams hinted at his own mortality. His nightly visions of dead persons, graveyards, and rivers crossed but not returned upon seemed to evince the presence of death—not only Urgyen's and Padma's, but his own.

As we have seen, Yolmo wa fear death primarily because it severs the "bonds" of love between family members. It is noteworthy, then, that when asked what came to his heartmind when Meme called back his life-forces, Mingma said "I was thinking that maybe my life will return, and, if it does, then I can live one or two more years and still do the things I wish to." Along with business concerns, these activities included participating in the lives of his children and grandchildren.

In my view, Mingma's illness derived from a complex of emotional distress sparked by the death of old friends. This distress was similar to, yet distinct from, Nyima's grief. As with Nyima, the same cultural constraints on emotional expression applied. And as with Nyima, an experience of loss catalyzed the distress. But Mingma's malaise seemed to intimate another loss, one that lay in the distant yet imminent future: the loss of his own life, friends, and family. Urgyen's death reminded Mingma of his own mortality and the inevitability of death. Though haunted by this fate, he had few means to express his despair or come to terms with it in himself, save to imagine that he lost his vitality "when walking at night, alone, on a road, in darkness."

*   *   *

Nyima and Yeshi, like Mingma, also lost their spirits, but for different reasons. Despite the range of experiences, however, Yolmo soul loss engages similar sensibilities. All three fell ill in similar ways. They lost their "passion" for life. Heavy pains wounded their bodies. During the day, confusion, frailty, and a lack of presence clouded the heartmind. At night, fragmenting moons, dilapidated houses, and downhill descents haunted their dreams.

"If you lose the spirit," said Meme, "you are like a dead person, living in the land of the dead."

There are other ways to bear pain in Helambu. Ghostly pains and dreams troubled Pasang. Dawa's right hand hurt in the wake of Urgyen's death. Others fall ill from "astrological plight," the wrath of deities, or the assault of witches. Yet it appears that "soul loss," in its varied forms (the loss of *bla*, *tshe*, or *srog*), has become one of the most prevalent forms of illness in the region of Gulphubanyang. Of twenty-four shamanic healings I attended during a twelve-month period, nine served to alleviate some form of soul loss. While it is difficult to assess the ethnographic literature, it appears that incidents of spiritlessness occur more frequently among Yolmo wa than among many other ethnically Tibetan societies, such as Tamang of central Nepal or Nyinba of northwestern Nepal.[35] And, according to Karma, the residents of eastern Helambu (where he was raised) do not lose their spirits as frequently as they do around Gulphubanyang.

Why do many of Meme's patrons fall ill in this fashion? To be sure, Buddhist theology provides much of the fodder for Yolmo understandings of spiritlessness. Many of the basic tenets of Buddhism—the acknowledgment of change, decay, and death, the presence of suffering, the stress on purity, the adept's revulsion of his body, and the focus on ethical conduct and right mindfulness—propel Yolmo concerns and sensibilities.[36] In turn, Yolmo imageries of loss, decay, and fragmentation correlate with the themes of many Tibetan folk religions. In Tibet, as in Helambu, one's "life" (*tshe*) may "scatter" or become "exhausted, weakened, or lost,"[37] and one's *bla* is "subject to wear and tear"—a deterioration reflected in the "cracking" of a necklaced turquoise representative of the spirit.[38] Tibetans also know of a *rlung rta* or "wind-horse": a "high" or "low" wind-horse corresponds to a person's general well-being and worldly luck.[39] In the Lamaist *gcod* ("cutting through") ceremony, in turn, the practitioner offers his body, limb by limb, to feed his demonic guests.[40] The tantric process reflects the Osirisian theme of corporeal dismemberment in shamanic initiations,[41] a spiritual rite of passage present in South Asian myths of divine dismemberment.[42] And MacDonald identifies a model of "creative dismemberment" among Tamang and Sherpa groups wherein the mythic dismemberment of a yak—horns, tongue, and hump—gives genesis to human clans.[43]

Yolmo wa are a Buddhist people who practice shamanic healings, and many of their concerns are common to a variety of Tibetan communities. At the same time, the Buddhist views and shamanic imageries that underlie Yolmo practices have fused into a particular constellation in Helambu, such that certain perspectives, and certain patterns of experience, have taken on a particular intensity. Notions of loss, for instance, appear to hold particular relevance for the everyday concerns of villagers. Why is this so? In my estimation, Yolmo experiences often conform to a pattern of social history, and the history of social malaise influences the nature of bodily malaise. In other words, the basic tensions of corporate life as they presently exist in the vicinity of Gulphubanyang predispose its residents to suffer from lost vitality.

We learned in an earlier chapter that a fear of fission and fragmentation troubles Yolmo social groups; this fear can enshadow the physiology of a body. The forms and tensions marking Yolmo experience (be they of body, household, or village) generate the aesthetic sensibilities that tell how these forms are held together (through balance, harmony, integration), how they fall apart (through loss, decay, fragmentation), and the tensions can that lead to their dissolution (fission, conflict, malevolent intrusions). In Gulphubanyang, the present threats to local collectivities are those of conflict, fission, and dispersal. Regional politics involve antagonisms between families and villages, and the economic situation has led more males to work for long periods of time in Kathmandu and India, increasing the frequency of separations in the region. In several villages, a "migration" of young men occurs during the Nepali trekking seasons (spring and fall). Women often must live without husbands for several months of the year, and sons and daughters "cut" from home at an early age to work or attend school. These events have created a sensitivity to loss, fragmentation, and decay.

Since the physiology of the body mirrors the physiology of households, families, and villages, bodies often assume a sensibility of loss when distressed. Each illness intones a distinct melody, from the "piercing pains" of witches to the fateful dirge of astrological plight. When troubled, however, Yolmo wa often respond with a posture of languid weariness. The body fragments, its vitality withers. "Soul loss" is the sensory correlative of fragmenting mosaics: the experience suggests what it feels like when a corporate form (body, house, family) begins to fall apart. By definition, "soul loss" occurs when life-forces part from the body, yet other losses (the death of a family member, the fission of a lineage) resonate with the formal architecture of this malaise and so can induce similar feelings of spiritlessness. In this way, form and feeling deeply pattern one another. The vicissitudes of form tie into the texture of feeling, and a loss of integration equates with a loss of a *sense* of spirit and vitality.

For this reason, among others, it is important to grasp not only what soul loss means to Yolmo villagers, but also what it feels like. With a heavy body or a waning spirit comes not only a way of interpreting a world, of giving meaning to it, but a way of being in it. These ways of being have their histories. Since the losses that bodies, families, and villages know of correlate with one another, Mingma's despair recalls the misfortunes that have occurred in the history of many Yolmo forms (from the fission of lineages to the loss of family members). Yolmo history can thus be "remembered," as it were, in the way a body feels.[44] Yet it is important to note that Yolmo bodies do not incarnate history *per se* in the concrete; they incarnate the rudiments of form which make that history possible. Since Yolmo bodies, households, and villages possess similar constraints on form, are guided by similar aesthetic values, and entail comparable destinies, the felt history of Mingma's body tends to resonate with, and so seems to comment on, the history of other Yolmo forms. Again, the resonance is not one of representation, with bodily pains symbolizing a history, but one of similitude, with the histories of bodies and families resembling one another (such that a vague sense of déjà vu shadows the ethnographer when he walks from hamlet to household).

A phenomenology of embodied aesthetics thus takes us a long way in assessing how and why villagers in and around Gulphubanyang lose their spirits, and what these losses feel like. Tensions between cultural representations and personal experience, or between different aesthetic sensibilities, can, under certain conditions, spark conflicts leading to illness. With Nyima, an ethos of emotional avoidance, driven by an aesthetic of purity and restraint, exacerbated her distress in the wake of Urgyen's death. With Yeshi, a difficult living situation, combined with cultural constraints on communication, led to a spiritless body. While a culture can be seen to "work" to alleviate or transform personal distress,[45] the spectrum of values that make up a culture (as I define it here) can also cause or exacerbate distress.

The sentience of Yolmo spiritlessness is also grounded within aesthetic sensibilities. Mingma's distress, for instance, related to a slow decline of physical strength and agility. He was just ill from old age, getting older, and afraid of dying, yet his life was eclipsed by a classic Yolmo irony: his heart-mind felt younger, but his body grew older and older. Mingma despaired of the mortality of body over mind; his body assumed a sensibility that felt that despair. For others as well, a loss of vitality accords with basic bodily dispositions, and so seems a natural, sensible way to fall ill. In Helambu, aesthetic sensibilities actively configure experience: feelings of malaise tend to fall into familiar patterns; they assume common structures, like disparate musical notes come to form distinct and well-known melodies.

The melodies recur. The felt immediacies common to Yolmo soul loss belong to the society as a whole. They echo within the tissues of a body, the confines of a household, and the aging temple of a village. Villagers' tales of loss and fragmentation are borne of the corporate forms of Yolmo experience, and so embrace the tacit sensibilities and tensions occasioned by those forms. A loss of spirit thus often takes on mythic tones—namely, the erosion of form. Despite varied histories, the bodies of Mingma, Nyima, and Yeshi become no more than felt variations of a basic chord: the cadence of loss.

Part II

Healing

6. The Art of Knowing

Yeshi lay on the well-worn edge of a wood cot. While her infant daughter clung to her breast, another child nestled against the wall, his runny nose hidden within the fold of a green shawl. Newspapers yellowing with age lined the surface of the mudstone wall. In one advertisement, a plump Brahman grinned over an open refrigerator; in another, an article on Georgia O'Keefe's "Erotic Flowers" blossomed onto a *Newsweek* center-fold. Photographs hung from the mantel above. Her parents posed, young, somber, and shy, in front of a black-and-white Alpine scene cut from Kathmandu cardboard. Her husband's nephew sported sunglasses, youth-ful pride, and a Nepalese cap among classmates in front of a schoolhouse.

It was an early May evening in 1988, along the outskirts of Chumdeli, on a hillock below the temple. Minutes before, Yeshi sat by the hearth and brewed a pot of salt-butter tea to serve to her guests. Now she gazed out on the night's proceedings and nursed her infant daughter. A few women with children sat around the hearth, talking among themselves. Yeshi's husband Tenzin tended to the fire as he prepared tea and heated beer. Her father-in-law, Kusang, lay, shirtless, on a mat "touching" the fire. A whirlwind of playing cards bustled amongst five adolescent boys gathered for the eve-ning. With a loud, expansive laugh, one of the youths rested the nape of his neck against the central pillar, which held, on a bent nail, a smoky, hand-worn drum.[1]

In the far corner from Yeshi, to the right of the hearth beneath the window, Meme sat on a straw mat. While he gossiped with Tenzin, Ku-sang, and their neighbors, he cupped a cigarette to his mouth. Each drag from the cigarette lit up the corner in which he had taken residence for the night. His black cap and coat, molded into a pillow, rested at the base of the wall. At his feet, cups of salt-butter tea and wheat flour sat atop a rectangu-lar serving tray. To his left, a tan sack, once used to store potatoes, held a leather belt strung with brass bells that spilled partly from the seams of the bag. And close to the fire, in the sacred, right-hand corner of the room, was a winnowing tray with a varied assortment of ritual implements.

Photo 14. The *gtor ma* altar.

The tray held the shamanic altar, which Meme was leisurely construct-ing. After the fourteen-year-old Serki and I molded each one of the rice-dough *gtor ma* cakes, we gave it to Meme who, after checking its specific features, set it within the altar. In all there were twenty-five cakes, each an offering to, and representative of, a god who, during the healing ceremony, embodied a specific cake and helped Meme to heal.[2]

While Meme arranged the elements of the altar, a young woman entered the house with a sleeping infant bound with cloth to her back. She greeted Yeshi's family, stepped toward the altar, and uncurled her hand to show a bundle of rice grains enclosed within a loose sheath of corn. She wanted, like other neighbors, to learn of any supernatural threats to her family; the rice was an offering to the gods to reveal the information when they "fell" onto Meme to divine.

"Please take this, Meme," she said. "It is for my family."

"Ah? . . . yes, my child," Meme said, with hands held out to receive the rice kernals. He added the rice to the pile set within the winnowing tray. The woman stepped back to the left of the hearth, content to share tea and conversation until Meme divined for the guests gathered.

Meme set the final *gtor ma* cake in the altar. He leaned toward the fire and squinted at the scratched surface of his wristwatch.

"Seven o'clock," he mumbled, then snuffed out his cigarette. The sun had set.

"Hand me the drum," he said. "It's time to work."

I unlatched the drum from the central pillar and gave it to Meme. He heated it over the fire to tighten the skin, then tested the skin's tautness with light taps of the wood drumstick. A low, sonorous sound echoed through the room. The kerosene lamp lit up the faces of those gathered in the room. I took my place to the right of Meme, who was ready to call the gods to divine.

What Is Healing?

Before entering further into the night, we must ask why Yeshi's family called Meme and what they expected from the healing ceremony.

Shamanic healing is integral to Yolmo ways of construing the interrelations between body, spirit, and society. Yolmo concepts of "health" are broader, more pervasive ones than many of those found in the modern West. Health not only implies well-being on an individual, bodily scale; it means that one's familial, social, and cosmic relations proceed as a harmonious whole. Yolmo villagers, like other Tibetan peoples, live in a universe that holds three distinct realms: the celestial land of gods, with its five directions (east, south, west, north, center), the telluric land of humans, and a subterranean "hell."[3] Each of these realms includes a variety of forces and beings, many of which can cause suffering among humans. Within the land of humans a gamut of ghosts (*shi 'dre, sri*) serpent-deities (*klu*), and forest shamans (*ri bombo*) can readily inflict pain on humans if the latter cross their "paths." In turn, a heavenly god may, if not worshipped properly, cause a "hindrance" (*bar chad*) to a person's life, or a hellish demon may wreak havoc in a household. In response to these threats, villagers try to live in ways that procure good health: they avoid the springs and waterfalls where *klu* are known to live; they feign off the astrological plight of *dasa graha*; they behave in a manner that will lead to beneficial karmic effects; and they honor the gods so as to avoid their wrath.

The last prerequisite underscores many attempts by Yolmo wa to heal. If a family neglects or offends the gods (by polluting their abode, for instance), illness may ensue. Shamanic healing subsequently appeases the offended god through incense or blood sacrifice. One man learned that a serpent-deity (*klu*) assaulted his wife because the family desecrated its underground abode. "Now we will have to satisfy this god," he told me. "Satisfy" here is the Nepali *bujhāunu*—"to cause to understand"—a verb that denotes the building of an agreement or understanding. This and other terms, such as the Nepali *manāunu* (to persuade, satisfy, cause to mind), characterize the relational, contractual nature of Yolmo healing.[4]

It is evident that Yolmo experiences of illness and health rest on premises distinct from those found in the hospitals of the modern West. Yolmo wa typically express ideals of health through images of spiritual, rather than physical, fortitude. The strength and vitality of life-forces greatly contribute to health. If a person possesses a full "life span" (*tshe*), he or she cannot be "touched" by illness or harm. "You might not even be killed by a bullet," Latu once boasted. A related notion of personal well-being is encapsulated in the pan-Tibetan concept of *dbang* or "empowerment." *Dbang* ("wang") actually refers to an "initiation" into Buddhist practice but has since come to denote in Helambu (as elsewhere) the "power" that the initiation bestows on the supplicant. (Latu and I sat one summer afternoon in the corner of a Tibetan monastery, for instance, in order to receive *dbang* from a prestigious lama from Bhutan.) For Yolmo wa, *dbang* refers most to the spiritual vitality that can be attained through religious practice. Shamanic and Lamaist rituals often work toward investing *dbang* within patients, for to possess the force is to be charged with power and vitality to the extent that illness and misfortune are easily defended against.

Yet to understand that human "empowerment" can be obtained also entails that it can be lost, and Yolmo villagers are often troubled by the potential loss and deterioration of vitalities, such as *tshe*, *bla*, and *dbang*. So while personal afflictions often relate to a waning of vital life-forces, healing works to counteract this spiritual entropy by rejuvenating body and soul. In Meme's words, shamanic rites "awaken" the patient's body—just as the forest shaman (*ri bombo*) heals severed tree limbs, cut down by woodsmen, by "awakening" them at night. The verb used by Meme was the Nepali *jagāunu* "to wake up, stimulate, arouse; give life, rejuvenate."

Since Yolmo bodies and souls are continually on the wane, there is a constant need for ritual regeneration. Often the deterioration of life-forces is an insidious process that weakens one's constitution without manifesting itself in physical symptoms. Villagers therefore participate in Lamaist and shamanic rites, even if they do not feel ill, in order to shore up remaining vitality before its loss causes significant harm. "Just as you go to the doctor for a checkup even when you're feeling well," said one young man of his participation in a Lamaist rite to consecrate "long life," "so we visit the lama once a year. It's just the feeling that the *tshe* may have gone that makes one want to receive the lama's blessing." Latu added, "It's like buying more sugar at the market before you actually run out at home."

Embedded within these notions of spiritual well-being are the aesthetics of everyday life that form and inform Yolmo sentience. A villager does not simply nurture the body; he must also live properly, with a sense of balance, harmony, and repletion, to assure that he remains healthy. And when there is the "feeling" of more discomfort than harmony in a body, by way of madness, loss, or pain, its owner strives to restore lost purity and fortitude. At first, a person attempts to smooth out the rough edges of his life. He eats, rests, honors the gods, cleanses body and heartmind, and perhaps visits the "hospital" to purchase some "tablets"—all in the attempt to "cut" pain from his body and restore diminished vitality. But if these initial efforts fail and illness persists, his family summons a shaman. Through his artistry, a bombo tries to recreate a sense of harmony, vitality, and completeness.

It is within this context that the rapport between shamanic and Western medicine occurs. Villagers have several options available when they fall ill: self-care, a shaman, the priestly lama, or a small medical clinic supported by a Kathmandu development project. Since the inception of this "hospital" in 1982, a steadily increasing clientele has stepped inside its doors to receive treatment for wounds, headaches, respiratory ailments, and a host of other services, such as vaccinations and eye examinations.

For villagers, hospital medicine remedies physical illnesses (a headache, broken bones, and bruises) without recourse to what Westerners would deem "spiritual" techniques. The concept of *sman* or "medicine" illustrates this practice. *Sman* ("men"), like Plato's pharmakon, is at once drug, poison, and remedy.[5] Alcohol is a "medicine" because it alters human physiology; witches do harm by mixing a "medicine" into a food that is then offered to unsuspecting guests; shamanic herbs and hospital "tablets" fix "ruined" bodies. *Sman* is a medicine to the extent that it transforms, for better or worse, human anatomy through physical means. For Yolmo wa, Western medicine falls along these lines.

Shamanic and Lamaist cures also alleviate physical pains, but by ameliorating the spiritual underpinnings of malaise. Whereas a villager may visit the clinic to receive aspirin to soothe a headache, he may also call on a bombo to divine its supernatural causes. The shaman can then cure the headache by "cutting" the cause from the body. This play between symptom and cause relates to Asian constructions of illness. As with the practioners of Ayurvedic medicine, a Yolmo wa must discern between contributory and primary causes: ritual impurities provoke humoral imbalances and thus physical malaise.[6] Working from this logic, villagers tend to think it a bit nonsensical to treat the physical manifestations of illness without treating spiritual causes. To heal bodies, shamans attend to spiritual forces. And while their clients might also patronize Western medical facilities, the spiritual dimension of their lives is always of chief concern. Yet despite the difference between shamanic and hospital practices, Yolmo wa do not see the two traditions as antithetical; as with other Himalayan communities, it is more a matter of appropriate use.[7] While Western medicine can cure "inner" illnesses, such as tuberculosis, "outer" illnesses, such as spirit loss, are the domain of the shaman.

Divine Knowledge

To heal Yeshi, Meme must divine the primary causes of her pains. Indeed, one of the most significant aspects of Yolmo healings is the knowledge that can be obtained through a shaman's oracular divination, a rite that takes place early in the evening.

The knowledge is hard to come by. In Helambu, there is much to self-experience, especially events of a distressful, fateful nature, that villagers cannot "know" in the heartmind. While the mirror lodged in the forehead bears a person's fate and constitution, its owner can never obtain knowledge of what is stored there. "Humans cannot find out what's written there," Latu conceded. "When we will die, we cannot know, not even the scientists." Yolmo wa cite a Nepali proverb that catches this dilemma— *babile lekheko, chhalale chhekheko, kasari dekheko?*: "Written by gods, covered by skin, how can it be seen?"

As much of the forces acting on a person are hidden from the heartmind, Yolmo wa often find it difficult to discern the cause or nature of distress. When villagers depicted scenes of illness to me, they often stressed that they initially were not aware they were sick. A demon (*sri*) covertly attacked one infant from a distance, sucking a little of its blood each night through a "straw" that extended from the vampire's haunt into the house; neither parents nor child learned of the attack until the son's flesh began to wither away. A man suffering from bad luck and a querulous mood did not know the causes of his troubles until a lama divined it was *dasa graha* (though his dog, sensing the evil within his master, snapped at him). And while villagers can easily diagnose spirit loss among children, it is difficult to do so when adults suffer from the malady. Indeed, if a person's "life span" (*tshe*) diminishes it may be months before the body feels the effects of the loss.

Symptoms, then, are the consequential signs of illness agents intruding on the body. Until painful symptoms signal a misfortune (business goes bad, blisters sear the skin, a cat prowls through one's dreams), a person remains unaware that something has gone wrong in his life. Only after he divines the cause of an illness can he know for sure what has happened and how to ameliorate it. Medical knowledge thus focuses less on afflictions per se than on interpreting the symptomatic manifestations of pathology.

Once a villager suffers the symptoms of an affliction, whether it be a lasting fever or physical weakness, he or she attempts to determine its cause. As I understand it, Yolmo wa typically regard an afternoon's headache or boils on the feet first as physical problems, and initially treatment is for the physical symptoms. A person attends to his or her health, eats nutritious foods, and rests body and mind. If the malaise persists for several days, however, villagers often suspect that supernatural forces might be involved and so move to discover a cause and cure.

An ill person can occasionally diagnose a malady on his or her own. I asked one woman whose son had fallen ill why she thought her child was suffering from the loss of his spirit (*bla*). "Because his pulse is fast and jumpy," she said, "and his eyelids are crisscrossed." Similarly, Nyima told me she did not need to divine the causes of her malaise because she herself knew that it was spirit loss, as evinced by a "heaviness" in her body and dreams of descending into a valley and walking through a cremation grounds. Despite lay methods available to make sense of lost vitalities and broken bones, however, an ill person is often unable to diagnose the specific cause and nature of his or her discomfort. While a villager's pains might suggest that a ghost rages in the stomach, he or she is hard put to determine which particular *shi 'dre* it is, where it lives, and what it wants—and thus which steps need to be taken to exorcise it.

Divination opens the door to such knowledge. Indeed, Yolmo patients, compared to healers, are thought to understand little of their bodies or the pain that can haunt them. Whenever I asked villagers to tell what they knew of illness and health, they matched their limited knowledge of ghosts, dreams, and life-forces against the vast lore of the shaman. "Why ask me, I'm not a bombo—why don't you ask your guru?" they often chided. I once asked a woman about spirit loss. "When the *bla* goes," she said, "we don't know. We're just sick. When we're sick, we call the bombo and through divination [*mo*] he tells us what's wrong. He tells us we have fallen down somewhere, that we have been frightened while at the river or while in the forest. We don't know ourselves." Another woman, queried on the difference between the loss of various life-forces, said, "We don't know this. We only sit and say where it hurts."

But even if a person says where it hurts, a shaman still cannot fully know an illness through a patient's words. Healers would argue that, since Yeshi's ability to interpret her pain through dream and sensation is impaired by psychophysiologic imbalances triggered by that same illness, her talk is "like the wind," ranging from hill to field without pattern. "The dreams of a sick person," Meme taught, "are not believable. She cannot have good dreams. What is shown may or may not happen." Freud might have listened for the symbols couched in his charges' symptoms, but Meme, sure of a layman's limits to self-knowledge, claims not to. From lost souls to astrological plight, only a lama or bombo can know the precise genesis, nature, and potential cure of a person's pain. This knowledge bestows power.[8]

A shaman's ability to divine the particulars of an illness rests entirely on his relationship with the gods. It is not the shaman who breaks epistemic barriers but rather the gods whom he has the talent for hosting within his body. Through the medium of the bombo's voice, deities reveal information about the world, knowledge that humans are otherwise incapable of obtaining access to. The spokesman for this transaction, a shaman learns much of what he knows through his relationship with a divine "guru" who teaches and empowers him.[9] When healing, Meme meditates on (*sgom*, "gom") the personal deity to elicit his protection and assistance; when traveling, the guru is "kept in the heartmind" to provide protective vigilance. The spiritual teacher also appears in Meme's dreams as tiger, yak, or bird to inform the student of auspicious times for healings and to reinstruct about any forgotten "learning," from the proper order of his mantras to the composition of the *gtor ma* altar. As the guru is passed from bombo to student, Meme taught me to worship the same guru that he did. On my departure from Helambu, he gave me the sacred *mala* rosary worn by lamas and bombos. "When you wear these," he said after consecrating the one hundred and eight beads, "you will have dreams of me and your other [divine] guru and will receive teachings during these dreams." Since leaving Nepal, I have often dreamed of Meme, who offers advice on the writing of this book.

Because a divine presence graces a healer's dreams, shamanic dreams often bear divinatory meaning. Unlike the dreams of lay persons, a shaman's dreams usually foretell of events to come not to the sleeper but to his clients. Omens of this kind have such significance that, when experienced, Meme can dispense with other means of divination; the dream sign, good or bad, includes all there is to know of a patient's prognosis. For instance, Meme might dream about a villager before that person falls ill, determining where a spirit has been lost by seeing its owner wandering into a forest. "I knew he would come and ask me to play the drum because I dreamed about him," Meme said to me on two occasions. If Meme witnesses good dreams, such as seeing his patient lie on his side, then the person in his care will get well. But if he dreams of streams, cremation grounds, airplanes landing in the village, or a person sleeping face up in a prone position (as when dead), the patient will not live long. If a shaman has significantly "bad" dreams, Meme concluded, it is not worth trying to cure for the patient will die.

Outside of his nightly rounds, Meme relies on several other divinatory techniques to "see" the cause and curative path of illness: pulse reading, rice divination, and oracular divination. As is common to Tibetan, Ayurvedic, and shamanic traditions,[10] Yolmo healers are known for their abilities to interpret the human pulse. When first encountering a patient, Meme touches his fingers to the left and right wrists to discern the nature of the body's "rivers" (n. *nadi*). When healthy, a person's pulse beats smoothly, rhythmically, neither soft nor hard for both left and right arms. But if the flow "separates," jumping back and forth, then the forest shaman is probably afflicting the person. A *shi 'dre* causes the pulse to "come out," to strike erratically, sometimes fast, sometimes slow. Among children, a lost *bla* due to fright quickens the pulse, making it race forward. Among adults, *bla 'khyer zin* slows the pulse to a dim, irregular beat—"like a watch," Meme said, "that does not tick properly." In other words, the aesthetics of integration, balance, control, harmony, and presence define the flow of the pulse; these aesthetics help Meme to divine the cause of illness.

By examining the pulse, Meme often can diagnosis an individual's pain. This was the case with Pasang. Usually, however, Meme can only develop a general understanding of a vague "harm." If asked, then, a shaman will perform a rice divination to confirm these ideas. The purpose of the latter practice is to come up with more specific information about a

Photo 15. Rice divination.

patient's illness. If Pasang's pulse suggests a ghost is harming her, through rice divination Meme can determine which *shi 'dre* it is, from which direction it attacked, what food it will eat in ransom for Pasang's flesh, and an auspicious time to heal.[11]

"I Show This to You"

A shaman's rice divination can thus reveal the cause of an illness and how to treat it. Often the cause is minor and the healer acts to correct it without needing to "play the drum." But if the illness merits a healing ceremony, Meme returns to the afflicted's home to perform a ritual cure on an auspicious evening.

With Yeshi, Meme performed an oracular divination to discover the causes and ramifications of her malaise. "That is something we don't yet know," Tenzin said when I asked how his wife lost her spirit; Meme therefore called the gods into his body.

Several preliminary rites, which took over an hour to perform, led to the divination of Yeshi's troubles. Meme began by "binding" his body (*lus mthud ge*, "li thumge") to various supernatural forces to protect it from the harmful invasion of ghosts, demons, and witches. He then consecrated the various elements of his altar and equipment by reciting the mythic origins of each ritual item: altar, drum, bells. He next offered incense (*gtsang rab*, "sanrap") to the gods and goddesses of Helambu and neighboring lands, including Tibet and India. The purification offering, in which Meme chanted a score of place-names and offered a cleansing incense, served to purify deities and their locales.[12] The gods, once purified and so appeased, were asked to embody the twenty-five *gtor ma* cakes set upon the altar, which itself represented the spiritual geography articulated by Meme during the *gtsang rab* rite.

After Meme beckoned the final deity to rest within the *gtor ma* altar, he transferred one of the gods into his body to divine. Beating his drum, he called one of the gods "who can see what is to come" to fall into his body. He beseeched the god with a lingering, melodious song that praised its attributes. "You are a great god . . . ," he sang. Slowly, Meme's body began to shake. Legs, arms, hips, and torso quivered beneath the beat of the drum as the god "fell" (*'bab pa*) into the body. The god's "breath" (n. *howa*, "wind" or "talk") entered his body through the fontanel *rter tshugs* to rest within the heartmind, which caused first the heart and then the entire body to shake "like the wind." While Meme continued to chant, energy built within his body until the shaking climaxed in a controlled, ecstatic frenzy.[13]

Soft whistles pierced Meme's clenched teeth as the god's "breath" stormed through his body. Meme had harnessed the god's energy, bridling its force yet permitting its speech to sound through his mouth. Soon the god spoke, beginning with a detailed portrait of his hagiography and majestic appearance, from golden armor and tiger pelts to colored skins and faces. The drum steadied to a rapid cadence, striking hard on the first note to sound the opening syllable of each staccato sentence—the pronoun "*Nga*" boldly sparking each declaration ("I . . . am")—and then trailing off as the words unraveled their meaning. After a series of pronouncements, tremors shook Meme's body anew and language collapsed into a frenetic drumming that slowed into another oracular cycle.

Minutes later the god's autobiography came to an end and the divination proper began. Throughout the room voices quieted and the whirlwind of activity ceased. The drumming held to a rapid pace (about six beats per second) as the words sounded from Meme's mouth. The beat struck hard at the beginning of each breath of words, with softer, quicker beats pacing Meme's words until the end of a statement, when the beats built up again and struck hard at the start of the next statement. The staccato breath of words came quickly, without too much affect and with the various syllables pronounced with a persistent singsong rhythm, the first syllable of each breath matching the force and volume of the first drumbeat and the subsequent syllables quieting down until the breath bottomed out into the rapid beat again. As the first divination "revealed" for the patron family (the second, for neighbors and kinsmen attending the event), Yeshi's family concentrated on the progressive denouement of the hidden causes of her illness, her heavy heart and body. Proper names were rarely noted but identities quickly grasped. At times, some revelation sparked a quick exchange among the spectators who sought to anchor the vision in their lives; at others, Yeshi's husband called out to the god "O lord, tell us what must be done!" Yeshi pulled the green shawl around her as she listened to the divination.

Of the god's prophecies that I witnessed, many were cryptic messages, the portent of which was uncertain. Who was implied and whether an action had occurred in the past or was destined for the future was often up for debate. On the occasion of Yeshi's healing, I listened to a lively discussion that followed Meme's "shakings," wherein he and the audience tried to make sense of the deity's words, gesturing with arms to the different cardinal directions noted by the oracle.

While Meme divined for Yeshi, I experienced my own "trance" (as noted in the first chapter) and so did not record the divination. I only know that the deities said that Yeshi suffered from the loss of her spirit (*bla*), her life (*tshe*) had weakened, and her infant child was threatened by the assault of a vampirish *sri* demon.[14] However, I did translate another divination performed at Yeshi's home that might make sense of the specifics of her malaise. The latter divination took place in October 1988, during a healing for Kusang, Yeshi's father-in-law, who suffered from a "diminished life" (*tshe nyams pa*). While Kusang did not look gravely ill, he appeared weak and frail. Toothless, shirtless, with ribs tight against his skin, he lay to the right of the altar and hearth and watched as the god entered the shaman's body. After completing the customary hagiography, the deity "showed" the following.

> In the back of the altar, white plants are erected.
> In the front, is the golden candle.
> In the middle, within the four corners of the altar,
> pure golden and silver rice is offered [for divination].

5 Concerning the bodies of the patron family,[15]
> I now divine.
> I am the student of Yurung Bon of the North.
> For the body of the male patron,
> for the body of the female patron.

10 In the head, there is the illness of the head,
> at the back of the head, there is the god of fire,
> in the front, there is the illness of numbness,
> the fever flames like a fire.

> Sometimes, there is the illness of dizziness[16]
15 when you fall into fierce anger.

> There are no other illnesses,
> no harmful effects of others.
> I show this to you.

A part of the life has decayed [*nyams pa*].
20   This occurred within the last seven months
and seven days.
During this time, you did not know in the *sems*,
you did not see with the eye.

The life [*tshe*] has decayed.
25   When the life decayed,
you had fallen into fierce anger.
Your flesh and bones have shrunk,
the bones have been absorbed into the flesh,
and the flesh absorbed into the body.
30   I show this to you.

Above, in the land of the gods,
[is] the main god in the center,
and the god(s) surrounding the center,
the Tree of Life [?], *Tshe Shing*.
35   To the Tree of Life perform an offering.[17]

If you cannot please this deity within the next year,
piercing pains [*tsher ka*][18] will occur in the back
and in the front of the body.

I show this to you. There are no other illnesses.
40   There are no harmful effects of others.

Dwelling in the East, *Dolakha Mai, Dolakha Bhinsen*:[19]
they will affect your young children.
When they affect your children,
you will not see with the eye,
45   you will not know in the heartmind.

I show this to you.
Perform a *puja* [ritual offering] to appease *Dolakha Mai,*
and *Dolakha Bhinsen*.
I am a clear [honest] guru from the land of the gods.
50   I am the student of Yurung Bon of the North.[20]

When traveling much fatigue falls on you,
whether you go east or west.
I show this to you.

In the heartmind there is much anxiety[21]
55   Upon the body much hair-pain has occurred.[22]

I reveal this to you. There are no other illnesses.
There are no harmful effects from others.

A god from above has fallen into your body.
It is bad to the flesh, it is bad to the body.
60   The bones are soaked with blood.
This enters into your mouth.

In your own flesh there are no illnesses to the blood,
but it enters into the bone of the mouth.

To yourself, when going in the direction of ————,[23]
65   much hair-pain occurs.
In the heartmind confusion persists.[24]

Concerning the bodies of the hosts, I reveal.
You do not know in the heartmind,
you do not see with the eye.

70   I am the student of Yurung Bon of the North. . . .

With the final words, the drumbeat became more pronounced and lingered for over a minute as Meme's body began to shake again. Up to this point, the oracle divined primarily "for the body of the male patron." Most likely, this was the old man, Kusang. According to the oracle, a gamut of wounds hurt his body: illness raged in his head [10–13]; his life span had diminished [19–26]; flesh, bones, and body were absorbed into one another [27–29]; fatigue, "anxiety," and "hair-pain" would burden the body in travel [51–55, 64–66]; and blood spilled from bone to mouth [58–63]. With this diagnosis came a prescription: to recover lost vitality, the patron needed to perform a ritual offering to "the goddess of life."

After the deity revealed Kusang's plight, he began another self-portraiture, which focused on other members of the family.

I am a god.
Within the past one or two months,
I have become disguised by entering into the body
of Yurung Bon of the North.

75   I am the interpreter of Yurung Bon of the North.
I translate what he says.

Within one body of the patron family,
there is an illness wandering in the front
and in the back of the body.

80   Within the body of a visiting relative/friend,
in the head, there is a piercing pain [*tsher ka*],
in the back of the head, the god of fire,
in the front, the illness of numbness [*bherne*].

There are no other illnesses.
85   I reveal this to you about the inner body.

Within the second half of the new year, the *Jo* [local
god, "lord"] living above Bharko, *Brtan Pa Rin Chen*,
affects the insides of the woman patron's body.

Do not abstain from ritually honoring
90   *Jo Brtan Pa Rin Chen* within one year.
This *Jo* may cause a hindrance [*bar chad*] to the
life. I cannot be sure.

I am the student of Yurung Bon of the North.
I see from the same direction that the sun shines.
95   I reveal about the inner body.

Within the body of the woman patron
dwelling in the foreign land,
there is much confusion [*yarpe marpe*]

in the heartmind caused by others.
100 Whatever illnesses, whatever harmful effects of
others, this is to be divined with rice.
For the woman, there is illness with many tears
falling from the eyes.

When the tears fall the heartmind is ill with
105 confusion, and she is unable to hold the *sems*.[25]
I show this to you.

In the hills and in the valleys *ginda* is set.[26]
In the heartmind there is much anxiety [*tsaba tsubu*].
This illness has occurred to the body.
110 I show this to you about the body.

The life has decayed.
When the life decayed, many tears fell from the eyes.
When these tears fell from the eyes,
she was unable to hold her heartmind.

115 I am a teacher who is clear within and without.
There are no other illnesses.
I am the student of Yurung Bon of the North.

Concluding the divination, the deity left his host's body, and Meme, tremoring slightly, marked the end of the possession with a steady, slow-paced drumbeat, which soon died out. Meme rested for tea and a cigarette and joined in a discussion of the divination's portent. Here the oracle revealed the hidden pains that haunted several family members: a member of the patron family [77], a visiting relative [80], and the woman patron [86–114].

Anger and Tears

I want to explore the processes of communication and knowledge intrinsic to instances of divination such as this. My intent is to chart Yolmo ways of knowing, and how these ways are put into practice, in order to assess how and what villagers can know of others, themselves, or a person's illness. Of particular interest are the tacit, embodied forms of knowledge realized by a shaman's revelations.

We find, in deciphering the pains described above, that Yolmo illnesses are embedded within a corpus of spatial relations. Spatial motifs animate Yolmo experience and thus the divination. The sacred spaces of the altar (back, front, middle [1–3]) mirror the fiery contours of the head: head, back, front [10–14, 81–83]. A Yolmo duality of body and mind divides pain into that which scars epidermal surfaces (the body's "hair-pain" [55]) and that which affects corporeal depths (internal "piercings" [37], the heart's distress [54, 98–99, 103–8]). We note the density of the body: pains haunt the body's front and back [37–38]; flesh, bones, and body collapse into one another [27–29]; blood spills from bone to mouth [60–63]. Bachelard offers a method to read such a poetics of space: "By following the labyrinth of fever that runs through the body, by exploring the 'seats of fire,' or the pains that inhabit a tooth, we should learn that the imagination localizes suffering and creates and recreates imaginary anatomies."[27] Could it be that, for Yolmo wa, these spaces draw the bodies of participants into the shamanic drama by attending to the felt immediacies of their experience?

Many of the narrative's spatial motifs touch on the relationship between knowledge and experience. The divinity divines through his omniscience: as a light penetrates a window to illuminate a house's interiors, the god examines the patient's "inner body" from "the same direction that the sun shines" [94–95]. The shaman's revelations compare to the vision quests of other Himalayan healers. The tutelary guardians of a Gurung shaman "fly out and search" for information pertaining to a patient's illness, giving the shaman "access to otherwise inaccessible regions."[28] Tamang shamans "'clarify' and 'reveal' or 'unveil' intractable worlds hidden from human sight."[29] And the Limbu shaman sends his tutelary spirit to predict the fate of his patron: "Look, guru, look closely, so the jungle does not prevent you from seeing; will his body be sick? Will he have a fever?"[30] While these diviners explore geographies real and symbolic, Yolmo wa delve foremost into the depths of the body.

Yet while the deity reveals much about the patient's "inner body," the attending patrons can not see within. They have no power to "see with the eye" or to "know in the heartmind," and so must depend on the god's revelations. The god comes to them without deception or dishonesty. Professing a character trait valued in Helambu, the god claims to be "a teacher who is clear within and without without" [115].

Of the god's many revelations, the most striking is the link between emotions and illness. Kusang learns that his illness—dizziness and a lost life—occurred when he "fell into fierce anger."

Sometimes, there is the illness of dizziness,
when you fall into fierce anger. [14–15]

The life has decayed,
When the life decayed,
you had fallen into fierce anger. [24–26]

Kusang had the reputation of being gruff and ill-tempered, a character trait that the oracle comments on. Though the causal correlation between emotion and illness remains ambiguous here (did anger cause the "life" to decay, or vice versa?), it seems likely that the man's rancor induced his malaise. Along with this etiology comes a censure for his outbursts. The divination, in chiding the disposition of its subject, reads as both revelation and homily.

The link between emotional and physical distress is noted in the god's later divinations as well. Within the heartmind of one patron "there is much anxiety" [54]—a restless, uneasy sense of internal suffocation. For the unnamed woman patron, "there is much confusion in the heartmind caused by others" [98–99]:

For the woman, there is illness with many tears
falling from the eyes.
When the tears fall the heartmind is ill with
confusion, and she is unable to hold the *sems*. [102–5]

The woman may be suffering from something akin to *tsher ka*, the pain of separation. We learn that she is "dwelling in a foreign land [97]," as a daughter-in-law would be, and that others have caused her confusion. Many tears fall from her eyes and her heart suffers from *yarpe marpe*—the wavering, tormented "up-down" thoughts common to Yolmo distress.

The assessment correlates with what I observed of Yeshi's life. I found her to be sluggish, without spirit. During her own healing, she sat numb and apathetic as Meme attempted to recover her spirit—a vitality apparently still absent from her body. It appears then that, by entering into trance, Meme identifies the contours of Yeshi's emotional life. He lends her a voice which, as a young Yolmo woman, she might not otherwise have access to.

But what, precisely, does the voice communicate? For one, it declares that Yeshi's "confusion" is not her responsibility; it is "caused by others" [99]. The etiology lifts the blame off Yeshi for her distress, particularly her inability to "hold" her heartmind. As we have seen, a Yolmo woman must constantly "catch" her *sems*, holding its contents within the body to prevent emotional spillage. By doing otherwise, she runs against local values and risks social censure. The god's explanation thus gives reason for Yeshi's folly and reprimands others (her husband's family, most likely) for causing the distress.

Meme situates Kusang's anger and Yeshi's pain within a realm of social discourse. He thus works to crystallize, comment on, and potentially re-dress the social conflicts that often underlie experiences of illness in the Himalayas.[31] By speaking through the "breath" of the divine, he lends an authority and impartiality to his visionary judgment, a diagnosis that would be inappropriate if offered through the profane role of farmer or neighbor.

In tracing Yeshi's illness to her tears and confusion, the deity's etiology embeds her illness within an idiom of emotional distress. As with Kusang, her "life" diminished because she suffered an outpouring of tears:

The life has decayed.
When the life decayed, many tears fell from the eyes.
When these tears fell from the eyes,
she was unable to hold her heartmind [111–14]

Though the causal link remains ambiguous, the experiential link seems clear: Yeshi's tearful anxiety and lack of control induced the loss of her "life."

The god conveys another message: only he can reveal that link. The patrons could not know even "in the *sems*" what lies within their hearts, nor how such distress relates to spiritlessness. They must pay homage to the divine (and hence the shaman) to learn of their inner bodies.

The divination thus offers insight into the realms of social and bodily experience. As for social knowledge, there are two major constraints to empathy and communication in Helambu. In a land that values privacy, personal integrity, and the control of personal desires, knowing of another's "inner thoughts" is a difficult task. And because the body hides its contents from the eyes of others, it is difficult to communicate personal distress to another when the heart is on fire. Consequently, spirits are lost without the awareness of one's neighbors.

Shamanic divinations thus provide a medium to express pain, distress, and anger to others. A healer, through his correspondence with the sacred, transcends the cultural limits to social knowledge; his divinations provide a discursive outlet to communicate or "cleanse" emotions that cannot otherwise be expressed in Yolmo society. As with Yolmo "songs of pain," his divinations affirm a bride's sorrows and the woe of marriage—to the community, no less, that generated the distress.[32]

By affirming distress, the shaman transforms it, molding the patient's unnamed suffering into a cultural language of sorrow and pain.[33] Social conflicts are given a tangible, objective form.[34] It is important to note, however, that the shaman's divination is not mere reiteration, simply mirroring what lies hidden within the heart; it is an "active interpretation," to use Nietzsche's words, which "molds" a patient's sense of body and home.[35] Meme fills the "inner bodies" of his patients with meaning and tears as much as a Yolmo artist (*mkhas pa*, "keba") colors his *thang ka* canvas with deities and icons.

This leads us to ask, to whom is the distress being communicated? To Meme's audience, no doubt, but this audience includes the patient. Yolmo deities hold that they reveal not only to others the link between emotions and illness; they also inform the patients. If we can believe Meme's "clear" gods, patients possess little insight into the causes of their distress before the divination. As the deity puts it, they do not "know in the heartmind," they do not "see with the eye."

Shamanic divinations thus are an education into self-experience, for they map domains of body and soul which patients do not have access to. Just as the shaman expresses Yeshi's inner world to others, so she learns as well. The subtle play between knowledge and bodily experience again has its roots in Yolmo sensibilities. As we have seen, the causes of illness often remain hidden from conscious view; life-forces are lost without one being aware of the imminent distress.

Meme, in turn, gives form to the vast regions of bodily experience that Yeshi's heartmind cannot readily approach. While certain sensibilities lead to harsh limits on personal and social knowledge, divination enables this knowledge to be tapped. Shamanic divinations make known the otherwise unknowable.

Epiphanies

Yet how does Meme come to know what is troubling Yeshi, Mingma, or Pasang? What does this knowledge consist of?

My sense is that the information conveyed through shamanic divination often relates to tacit forms of knowledge latent within the bodies of patients and viscerally assessed by healers. Yolmo wa hold that a wealth of information can be gleaned from the flow of a pulse, the lines of a palm, the wrinkles around the eyes. In addition to these potential reservoirs of knowledge, more implicit realms of meaning lie within the body. Knowledge registers in the way a body moves, hands tend a fire, or pain pierces the flesh. As all pain relates to a system of aesthetic value, the images, sensory patterns, and bodily dispositions that mark moments of malaise engage certain sensibilities. These sensibilities make up the sensory grounds of experience and imply specific ways of being, from Pasang's pains to Yeshi's slumber.

Somatic sensibilities exist on a tacit, visceral level; usually, villagers are only vaguely aware of the forces and tensions that occasion them. It is for this reason that the afflicted ask shamans to divine the causes of their malaise. Yeshi feels lousy, though she does not know why she feels that way nor how to express her concerns to others. She only senses a silent melody lingering within her limbs.

Through divination Meme intones the melody; he lends image to a felt sensibility. Like an expert critic evaluating a painting, he assesses Yeshi's discomfort for its aesthetic portent (its tone, texture, and overall mood or spirit), then conveys what he senses of the situation through appropriate imagery. Yet a shaman's skill primarily lies not in the ability to perceive sensibilities but rather in his ability to grasp the rudimentary forms and tensions that occasion them. Since certain cultural forms and tensions lead to certain sensibilities, Meme, by sensing how Yeshi holds her body (head down, eyes away), can divine the underlying forms and tensions intrinsic to her situation; he figures a lost life caused by confusion, anxiety, and familial strife. Pasang's sullen pulse and pains, in turn, tell of the assault of a ghost. And as the physiologies of Yolmo forms (body, house, village) tend to mirror one another, a shaman seems able to gain a fair estimate of the problems troubling a family by canvassing the physiology of a troubled family member. The aesthetics of Pasang's pulse, for instance, spoke to Meme of ghostly harms.

Since patients do not fully realize, but only sense, how aesthetic sensibilities take form in their lives, a divination often appears like an "epiphany"—an image that "shows" (from the Greek *phainein*) the truths of a situation. James Joyce used this word ("the revelation of the whatness of a thing") for those moments when a scene or image captures the underlying forms and tensions of a situation.[36] Since epiphanies in Helambu can resonate with a patient's basic bodily disposition—his or her "feel" for a situation—a divination often seems to reveal, in uncanny, extrahuman terms, the "truths" latent in an old man's fatigue or a bride's despair. Most often, the truths reveal the physiology of conflict. But since that physiology is often a product of the tensions of Yolmo life, the truths tend to go beyond the specifics of one woman's pain and manifest the tensions themselves. The divinations thus address what Yeshi, Kusang, and Meme feel in their bones. It may be that the participants in a healing take the revelations to be truthful when the language "really reaches" them, to use Gadamer's words: when they "recognize," rather than simply "recall," basic truths of their history.[37]

While a divination can reveal the truths of a situation, this does not make acknowledging either the truths or the situation any easier. I found it difficult to talk with villagers about the specifics of Meme's divinations, in part because the oracles were considered sacred, in part because villagers seemed hesitant to discuss their portent. When I recited to Latu some passages of the divination noted above, for instance, he denied any causal link between illness and emotional distress. "The woman is crying because she doesn't feel well" he said, suggesting a link between Yeshi's tears and the loss of her life. The old man, in turn, was angry because "that's how one feels when one gets sick." When I interviewed the benefactors of other healings, such as Nyima, they similarly did not link their malaise to the emotional turmoil felt in their lives, save for the "fright" thought to induce spirit loss.

Although villagers are reluctant to discuss the specifics of divinations, they do seem to consider some revelations to be more fitting, more "truthful," than others. Nyima, for instance, had two divinations performed to assess her feelings of malaise: she considered only the second ("a lost spirit and the assault of a ghost"), which led to the recovery of her spirit, to be an accurate assessment of her pain (the shaman who performed the first divination, in contrast, "worked falsely"). A divination is accurate, it appears, if it strikes a chord with a patient's experiences—if it conveys the tacit qualities of a patient's situation. A goodness of fit thus exists between an accurate divination and the aesthetic demands of a situation: the interpretation that a situation of malaise calls for. Divination is fundamentally an aesthetic act. Truth relates to value.

Yet a good divination need not be especially precise. Yolmo divination is less concerned with a precise semiotics of illness, whereby villagers rely on a set typology to trace specific kinds of pain back to specific causes, than it is concerned with an aesthetics of experience, whereby Meme uses the associations, bits of meaning, and formal resonances that a divination conjures up to engage an "affecting presence." For Robert Armstrong, an affecting presence involves the range of emotions, allusions, and dispositions that a work of art evokes.[38] With Meme's more artful divinations, it is their open-ended, subjunctive qualities—the histories engaged, the potentials evoked—that effect presence. Like a well-told tale, a good divination emits flickers of meaning and connotation, the portent of which is filled in by (and so engages) its listeners.[39] When Mingma fell ill, he sought a divination that confirmed his felt experience. He came to express his plight not only through declarations ("I am afraid of dying") but also through intimations of loss, darkness, and downhill descents. Those intimations carried emotional force. The decoding of his plight ("The shaman told me I had the same illness as the man who died") engaged tacit sensibilities that reaffirmed a style of living and so a "natural" way of aging. They also bestowed on that particular tale of aging a uniqueness and an importance in the moral order, a sense that his solitary jaunt was real and powerful and quite possibly latent in the lives of his neighbors. Like a ghost, Mingma's tale came to evoke a presence that could not be touched or seen but that could be sensed and appreciated (and even feared) for what it implied.

The assessment of Mingma's and Yeshi's distress suggests that both shaman and patient use the divinatory resources at hand to negotiate meanings for pain. Pasang sat passively as her father-in-law and Meme decided her fate, filling her body with meaning, giving voice to its pain. Yet while Pasang accepted the naming of her illness without advancing a word herself, her silence was illusory. The fact that she fell ill and embodied her distress in a particular way suggests that her pains came to define her malaise in a sensible, interpretable manner. Her sullenness presented a meaningful way of being ill. Meme's divination thus was not performed by him alone, but involved an interpretive duet between patient and healer. Pasang lived a sense of malaise and Meme assessed and gave tangible form to this sensibility.

Yet why can only shamans divine? It appears that shamans are particularly sensitive to bodily dispositions and have the ability, in trance, to convey the underlying forms, tensions, and sensibilities intrinsic to a situation. Meme has the ability to "read" the pulse of a family—the diffuse tensions that can haunt bodies and households—as if the extraordinary state of trance enables him to both hear and voice the basic chords of Yolmo experience as they take form in the particulars of one woman's song of pain. What part of Meme's corporeal mosaic is sensitive to this music? Not his heartmind, for he would then know the causes of malaise in his waking, daily life and have no need to call on the gods. Yet since oracular revelations sound from his own throat, the understanding must emerge somewhere from within his form. My sense is that the revelations issue from his body. A shaman's body admits a certain potential for empathy, an empathy of form, where one body makes sense of another. Meme, who has himself experienced various sensibilities, can interpret a patient's malaise through the conduit of his own body. It may be that his body, by participating in the everyday activities of a family before and during a healing ceremony, begins to pick up on the tensions and rhythms that characterize the physiology of that family; he then crafts this kinesthetic knowledge into tangible images that identify the sources of malaise. Yolmo divination, like Nietzsche's art, is "applied physiology."[40]

Trance is the primary medium through which the body speaks. Meme can only know the "unknowable" when hosting the gods within his body, with the aid of his guru, and so villagers (including Meme) attribute his revelations to the gods. Indeed, an oracle's power to tap into the primal veins of Yolmo experience leads to the sense that inhuman forces are involved. In a sense, I come to the same conclusion. Through divination, Meme's body serves as a conduit that sounds the basic chords of Yolmo experience—chords that course through households and villages and take form between bodies, belonging thus to no single person.

Yet while I have found the shaman's gods to possess genuine force and presence, I take the divine to arise out of embodied knowledge. "Those who know everything," the gods stand for all that human heartminds cannot obtain insight into through secular means. Invoked when someone lies sick, their job is to make known what cultural values do not permit its members to know in their everyday lives. Forging a body's sense of distress into ghosts, lost spirits, and bodily harms, the divine thus forms part of a cultural circuit of knowledge. This circuit transcends individual bodies. It encompasses interactions between bodies, households, and the environment. It draws from and contributes to collective experience. It courses through the laughter of a tea shop, the dreams of a shaman, and the "rivers" of a body. Its value lies in its collective aspects.

We may recall Bateson's epistemology of the self: "The total self-corrective unit which processes information, or, as I say, 'thinks' and 'acts' and 'decides,' is a *system* whose boundaries do not at all coincide with the boundaries either of the body or of what is popularly called the 'self' or 'consciousness.' "[41] If we compare Bateson's epistemology to Yolmo ways of knowing, we find that Yolmo "self-systems," though more expansive than Western versions, include aspects of bodily and social experience exceeding the purview of the heartmind—to the extent that the phrase "self-system" itself seems inappropriate. Perhaps we should speak of a "societal-system" or of an "ecology of knowledge."[42] The flow of Yeshi's pulse, the forest shaman, Meme's guru, and the gods of the five heavens all form part of, and work toward, that ecology. There is much that a villager cannot know in the heartmind, but the larger ecology still "knows" about such matters at some tacit level, particularly if we include in this system the visions of shamans and the workings of the gods. When distressed, the system communicates what it knows through tacit sensibilities and divine musings into previously unarticulated aspects of human experience.

The function of the diviner, in sum, is to transcend the boundaries between Yolmo bodies and thus to breach the borders between tacit and apparent realms of experience. Since shamanic knowledge comes most into play when someone is sick, the gods are telling villagers most about the corrective mechanisms necessary for health. Indeed, the cures are in large part epistemic ones. To divine is to heal. While aesthetic sensibilities inhibit certain understandings of self and other, those constraints can spawn pathologic side effects. Yolmo wa, cut off from certain realms of personal and social knowledge, are at a loss when anxiety, confusion, or tears cloud the body. Meme's art is to tap into the collective circuit of knowledge, map uncharted regions of experience, and give image to pain by voicing the music of the gods.

7. Metamorphoses

After the final deity left his body, Meme set the drum on the floor, took off his belt of bells, lit a cigarette from an ember, and relaxed his body against the central pillar. Tenzin handed him a cup of tea and a plate filled with steaming rice, lentils, and potatoes.

"Please, Meme," Tenzin asked, with hands held low. He then scooped rice from the cooking pot and dished it onto other tin plates. He passed the plates to the neighbors in the back corners of the room, then gave Yeshi a small amount of rice and lentils.

"Eat," he said, and placed the food close to her side.

As my hands struggled to scoop rice from plate to mouth, I watched Yeshi gaze at the food for a moment, nibble a handful of rice, then push the plate from her body.

Meme licked his plate clean and walked outside to wash his hands. He stepped back into the house to smoke another cigarette, then joined the ongoing conversation, much of which concerned the portent of the deities' revelations. He took heavy drags from the cigarette, snuffed it out on the mud floor "below" the altar, gazed at his wristwatch (ten-thirty), donned his belt, and lifted the drum off the floor.

Once Meme divined the causes of Yeshi's malaise, he tried to alleviate her pain in the "main work" of the healing: the exorcism of harms and ghosts from body and home, and the retrieval of lost life-forces. Through my participation in Meme's rites, and by talking with patients during and after them, I have found that the theories of ritual healing which dominate current anthropological thinking—from psychological to intellectualist and symbolist positions—take us only so far in explaining if and how Meme's rites do, in fact, alleviate suffering. While these theories focus either on the meanings of rituals or the thoughts and beliefs of their participants,[1] they fail to grasp what it might feel like to have ghosts and pains cut from the body. They do not take into account the presence of bodies.

In coming to terms with Meme's rites of exorcism, as we shall do in this chapter (with the soul-calling rites addressed in the next), we could ask what the rites of exorcism "mean."[2] We could ask who the demons are, what they "symbolize."[3] But even if we could find credible answers to these queries, which is questionable,[4] they would not help us to grasp how the rites work. Only by attending to the sensory dimensions of the rites—how Yolmo bodies move, feel, and know—can we appreciate their experiential force and so gain insight into the nature of Yolmo healings.[5] To begin to develop such an appreciation, we must return to Yolmo uses of space, rudiments of form, and imageries of healing. At the same time, we must bear in mind the basic dilemmas that trouble the anthropology of ritual. How can we gain a sense of what Yeshi experienced of Meme's exorcisms?[6] How can we write about a shaman's dance, the stirrings of ghosts, or the smell of pain—events that linger on the "hither side of words" and cannot be readily described through words?[7]

Protection

Meme's rites of exorcism relate directly to the ways in which he and others make sense of space. We have seen that spatial motifs influence how Yolmo villagers construe and experience their bodies and their environment. A body implies a plenum of icon, organ, and pain. Motifs of inside/outside, right/left, and high/low (themselves rooted in the structuring structures of the house) course through Yolmo bodies to code knowledge, morality, and gender into spatial form. Yeshi's body mimics the parameters of the house and the contours of the cosmos: the five directions color her fingers, bones, and torso. The homologies between body, house, and cosmos create a hall of mirrors through which the participants of Yolmo healings pass: body resembles house resembles cosmos.

The conceptions of space that structure how Tenzin cooks a meal, Yeshi feels pain, or Meme calls the gods also influence the language that they use. The Yolmo "geometry of ordinary speech," to use Avrum Stroll's term,[8] maps bodily experience on to a plane of spatial relations. High and low, up and down, inside and out, right and left, back and front, near and far—such are the idioms on which Yolmo wa coordinate not only their physical movements (entering into a home, ascending a hill) but their moralities and social relationships (polluting feet; "inner" knowledge). This language gives form to gender relations (male and female sides of the house), dreams (descending into a valley) and illness (spirit loss). In many ways, spatial relations compose much of the grammar of Yolmo experience.

Meme relied on some of that grammar when healing. Once he began to play the drum, the profane melded with the sacred. Cadences of imagery pulsed through the room. The corners of the house became fused with the four sacred directions. The central pillar, heavy with coats and oil lamps, stood for the *axis mundi* leading to the central heavens. The cosmos became further refracted within the shaman's altar and body. East, south, west, north, center: the altar embodied, the body enshrined. The hues of the five directions (yellow, white, red, green, blue) similarly colored Meme's bones. When facing the altar, his back to door and spectators, Meme faced east.

The door marked the threshold between interior and exterior, light and dark, and "inside" and "outside" people. The house, which resembled Yeshi's form, included the motifs of inner and outer on which Yolmo experiences of healing and illness take form. Ghosts are exiled from the house, life-forces return to the flesh, and a person's renewed health is defined by an aesthetic of purity and repletion.

The "binding" of Meme's body, which drew on Yolmo conceptions of space, outlined his curative approach to the body. With this preliminary act, he meshed his body with supernatural forces to create an impenetrable shell around his form.[9] "It's like putting up fences," Meme taught. "Just as the police live with their weapons, so we need to tie our bodies, tie the four directions, to protect ourselves from witches and ghosts. If we don't bind a circle, witches and ghosts come and hurt the body."

Holding the drum upright in his right hand, Meme made a circular motion with it above the ground, first clockwise, then counterclockwise, then stuck the handle of the drum into the ground after completing each circle. The action served to "fix" and "pierce" the evil to be exorcised.[10] Motioning with the drum, he mumbled:

In outer space, a wall of iron
In midspace, a wall of bronze
In inner space, a wall of crystal

"Wall" is the Tibetan *ra ba* ("rawa"), a "fence" or "enclosure" often summoned to enact a protective barrier.[11] The spatial dimensions of "outer" (*phyi*, "chhi"), "mid" (*bar*), and "inner" (*nang*) denote concentric walls that encircle the shaman's body (see Figure 5).

Meme continued:

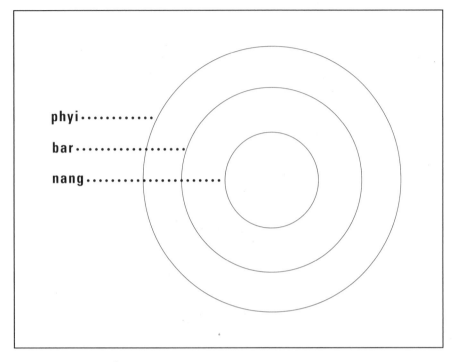

Figure 5. Spaces of protection.

On the right, bind the Great White Khyung
On the left, bind the Great Golden Khyung
In the back, bind the Great Red Khyung
In the front, bind the Great Green Khyung
Above, bind the Great Blue Khyung

"Bind" is *'khril* ("thil"), a Tibetan verb that means "to get coiled."
Khyung is the eaglelike mythical Garuda bird of Tibetan and Indian lore
(represented in the *gtor ma* altar by a predatory bird with a snake ensnared
within its claws).[12] The chant thus "bound" the five Khyungs to Meme's
sides as a snake coils around an arm.

The chant ended:

Around the body, burn an everlasting fire
On the right, bind a wheel of water
On the left, bind a wheel of fire

Om a hung guru sgom
guru sgom pai tangma 'khril

The magical words "*om a hung guru sgom*," which mark many of the bombo's mantras, bear the literal significance of "Body, speech, mind, meditate upon the guru." On a profane level *sgom* ("gom") means "to fancy, imagine, construe in one's mind."[13] But the verb also implies a Tantric process, common to Tibetan peoples, whereby the meditator creates a magical reality by mimetically envisioning it.[14] Through magical chants, shamans enact transformations, grafting the imaginative onto the real. To throw a ghost or trap a witch, one mumbles mantras. It is less important that a healer (or patient) understand the mantra than that it be spoken effectively. Here, Meme summoned his tutelary spirit by invoking the tripartite embodiment of existence: body, speech, mind.

Yolmo healers are quick to say, however, that voicing the mantra is not enough in itself. Meme needed to envision the imaginary scene being invoked. With each mantra came a specific (and highly secret) *dmigs pa* ("mikpa") or "imagining," that, when envisioned by Meme's heartmind, enacted the effect mimed through words. "Words won't work by themselves," Meme once said, hoping I would pay a thousand rupees to learn his *dmigs pa*. "It is through the *dmigs pa* that we call the gods. Unless you know the *dmigs pa*, it's just words. No pains leave without it."

Words thus couple with images to effect transformations. When "throwing" a ghost, Meme imagines a place "far, far away" in which to banish it. To "bind" the body, said a younger shaman, "We meditate upon [*sgom*] the four corners, and the sky above [*dbus*, "ui"]—we bind this, for protection. Then ghosts cannot enter inside." This healer paraphrased his own "binding" mantra with the words:

Bind the four corners,
bind heaven, bind hell,
bind the four windows of the four directions,
place iron thorns, copper thorns,
a fire of bamboo at the four corners,
enclosing this place

The image of protection is basic to Yolmo notions of health and healing. "On the right, left, front, back, above"—the shaman's body is bound as a house holds boundaries. His mantra erects inner, middle, and outer "walls" around his form. In creating this impenetrable defense, a shaman's body manifests a Yolmo ideal: it is bounded, enclosed, and protected. Meme's imaginings thus tend to Yolmo rudiments of form. There is a "goodness of fit" between shamanic imagery and a core Yolmo experience, an experience of form founded on a play between inner and outer, ingress and egress, stoppage and flow.

The play between shamanic image and experience spills over into the patient's world. In reciting this and other mantras, Meme mumbled them into the nape of his drum, wary of those who might try to steal his magic. When Yeshi listened to the opening chants, she probably possessed only a dim sense of their specific portent. As with most patients, she might have thought that when Meme bound his body, he also protected the house from unwanted intrusions of malevolent forces. As one woman told me, "The bombo protects our home so neither ghosts nor witches can enter."

The theme of protection lends image to many experiences of healing. Patients often understand healing to be founded on a protection of bodies and homes. Ghosts are thrown, deities appeased, and anatomies cleansed— all in the hopes of defending the body from further harm. The defense crystallizes in the construction of protective *srung ga* amulets, which often takes place during the healing ceremony. This, the "bombo's medicine," works to shield the bearer (usually a child or mother) from demonic onslaughts; the amulets prevent ghosts and witches from "touching" the body. "They keep the ghosts outside," said one man, "so that they cannot come inside." Similar to the "binding" of Meme's body, the amulets conjure a house of fire around the skin.

Shamanic rites of protection demarcate the geography of Yolmo forms, accenting what belongs within a body or household and what does not. The core experience pivots on an image that is instantaneous, mimetic, without narrative time. My understanding is that Meme, by giving imaginative form to the experience, conveys the felt sense that body and house are more bound than open.

In turn, by stopping the flow between inner and outer, Meme not only maintains the boundaries of the body but refigures them. Earlier, we found that tensions inherent in Yolmo social life (conflicts between values of autonomy and interdependence) shape experiences of form as being founded on a tense dialectic: a continuous flow between body and environment (inner and outer) and a need to block this flow to accent and so maintain the boundaries of the body. Yolmo healings secure the latter need. In closing the "windows" of the corporeal abode, shamanic protection shores up a body's borders. And if Yolmo shamans protect and "cut" the patient from ghosts, witches, and demons, then their rites address tensions intrinsic to Yolmo experiences. Illness results from the malevolent actions of one's neighbors; Meme works to heal ruptures between person and society. Yolmo healings, by refiguring the body, clarify the boundaries between person and community. They thus inform Yeshi that, though a social being caught in a web of interdependence, she is, in fact, an autonomous, distinct person. And as her body resembles the household, the rites fasten the windows of the latter form as well.

Movement

Rites that worked to "cut" Yeshi's pain, performed after the oracular divinations, similarly attended to the spaces of her body. Meme "transferred" Yeshi's harms into a chicken by brushing it against her head, back, arms, sides, legs. He then killed the chicken and "fed" its blood to various deities figured in the *gtor ma* altar: the sacrifice bound the gods into helping Meme, and Tenzin examined the entrails of the lifeless carcass to see if the internal "signs" (*rtags*, "tak") of illness within the chicken's body corresponded to Yeshi's wounds as divined by Meme. Tenzin found a swollen red appendix that "showed" that Yeshi's life span (*tshe*) had, in fact, weakened.

While the chicken sacrifice removed physical pain from the body, other rites of exorcism "cast" harms, and the supernatural agents responsible for those harms, from body and home. To exorcise the *sri* afflicting Yeshi's child, Meme donned a white dress and danced and drummed around Yeshi (and her child) in complete circles with a dog's skull attached to his toe (see Photo 16). Meme attracted the ghost to the skull, "bound" it within the cranium, then "dragged" the skull outside and buried it into a hole at the base of the steps leading from the house ("It can never come out again," Meme once boasted, "for life after life!").

To suck "harms" (n. *betha*) from Yeshi's flesh, Meme called the heart-mind of a tiger (*khyim srung*, the "House-Protector") into his body, crawled around on all fours, sniffed the surfaces of Yeshi's back, neck, arms, and legs for hidden pains, then "removed" these harms by "biting" her skin for several seconds and spitting bloody fluids and foul-smelling insects and earthworms into a bowl.

Meme forced the magical "arrow" (n. *bān*) of any witch, shaman, or

Photo 16. Pressing the *sri*.

enemy to "come undone" by slapping a set of leafy green branches soaked with hot water against the backs, arms, and legs of Yeshi's family members as they sat sequentially by the door, facing outside, with hands held in prayer and steam rising from their clothes. Mantras assured that the water felt cold to humans but scalded and "triumphed over" ghosts and evil spirits.

In Yeshi's healing, exorcisms realized a basic act: they achieved displacements from interiors to exteriors. To expulse harm from the body, Meme

removed
transferred
threw
sucked
cleansed
cut
separated
(and) untied

ghosts, harm, and impurities from Yeshi's flesh. Sacrifice "transferred" pain from her body into the chicken's organs; the "tiger" sucked bloody fluids from her limbs; the water-cleansing removed harm from the surfaces of the skin. In more metaphoric terms, the healing "cut," "separated," or "untied" illness from the body.

While these actions sparked displacements from inner to outer, others effected movements from high to low. On other occasions, Meme buried a *sri* ghost beneath the earth and "threw" a ghost into the valley below. Other rites enabled him to "step over" and so dominate a malevolent spirit (just as the passage of one's feet over another occasions pollution and disrespect).

Villagers often spoke of the kinetics of healing when discussing the curings they were party to. "The tiger bites me," one woman said when I asked her what happened during the rite. "He sucks away the pain-distress [n. *dhuk pir*]. By biting, he picks up the pain." "I did not feel fear," another recalled of the hot-water spraying, "but I felt my disease [n. *rog*] was going out. I prayed, at the time, 'May my disease just go out.' I felt comfortable, better, as if my disease was leaving." "The bombo threw the ghost from my body"; "My bad luck was cut"; "Meme removed my pain"; "He stepped over the *sri*," others recalled.

The stress on displacements—and the corollary sense of change—

Photo 17. "The tiger bites me."

suggests that the actions have powerful effects on a patient's sense of health. Yolmo healings thus pivot on what Bourdieu calls "the language of the body,"[15] for ritual processes mirror the displacements, movements, and postures engaged in the everyday life of the flesh. As Bourdieu remarks of the mimetic propensity of Kabyle ritual, "The most characteristic operations of its 'logic'—inverting, transferring, uniting, separating, etc.—take the form of movements of the body, turning to the right or left, putting things upside, going in, coming out, tying, cutting, etc."[16]

With a few modifications, the same could be said of Yolmo wa. In Helambu, exorcists plot strategies of healing on the map of felt experience—a map marked by thresholds, openings, and closures. There is a goodness of fit between the kinetics of healing and Yolmo experiences of form. Healing rites catalyze an ontology of experience patterned by a play of flow and stoppage, ingress and egress: ghosts are thrown, life-forces retrieved, and body surfaces cleansed and protected. The rites try, through the magic of mimesis, to cleanse the body by returning it to the most primal of Yolmo experiences—that of bounded, untainted form.

We discover, in turning to the area literature, that movements through space define ceremonial forms throughout the Himalayas. Tamang work to "cast their grief" at the conclusion of funeral rites.[17] A Kham-Magar shaman washes "impurities" and "evil omens" away by setting them within a tiny boat that is set adrift on a river: the shaman sings of the boat's itinerary as the evil floats away.[18] Sherpa remove "bad smells" from their bodies during a funerary exorcism by passing a lump of dough over their bodies and then discarding it.[19] Tibetans "throw" malevolent spirits and rely on ritual "sucking" to remove harm and illness from the body.[20]

In my estimation, anthropologists have overlooked the experiential force of such transformations in Nepal, Tibet, and elsewhere. No theory ties the ritual structure of exorcisms to indigenous patterns of bodily experience. In Helambu, the rites crystallize an ontology of experience predicated on expulsions from the body. The tiger's bite and a ghost's retreat change a patient's sense of her body.

The changes are borne of common needs. There is something archetypal about the sweep of an arm, the bite of a tiger, something vital about a ghost tossed into the night or a demon buried in a hole. The acts employ basic urges of a body. There is the urge to cry. To defecate. To sweat out impurities. To cleanse the body. To throw away. To run from a bad dream. To cast out grief. To abscond from pain.

There is the urge to exorcise.

Exorcisms belong to the realm of spectacle, of gesture, of feeling, of magic—much like the theater of "cruelty" that Artaud sought to counter Brecht's theater of allegory and intelligence.[21] Yolmo exorcisms entail more than beliefs or ideas. They are more than symbolic actions. They are less dependent on "key," "dominant," or "transactional" symbols[22] than on key kinesthetic actions. There is little that is symbolic about the ghosts and harms that Meme casts out. They do not stand for anything but themselves (though they may, at times, be associated with pain, misery, and anxiety). Ritual exorcisms do not work from a logic of symbolic identity, wherein a sign (ghost) comes to represent a referent (negative emotions, sexual angst). Rather, they engage a principle of kinetic action, wherein movements through space change how a body feels. "I felt my disease go out," says one man. It is precisely this felt sense of healing, of pain leaving the body, that Meme seeks most to achieve.

So while exorcisms among Sherpa groups might reflect or rhyme with symbolic motifs specific to those groups, from structural tensions (greed and selflessness, for Ortner[23]) to psychosexual conflicts (repression and guilt, for Paul[24]), that is not their function. Their purpose is to cast evil and harm from a body, a house, or a village.[25] In terms of healing, it is much less

Photo 18. Throwing a ghost.

important what a ghost means (if it "means" anything at all) than that it be successfully thrown. Neither Meme nor Yeshi are interested in "getting behind the demons," as Freud suggested psychoanalysts (and so anthropologists) should be.[26] They just want to be rid of them.

To get rid of demons, Meme must touch Yeshi's skin. The kinetics of healing imply tactility, a kinesthesia of touch. Meme coils a wall of fire around his skin. He brushes a chicken against Yeshi's legs, arms, and neck. He slaps hot water against her back, thighs, arms, legs. He makes her sit on the floor to watch the *sri* encircle her child. He places her foot atop a dog's skull to "step over" that ghost. He sucks beetles from her skin.

If the rites heal, their transformations are of a sensory nature because the rites are. The kinetics of healing do not take place within some abstract realm of ideas, symbols, or heartmind; they are realized at the level of a body that (following Plessner) Yeshi not only "has," but "is."[27] The rites do not influence some "I" or ego detached from the flesh. They work directly with the body through gestures, smells, and sensations. This is why the brush of a hand or the tastes of pain succeed where abstract words fail: it is the sense of cleansing, of expulsion (rather than just the idea), that adds to human sentience.

The lesson applies to shamanism and writing alike. Meme's task and the task of an ethnographer are not dissimilar. Meme must convey the felt sense that ghosts are leaving Yeshi's body; an ethnographer must portray, as he or she understands it, what that departure feels like. Both tasks require a bit of magic ("Words won't work by themselves"). Both are prone to failure.

If either shaman or writer has any chance of succeeding, they must draw on the sensibilities and rudiments of form that give life to personal experience. Sensations are basic to ritual healing, but those experiences only make sense to participants through the values and grammars specific to a people. For Yolmo wa, we have seen, a body cleanses itself of painful harms by experiencing, through direct, visceral means, the removal of those harms. I do not quite grasp how this magic works (and fear that the words to best depict it have alluded us here), but I do know that it requires the sensory presence of a person's complete being. "If the patient is asleep," Meme once said of the rites, "she won't get better." If the body is asleep, if it is not touched, moved, or prodded, it can barely feel, listen, or remember. To alter Yeshi's sensibility (the way her body feels), Meme must work within a plane of feeling, sweeping pain from her skin, cutting ghosts from her bones. And soon there may be no pain, no pollution, no ghosts.

8. A Calling of Souls

By midnight, most neighbors had returned to their homes after eating a meal made with the sacrificed chicken, and took with them their newfound concerns over their families' welfare. Only Yeshi, household members, and close family members stayed up past midnight to help Meme.

Meme had divined the causes of Yeshi's distress, appeased the gods, thrown the *sri* from her home, and cleansed her anatomy of "harm." Despite these healing endeavors, her body remained weak and lacking. Life-forces that usually supported her body remained apart from it. To fully heal, Meme had to recover these vitalities by "calling" them back into the body.

Enhancing the Life

He first performed the *tshe grub* rite to "enhance" (*grub*, "dup") Yeshi's life span. To achieve this, Meme beseeched various gods and goddesses to return the "life" that had fallen into their hands. These deities then turned the *tshe* over to *tshe yid bzhin norbu*, the Buddha of Life, who dropped it, in the "image" of a small white "snow-flower," onto Meme's waiting drum.

As Yeshi and her family sat attentively, Meme began by invoking his tutelary deity in time to the slow beat of the drum:

> Imagine the guru.
> Body, speech, mind, imagine the guru

He then commenced, in a voice as sinewy as it was melodic, a ritual litany that likened the hoped-for expansion of Yeshi's life span to the gradual waxing of the moon.

> Like the white moon of the first day shines,
> upon the lower realm of the *srin po*,
> may the life shine here

Like the white moon of the second day shines,
upon the upper realm of the *klu*,
may the life shine here

The *srin po* ("simbu") is a lowly demon, an evil denizen dwelling in subterranean depths beneath those of the "serpent-deity" *klu* ("lu"). Yolmo wa imagine these lands to lie within the patient's body: the soles of the feet mark the *srin po*'s abode, the calves embody the *klu*. The song thus evoked two processes: it narrated the ascendency of the "life" through the running simile of the waxing moon, and it charted this ascendence on the distinct parts of the human body in a hierarchical movement from foot to scalp. Like the new moon's sliver of light, the *tshe* at first expanded as large as the feet in proportion to the whole body. On the second day of the new moon, the life shined up to the calf. And on the third:

Like the white moon of the third day shines,
upon the golden mirror of the knee,
may the life shine here

It is the singing of the body—from foot to calve to knee—that most captures the imagination of the healing audience. When I asked villagers the portent of the shaman's litany, they invariably noted that "In calling the life, the bombo names all the parts of the body: legs, mouth, ears. . . ." When I played a tape recording of one session to Latu, he choreographed the moon's ascent on his body with an upward migration of his hand. "Listen, it has reached the calf! . . . Ah, and now it touches the stomach!"

Unlike many of Meme's chants, the *tshe grub* litany is understood by all. Indeed, to be effective, members of the audience must participate in its unfolding. After Meme sang of the first three days, the members of the audience chorused a refrain to invoke lost life-forces (Yeshi mouthed a few of the words).

Dorje, assure that my life does not perish,
life here, *brum, yu brum, bla brum*

Participation was key. Both Yeshi and audience helped to recover the lost life.

Meme continued his ascent on the body, voicing a lengthy melody that often did not pause between the different "days" yet stopping at times to enable his audience to chorus the above refrain. As Yeshi attended to the moonlit song, Tenzin told her to imagine a snow that gradually descends on her body, blanketing it in purity and whiteness.[1]

> Like the white moon of the fourth day shines,
> upon the patterns of the crystal [hip bone],
> may the life shine here
>
> Like the white moon of the fifth day shines,
> upon the sack of the stomach,
> may the life shine here
>
> Like the white moon of the sixth day shines,
> upon the prayer flag of the life [appendix]
> may the life shine here
>
> Like the white moon of the seventh day shines,
> upon the hilly clouds of the lungs,
> may the life shine here
>
> Like the white moon of the eighth day shines,
> upon the golden *stupa* [shrine] of the heart
> may the life shine here
>
> Like the white moon of the ninth day shines,
> upon the golden box of the lips,
> may the life shine here
>
> Like the white moon of the tenth day shines,
> upon the golden flute of the nose,
> may the life shine here
>
> Like the white moon of the eleventh day shines,
> upon the forehead's mirror of fate,
> may the life shine here
>
> Like the white moon of the twelfth day shines,
> upon the crown of the head,
> may the life shine here

Like the white moon of the thirteenth day shines,
upon the meadow grass of the hair,
may the life shine here

Like the white moon of the fourteenth day shines,
upon the *snang ba mtha' yas* of the *rter tshugs*,[2]
may the life shine here

These bodily parts, it should be stressed, were continously likened to
the expansion of the moon until its fourteenth day. For Yolmo wa, the
moon illuminates the waxing and waning of powers both spiritual and
physical. Its demise (*mar ngo*, "marno"; "down-face") denotes death and
decay; its rise (*yar ngo*, "yarno"; "up-face") conjures images of strength,
vitality, and completion. Combining both themes, the lunar cycle hints at
the incessant play between fertility and decay, life and death. A bombo
mediates between these forces, and the full moon is the shamanic image par
excellence, a moment of ecstasy, health, and transcendence. Many shamanic
pilgrimages move to celebrate the night.

Asian societies have likened the human soul to the moon for time
immemorial. The ancient Chinese looked to the changing phases of the
moon to understand the periodic birth and death of the human *p'o*—its
"white light" or soul.[3] Tibetans chart the association within their physiology, for the soul "undergoes a regular monthly migration" within the
body.[4] At the new moon, the soul resides in the sole of the foot and then
"rises higher each day . . . to reside at the top of the head on the fifteenth and
sixteenth (at full moon), and return afresh to its initial position."[5] In
general, a person's life-forces are thought to wax and wane like the moon.
"Periods of deterioration" (*nyams*) induce weakness and illness; healing
increases the strength of a life-force.[6]

A similar imagery was at work for Yeshi: Meme aspired to make her life
as round and complete as the moon on the fifteenth day. For one patient,
the function of the *tshe grub* rite was "to make the life like the shining full
moon." And in Latu's words, "The *tshe grub* prayer is like a blessing—that
your life should be like this. Half is not good."

Before celebrating the full moon, Meme needed to implore the various
deities to hand over Yeshi's life if it was in their possession. He began the
search by calling on the five primordial shamans (*bon*) from the cardinal
directions.[7]

The four great *Bon* of the four islands
   of the four directions:
Pau Bon of the East,
   deposit the *tshe* from your hand. . . .

Meme likewise cited a litany of deities, noted their place in the five directions, and asked them to "deposit the *tshe* from the hand." His intent was to recover the lost life if it had fallen into their hands. The four *Jo* and *Jomo* of the four directions, the King of Tibet, the Queen of India, the gods "of this land," "White Father God" and "Black Mother Goddess"—Meme called over sixty deities as he toured the sacred geography.

"Ah, we have now touched the north!" said Meme, lifting a finger toward the Himalayas upon hearing a tape recording of the litany one afternoon. "And now we reach above!" he added, nodding his chin toward the central pillar as the prayer continued.

The celestial pantheon complete, Meme ended the prayer by conjuring vital images of the full moon.

Like the white moon of the fifteenth day shines,
deposit the life
Like the sun shines in the mountains,
deposit the life
Like the shining white rhododendrons
in the land of *Ne Chari Kungri*,
deposit the life
Like the snow-flowers which fall
from *dbus rnam par snang mdsad*,[8]
deposit the life

Deposit the life lasting seven hundred years,
the life of the Jewel of Knowledge [the Buddha]
the life of the King of China,
the life of the Jewel of Knowledge,
deposit the life from the hands,
bhrum!

On ending the litany, Meme turned his drum so that the skinned surface lay horizontal and drummed on the bottom surface while reiterating the names and locales of deities. "If the patient is not going to get well,"

Meme cautioned, "the life does not come, and the patient won't live much longer." But if the rite is successful, the *tshe* falls "like a leaf from a tree" and lands on the drum surface in the "image" of a small "snow-flower."

As the flower was no larger than a speck of dust, Tenzin, Serki, and I scanned the drum surface with flashlights in the anxious hope of locating Yeshi's life. Yeshi sat silently on the mat. After several minutes, we spotted the tiny "flower" bouncing on the drumskin. Meme turned his drum toward the altar and, while still drumming, dropped the *tshe* into the *pāthi* (measurement) bowl that held the grains, phurba, mirror, and *rtags dar* flags. The bowl served as a "safe-keeping" vessel for the "life" until Meme returned it to the body.

Hooking the Spirit

After Meme recovered Yeshi's life, he attempted to return the *bla* to her body. Earlier, the oracular divination revealed that Yeshi's "spirit" was lost. Since that loss, she lacked the volition to eat, work, travel, and talk with others. To recover the lost vitality, Meme searched in the various locales where the spirit might have strayed, venturing in the heavens, hell, or the expanse of hills, valleys, or forest of Helambu itself.

Tenzin prepared for the rite by constructing, on a blanket a few feet behind the shaman's altar, a swastika made from rice grains (if the patient is female, one creates a swastika; if male, a *dorje*; see Figure 6).[9] He placed *chang*, rice, curd, meat, and an egg on a board in front of the blanket in a display reminiscent of Lamaist food offerings. Yeshi sat directly on the swastika symbol. "A woman must put her left foot onto the sign first," her husband told her. "Men begin with the right." Yeshi draped a white shawl over her head and body and clasped her hands together as in prayer.

Meme picked up the drum and called the fierce *khyung*, the eaglelike Garuda deity of Buddhist lore,[10] and its four "bodyguards" (*shyamar*) to his assistance.

Earth Khyung, *Rinchen Khyung*
Sky Khyung, *Garuda Dorje*
Twenty-one Khyungs
Thirty-five Khyungs
Forty-five Khyungs
Fifty-five Khyungs
Sixty-five Khyungs!

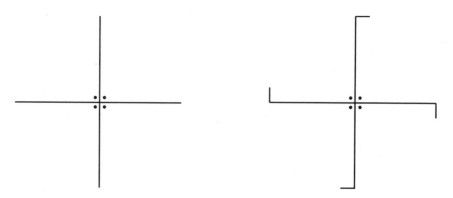

Figure 6. *Dorje* and swastika.

The *khyung* responded to the call, and Meme's heartmind left his body with a joyful, ecstatic shout and glided through space, clinging to the bird's chest as it escorted him in the search for the lost spirit.

All was silent as Meme searched "above." His body was still. The audience waited. Yeshi prayed. Meme traveled through the air, scavenging "like a hawk" in search of the displaced spirit. From time to time, he confronted evil spirits—a witch, ghost, or angry god. In a struggle to escape their clutches, his body shook, causing the bells strapped around his chest to ring out.

"We must go like thieves," Meme taught one afternoon, "without evil spirits knowing of our presence. Otherwise, they will attack. We go like a hawk hunting a chicken, looking far away, then coming to snatch it away. Sometimes along the way a tiger comes to cover [attack] us. Sometimes an ox comes to hit, some dogs come to bite. We get startled."

With each healing, Meme looks everywhere for the spirit, "in someone's house, in the jungle, in the land of the dead, the land of gods, above, below." "Sometimes we need to search along cliffsides, jungle, heaven, or hell," Meme said. "Unless we see the face, we keep roaming. If we see the face, immediately we can catch it. But we don't take it by our hands. It is snapped up by the claw of the *khyung*."

Since Meme often spies the vagrant spirits of others, he must see the patient's face clearly to bring back the correct *bla*. Often the search invokes a treacherous journey, as Mingma recounted of his own healing: "Meme found my spirit in the land of the dead [*shi yul*], but he had great difficulty in bringing it back, for something was pulling it away from him, not wanting to leave. He was frightened by seeing ghosts and other evils."

Photo 19. Hooking the spirit.

Save for Meme's tremors, silence filled the room for several minutes. Suddenly, Meme began to shake and chant fiercely: he had "hooked" (*'gug*) the spirit and was returning with it! The participants of the healing shouted out in celebration, and Tenzin and Serki passed the incense bowl around Yeshi's body, three times clockwise, three times counterclockwise. The act cleansed Yeshi's body of lingering harm and created a protective circle around her form. Another man raised the *pāthi* bowl (containing the *rtags dar* and recently recovered life) to the crown of her head, then touched it to her scalp, two shoulders, chest, hands, two knees. Through this act, Yeshi recovered the newfound "life" and the "power" (*dbang*) bestowed within the bowl. "You need to touch everywhere," Meme once advised, "to assure that the spirit returns to the body, and to give power to its different parts."

The spirit, "hooked" successfully, fell onto the drum surface in the "image" of three white "flowers" the size of specks of dust. After each flower appeared, Meme dropped it into one of the foods set on the tray (egg, meat, curd) as Yeshi lifted it to her mouth to eat. In consuming each of the foods, she reincorporated lost vitality. Meme then took the magical "dagger" (*phur ba*) from the altar and touched it to Yeshi's forehead. He did the same with some butter, affixing it to her forehead to bestow further power within her body. He then replaced the *phur ba* within the *rtags dar* bowl and told Yeshi to hold the bowl. Yeshi took the bowl to her cot and placed it on the shelf above her head. The resting place had significance, for Yeshi's "spirit" was said to be "above, in the body."

The *bla 'gug* rite ended with a flurry of profane activity. Meme removed the bells from his chest and recounted where he found Yeshi's spirit. "I had to rescue it from the land of the dead!" he said as his fingers reached for a cigarette. Tenzin gathered the scattered rice grains of the now defunct swastika symbol into a bowl and cleaned the floor of lingering debris. Yeshi lay with eyes closed, arms beneath her shawl.

A Sense of Healing

Since the first nights of my apprenticeship, I have been trying to understand if, how, and to what extent Meme's soul-calling rites work to rejuvenate spiritless bodies. My present understanding is that the rites do, at times, have a positive effect. When they are effective, they work through indirect, tacit means—the less obvious aspects of ritual[11]—to lighten a heavy body or "brighten" a weary heart. Simply put, Meme changes how a body feels by altering what it feels. His cacophony of music, taste, sight, touch, and kinesthesia activates a patient's senses. This activation has the potential to "wake" a person, alter the sensory grounds of a spiritless body, and change how a body feels. A successful soul-calling rite recreates the sense of "presence" intrinsic to Yolmo experiences of well-being.

My understanding of Yolmo soul-calling rites, in which the sensory dimensions are pivotal, goes against the grain of anthropological accounts which privilege the ideational, rhetorical, or symbolic aspects of ritual healing. My thinking on the subject has evolved out of a dissatisfaction with the tenets of such approaches, for they do not seem able to account for the ritual techniques or the effectiveness of ritual among Yolmo. A discussion of two of the most dominant explanations of the effectiveness of ritual healing—the "intellectualist" and the "symbolist" positions—might show the reasons for my dissatisfaction.[12]

The intellectualist position of British social anthropology, developed most recently by Skorupski, holds that the shaman's and patient's concern for efficacy is an intellectual one.[13] The shaman acts in order to instill a faith and belief in the patient's mind that something can be done to ameliorate his malady.[14] Such acts work because they have worked in the past and are expected to work in the present. As Malinowski suggests, ritual acts are geared not to mean something (for the acts can even be "meaningless") but to enact something.[15] Through this enactment, the patient is said to gain faith in the curing process and begin to think differently about his or her condition.

In contrast to the intellectualist stance, "symbolist" positions, the products of French structuralist and American semiotic approaches to ritual performance, contend that curing rites work chiefly by provoking transformations either of the worldview held by a patient or of the symbolic categories that define the experiences of that patient.[16] A healer typically evokes symbols or metaphors that provide a tangible "language" through which the patient can express, understand, or transform the personal or interpersonal conflicts underlying his or her illness. These orientations follow the spirit of Lévi-Strauss's classic paper "The Effectiveness of Symbols," which argues that a Cuna shaman's articulation of a mythic realm effects transformations in the physiology of his patient.[17] Dow, for instance, outlines the "universal structure" of symbolic healing: a healer attaches a patient's emotions to "transactional symbols" and then manipulates these symbols to help the patient transact his or her emotions.[18] Kleinman articulates a "structural model of healing" that builds on the notion of a "symbolic bridge" between personal experience and cultural meanings: a healer manipulates "mediating symbols" to effect change in a patient's emotional reactions.[19] And Kapferer, despite his focus on dramaturgy, holds that the symbolic forms of Sinhalese demon exorcisms "link the inner experience of the subject with the objective structure of the rite. Through the manipulation of these mediating symbolic forms, the inner experience of the subjects can be made to parallel the transformations taking place in the objective structure of the rite."[20] A patient is thereby "progressively reordered" and his or her subjective awareness "reconstituted."[21]

While both the intellectualist and symbolist positions have helped to explain the structural logic of many religious rites throughout the world, I find neither to be particularly useful in explaining how or why Yolmo shamans heal. The intellectualist position, for instance, does not account for why Yolmo shamans go to the extent that they do to recover a patient's vitality. According to this model, ritual acts aim to achieve what they purport to achieve (here, returning life-forces). Meme needs only to call the patient's spirit back to instill the personal conviction that something substantial is being done to improve his or her condition; he does not need to enact a vivid and lengthy rite. And yet he does. In an attempt to explain why he does so, I want to suggest that how a Yolmo shaman searches for a spirit is as important as actually finding it.

At the same time, I do not believe that Meme recovers a spirit primarily through the use of metaphors, symbolic transformations, or rhetorical tropes, as recent studies of "symbolic healing" hold. Although these representational models, which have dominated ethnographies of healing since Lévi-Strauss, apparently identify the general structure of ritual healings in a variety of places, they cannot account for a Yolmo calling of souls. It is true that Meme's rites achieve their efficacy through the "transformation of experience":[22] Yolmo healings imagine a symbolic ascent from weakness to strength, fragmentation to integration, deficiency to completion, disharmony to harmony, defilement to purity. Yet the symbolic shift from illness to health is not the method but simply the consequence of the rites. Soul-calling for Yolmo wa is less like a mythic narrative, progressing from one stage to another, than an imagistic poem, evoking an array of tactile images that, through their cumulative effect, evoke a change of sensibility—a change, that is, in the lasting mood or disposition that constitutes the sensory grounds of a person's bodily experience. Seen in this light, it is more the visceral impact of the poem, rather than its metaphorical structure, that effects change.

This impact ties into sensory experience. Meme's craft involves a healing of bodies, of sensibilities, of ways of being in the world. His soul-calling rites might change how a patient thinks of his or her condition, and they might even alter the symbolic categories that define that condition. But if the rite is to be considered a successful one, it must change how a person feels. This is because Yolmo criteria of efficacy rest on the lack or presence of visceral evidence that the body feels better in the days following a rite. These rather experiential criteria relate, at least in part, to Yolmo epistemologies of illness and healing. In illness, a villager cannot know the cause or course of his or her plight until its signifying symptoms (bodily pains, bad dreams) become manifest. Similarly, since the spirit is an intangible force, a villager can only determine its return by interpreting how body and heartmind feel in the hours and days subsequent to a rite.

"After the spirit returns," Lakpa, a middle-aged Yolmo woman, told me in the wake of a soul-calling rite performed on her behalf, "we feel like eating again. Energy returns. After two or three days, the body feels light, the heartmind brightens, it becomes clear, lucid. The eyes become brighter." Others spoke of similar responses. "When the spirit returns," Nyima said of the soul-calling rites, "it feels like a jolt of electricity to the body. . . . The body feels good, and we feel good in the heartmind. After it returns, you can sleep well." "We have the sensation that the spirit has come back," said another man. "When the spirit returned to my body," Dawa said, remembering a cure for spiritlessness, "I felt well. I felt happy, comfortable. I felt a little bit lighter by the next morning. Slowly, slowly, within ten, fifteen days, I was fine."

A Yolmo patient can take a healer's word that he has recovered the spirit, but such talk, I was told, is occasionally "like the wind," and villagers sometimes consider a shaman's "rhetoric of transformation"[23] to be mere rhetoric. "The shaman knows for sure whether the spirit returns or not," Lakpa added. "Or so they say. Shamans and lamas tell us 'The life has come back,' but we don't know this, we can't see this. When we feel better, then we think it has returned." A patient, therefore, cannot be sure whether the spirit has returned to the body until the sensibility of soul loss (heavy body, weak eyes, weary heart) has been "cut." The visceral sense of renewed health, which usually takes hold in the hours after a rite and must last if the rite is to be considered successful, is the major criteria upon which villagers judge rites efficacious or not. In Helambu, a person does not feel better after being cured; she is cured after feeling better.

Whereas all rites, by definition, effect symbolic transformations (and so, in Kleinman and Song's terms, "cannot but heal"[24]), Yolmo wa do not consider all rites to be efficacious. This fact suggests that if we are to develop a model of Yolmo healing, the model must not simply sketch out possible mechanisms of healing but also tie into the ways in which patients know themselves to be healed.[25] In an attempt to develop such an understanding here, I shall build on the work of several anthropologists who emphasize the performative and dramaturgical aspects of ritual healing.[26] While this research attributes ritual efficacy to a variety of factors, from acts of catharsis to resolutions of social conflicts and the ritual reframing of cultural realities, a constant concern is for the ways in which dramatic actions and aesthetic performances engage participants and evoke emotional responses. To date, however, this work has focused more on the social and psychological rather than visceral dimensions of such engagement.[27] There is therefore something at work in Yolmo healings that this literature has yet to fully account for: namely, the presence of bodies in the rites and the extent to which ritual performances work directly to change how patients feel.[28] In the following pages, I want to address these concerns by outlining how Meme might work in the soul-calling rites to lighten a heavy body (the next chapter asks how effective are the rites). In essence, I argue that Meme's chants tend not to represent past experiences; rather, they activate the senses to spark sensibilities distinct from those of malaise. These newfound sensibilities tie into Yolmo aesthetics of experience, for they engage senses of presence, vitality, harmony, and repletion.

"Wild" Images

Meme's search for Yeshi's soul parallels shamanic itineraries in other Himalayan lands. A Bhuji shaman lies in a burial ground and "calls to the soul as if it were a child, luring it from the clutches of its captor or enticer."[29] A Gurung shaman ventures on an elaborate search of cosmological domains, first calling out the names of goddesses "of rock, soil, rivers, and trees" to ask if the soul has been hidden in these domains and then enticing the soul from the land of the dead.[30] Tamang healers journey to divine and reveal "hidden" lands to recover lost shadow-souls[31] and Magars descend into the "underworld" to overtake a soul before it reaches "The Waters of Forgetfulness."[32] These searches mirror the ecstatic journeys of Asian shamans, who typically hunt for stray spirits "through mountains and rivers and on into the land of the dead."[33]

Of particular interest is the way healers carefully communicate to the patient concrete details of what they see during their flights: from river to forest, they sing of their journeys. A Kham-Magar's chant successfully mentions a half-dozen hamlets, two river crossings, a cave dwelling, a monastery, a sacred shrine, and a "place of origin and fertility."[34] A Tamang shaman calls out places where lost souls can "get stuck":

> In a heaven of the homeless,
> In a heaven of confusion,
> In a heaven of distress,
> In a heaven of rumorous gossip,
> In a heaven of cannibals,
> In a heaven of closed mouths,
> In a heaven of licentious sex.[35]

If the healer does not leave his body in an ecstatic search for the patient's spirit, he calls out to it, imploring the spirit to return as Meme beseeches his gods to "deposit the life from the hand." The calling of the soul occurs throughout the world.[36] Mexican *curanderos* admonish the patient's lost soul to return by calling, for example, "Juliana, Juliana, come back, come back!,"[37] and a Siberian shaman, attemping to reclaim the soul of a sick child, calls "Come back to your country! . . . to the yurt, by the bright fire! . . . Come back to your father . . . to your mother! . . ."[38]

Often these requests, which in Asia date back at least two thousand years,[39] take the form of elaborate litanies. The Ancient Chinese "Elegies of Ch'u" narrate a "summoner's" ornate invocation to the strayed soul of a sick king to leave "the earth's far corners" and return to its "old abode":

> O Soul, go not to the north!
> In the north is the Frozen Mountain,
> and the Torch Dragon, glaring red;
> And the Tai river that cannot be crossed,
> whose depths are unfathomable;
> And the sky is white and glittering,
> and all is congealed with cold.
> O soul, go not to the north!
> There is no bourn there to your journeying. . . .[40]

In Tibet, Lamaist lurings of the soul assume a similar form: an elaborate, imagistic litany portrays a tangible expanse on which the soul's travels are plotted. In a Lamaist "calling the *bla*" rite, the summoner enumerates a divine pantheon similar to the gods surveyed within Meme's *tshe grub* rite:

> . . . Ye, the fire god, *rakshasas*, the wind gods,
> and the powerful ones in the four intermediate points,
> Ye gods of the earth below,
> All ye gods of the ten points of the universe,
> If ye have snatched [the soul]. . . .[41]

The litany climaxes with a bystander shouting at the top of his voice:

> Soul and life of such and such a person,
> of such a family,
> of such and such an age,
> bearing such and such a name,
> whether thou hast come to a royal palace,
> or a mansion of a nobleman,
> or a Buddhist temple,
> or a place of worship. . . .[42]

We can better realize the chant's power if we mold its conclusion into projective verse:

> . . . or an island or islet,
>   a rock or a cave, or
>   a thoroughfare, or
>   a place noisy with human activities, or
>   a place inhabited by malignant spirits or
>   mischievous demons,
> or whether thou art traveling or
>   drifting in the wind or
>   floating on the water, or
>   scattered about,
> whether thou are snatched away or
>   carried off,
> I bid thee come back.

Yet in contrast to Charles Olson's "Projective Verse," where "ONE PERCEPTION MUST IMMEDIATELY AND DIRECTLY LEAD TO A FURTHER PERCEPTION,"[43] the lama's chant presents a different logic of perception. There is no staircasing of impressions, no evolution of experience. The chant turns on a point by point appeal to the imagination. Each image, standing alone, acts as a lure. The *sems* leaps from island to islet.

The curative power of the chant, I am arguing, ties into its style of presentation, and so how patients respond to that presentation. On many occasions, Himalayan healers do not say whether or not they have found the souls they are looking for. In my estimation, they do not need to, for, in contrast to the intellectualist position, it is the search, rather than any ostensive result ("The spirit has come back"), that is of fundamental importance.

To better appreciate what makes the search itself so effective, we can compare Yolmo poetics to certain tenets of modern European literary theory. In his 1979 paper "The Metaphorical Process as Cognition, Imagination, and Feeling," Paul Ricoeur draws upon Marcus B. Hester's theory of poetic metaphors:

> Describing the experience of *reading*, [Hester] shows that the kind of images which are interesting for a theory of poetic language are not those that

interrupt reading and distort or divert it. These images—these "wild" images, if I may say so—are properly extrinsic to the fabric of sense. They induce the reader, who has become a dreamer rather than a reader, to indulge himself in the delusive attempt, described by Sartre as fascination, to possess magically the absent thing, body, or person. The kind of images which still belong to the production of sense are rather what Hester calls "bound" images, that is, concrete representations aroused by the verbal element and controlled by it.[44]

It is such "bound" images, Ricoeur suggests, that cohere with and add to the larger metaphoric structure of a poem and "bring to concrete completion the metaphorical process."[45] That process eventually leads to "a model for changing our way of looking at things, of perceiving the world."[46]

Ricoeur's discussion of "bound" images aptly documents the metaphoric process of Western poetics, a process that recalls the transformations of experience that symbolist accounts of healing portray.[47] At the same time, his dismissal of "wild" images, images that do not fit into a larger structure of meaning and so "distract thought more than they instruct it,"[48] reflects the rage for order in much of modern European poetry and criticism. In their influential treatise *Understanding Poetry*, Brooks and Warren declare that "poetic imagery must not be idle and meaningless, dead or inert, or distracting and self-serving, like some foolish ornament that merely calls attention to itself. Every bit of image ought to 'make sense' and to aid the poem in *its* making sense."[49] Baker advances a similar view in his assessment of Coleridge's theory of poetry.[50] "Images," Baker writes, "are not pillars supporting vacancy, but caryatids sustaining weight; they are not empty caskets, but barrels containing meaning."[51] Poetic images, in other words, must not be empty, light, or distracting and self-serving, like some foolish waif prancing about in the house of Order.

Yet "bound" images do not seem especially relevant either to the technology or to the effectiveness of Himalayan soul-calling chants. Rather, it is precisely those "wild" images—images that "distract" and "interrupt"—that we encounter time and again and that, I contend, work most to "wake" spiritless bodies.

To be sure, "bound" images are to be found in the Himalayas. In Helambu, for instance, the *tshe grub* rite likens the body to a waxing moon, and funereal songs of pain rely on a careful play of tropes. Yet Himalayan healers also value the iconic, the mimetic, the nonmetaphoric, and the wild. By "wild," I mean those Himalayan images that leapfrog into the imagination and so engage the listener not through any threaded storytelling but through a random and roundabout slideshow of perceptions: a rock, a cave, a thoroughfare. Through this slideshow, the chant excites the senses and entices the imagination in a particular way.

Which way is this? The poetics common to the chants seems one not of "contemplation," but of "distraction," to again fall back on words drawn from my own heritage—this time those used by Walter Benjamin in his history of Europe's "unconscious optics."[52] In contrast to the canvas of a painting, which, for Benjamin, "invites the spectator to contemplation; before it the spectator can abandon himself to associations," the movie frame is "based on changes of place and focus which periodically assail the spectator."[53] The soul-calling chants bear a charge and tactility similar to the film. "No sooner has [the spectator's] eye grasped a scene than it is already changed. It cannot be arrested."[54] Benjamin records the unsettling effects the new media had on European sensibilities; we can attend to the visceral impact of a similar sort of "distraction" in the Himalayas.

In my own encounter with the chants, I find that the images are predominantly open, unbounded ones; though they may distract, they also demand, by their very lightness, an attentive ear. The "Frozen Mountain" to the north, a sky "white and glittering"—the images succeed one another without any sense of denouement (the French "untying"), though there is an element of intrigue. The images do not build on one another toward a greater whole of meaning. They do not add to a narrative progression, with a precise teleological goal. The images do not engage their audience by pulling them into a narrative web, which Iser identifies as one of the tasks of Western literature.[55] Rather, they engage their listeners by the very lack of narration. There is no "directedness" in the litanies.[56] We lack a sense that the story is going somewhere (or even that there is a story). The endings of many chants, which often close with a final invocation to or for the lost soul, remain incomplete and provisional, as if the images throughout, both singularly and as a whole, do not work to round off a controlled and bounded fabric of sense. Instead, the images seem to invite an inconclusive dialogue, an interaction that consists of an initial summons to be answered by the patient and a fictive sketch to be completed by the patient's imagination. And so the suspense created by the chants is not one that is answered by the litanies themselves (as a Greek tragedy answers its own questions). The suspense can only be answered by way of the audience's own participation in a chant. Through this participation, the chant hooks a patient: it draws a body out of its spiritlessness to invoke a sense of presence, volition, and attention.

Indeed, it may be that the more bounded, closed, or weighted the imagery, the less chance there is of revitalizing those who hear them. If the fabric of sense was a closely knit one, the patient would be less inclined to anticipate, attend to, or interact with any novel stimuli in his or her environment; the more bounded the meaning of the chant, the more established the imagery within an expected context, the less need there is for the patient to break out of his slumber and actively step into the geography of its images. By necessity, then, the images remain open, unbounded, wild.

The open, unbounded quality of the images appears similar to the polysemic "fan" of meanings that Laderman, following Turner, identifies as the curative agent in Malay birth incantations: "Incantations cure by analogy, not through their specificity but by their 'fan' of meanings, their multilayered nature and the ambiguity of their symbols."[57] For Schieffelin, the tension and suspense cultivated through a Kaluli curing seance leads its participants to experience a sense of "inconclusiveness and imbalance."[58] This experience forces people to make sense of the performance and thus to "arrive at a meaningful account of what is happening." In so doing, they "complete the construction of its reality."[59]

Yet while the use of ambiguity to draw people into a performance appears basic to a variety of ritual settings, the reasons for such engagement can vary. While Schieffelin's Kaluli become engaged in a performance so as to "reach fundamental symbolic understandings and arrive at solutions to their problems,"[60] it appears that, in the Himalayas, the engagment itself is meant to be curative. The priestly chants do not necessarily facilitate any social construction of reality, but rather help a patient to participate, anew, in the everyday. This participation is the singular antidote for soul loss—a sense of spiritlessness defined by a very lack of engagement. The Tibetan litany reported by Lessing, for instance, compels an experiential pointillism; it attends, imagistically rather than narratively, to tangible features of the cultural landscape. Its aesthetic form—imagistic, tactile, precise—prompts attention, awareness, and presence. Each image stands alone in a complex field of tensions such that it is the complexity and tension of the perceptions that engages the dispirited. The heartmind opens up to a world exterior to itself and "noisy with human activities," and the heavy slumber marking soul loss can be countered.

This sort of ritual attentiveness, at once imagistic and sensorial, is vividly felt in the soul-searching procedure of a Himalayan shaman as reported by Hitchcock. "A Matwala shaman performs a ritual to cure a patient who is unconscious. During the course of the ritual he sings a song in which over 100 local flowers, bushes and trees are mentioned. After this he calls a *deuta* [deity], becomes possessed, and lies down unconscious before his unconscious patient. His interpretation of this last portion of the ritual is that the *deuta* is conducting his soul among the plants named in the song, for somewhere among them the soul is hiding. After some time the shaman awakes and ritually restores to the patient his lost soul."[61] Hitchcock adds "It is not the plant that holds the soul prisoner, but one or more evil spirits, who use the plant as a hiding place. The shaman has to do battle with these spirits in order to wrest the soul away. . . . The context takes place on earth, or just beneath it, among roots."[62]

Though no details are given, and the meaning of the term "unconscious" remains unclear, the imagery reveals an (under)world of sensorial experience. We see the green plants, taste the damp soil, and touch the sinewy roots. What effect, if any, could this vegetal imagery have on an "unconscious" patient? Perhaps by delving into plant and root the shaman induces the patient to attend to an expansive and richly colored scenario exterior to his own sluggish sensorium. He thus rejuvenates a body by rooting it within a garden of imagined sensations.

Often the domains articulated by healers focus on the creature comforts of Himalayan life (shelter, food, family) in the hopes of luring the soul to return "home." As soon as Lessing's Tibetan bystander addresses the wandering soul from the rooftop, he shouts out the favorite dishes or entertainments of the patient: "Come quick and eat this. Come quick and enjoy that. Come quick and do this."[63]

The images, less wild now, continue to rely on a poetics of presence. The Tibetans begin with the ten points of the universe, search the thoroughfares for winds and demons, then zero in on the hurried activities of the patient's backyard. The rite progressively focuses on the present, the felt, the immediate. By focusing on the everyday, the patient returns to the commonsensical.

One senses, at times, that the healer treats the soul like a wayward child, enticing it to return home by offering the familiar sweets of everyday life. Bawden notes that, to lure a Mongolian soul back to its body, "the attractions of his familiar surroundings are held out to him."[64] The ancient Chinese summoner described luscious delicacies (stewed turtle, casseroled duck) in the hopes of wooing the king's strayed soul to return to its "quiet and reposeful home," which itself exudes "high halls," "stepped terraces," and "lattice doors."[65] In the soul-calling rites, it is through the very process of directed attentiveness, in which images call attention to themselves, that a patient revitalizes. With the king's life on the line, the Chinese soul caller invests in the poetic punch of an ornate, sensate patter rather than in any binding metaphors.

That the rites aim to induce sensory attentiveness is further evinced in more recent chants, some two millenium after the "Elegies of Ch'u," whereby Tibetan and Mongolian Buddhist lamas lure vital souls by delineating what exists "HERE," in the immediacies of the patient's world:

> Your parents are HERE.
> Your brothers and sisters are HERE.
> Your friends and neighbours are HERE.
> The three white and three sweet foods are HERE.
> If you would drink tasty beer, it's HERE.
> If you would eat fat meat, it's HERE.
> If you would eat boiled-down [thick] food, it's HERE.
> Plentiful, sweet tasty food is HERE.
> If you would wear good clothes, they're HERE.
> If you would ride a good horse, it's HERE.
> Don't go there, there! Come HERE, HERE!
> Don't follow to the land of the deathlords!
> A-bo-lo-lo, come HERE![66]

The incessant "here" suggests that the healer seeks to recover lost vitality by picturing the taste and feel of the present. Fat meat, tasty beer, and a fine horse lie at one's side, close enough to touch. I have indicated the radical need for presence in Yolmo life and how a sense of "hereness" is lost when the spirit is lacking. Could this sensibility be salient in other Tibetan societies? If so, then a calling of souls works to ground the patient in the "here and now" by selectively attending to the concrete, sensorial features of his or her environment.

Indeed, it is not just the itinerant "soul" that lends an ear to the healer's litany: the patient listens as well. As with the Lamaist chant recorded by Lessing, the healer realizes the sensorial fissures of the patient's environment to change how body and heartmind feel and function. "Your parents are here, good food is here, it is safe to come out again," the litany seems to say, as if to coax a frightened child out of a hiding place. The rites, by attending to the patient's immediate environment, provoke a stance toward that environment and instill a willful attentiveness that is absent when the soul is lacking.

A Healing Geography

In Himalayan soul-calling rites, the soul returns to the body by attending to what lies outside its corporeal abode. A similar preoccuption with the patient's environment lies at the center of Yolmo healings. Meme calls forth a distinct spiritual geography throughout an evening of shamanic healing. By articulating this geography, he works to recover lost vitality through methods similar to those noted above: a selective attention to detail, an evocation of the senses, a mimetic presentation of a tangible reality, an invocation of the "here," and the use of wild images to induce attentiveness. Image by image, a Yolmo healer anticipates finite features of a patient's world in order to situate him or her more sensibly within that world.

Meme begins a healing ceremony by consecrating the various items of his altar and equipment by reciting the mythic origins of each ritual item, such as the five "stems" set within the altar's "god-curtain":

From the east, a stem of gold
From the south, a stem of copper
From the west, a stem of iron
From the north, a stem of turquoise
From the land of the gods above, a stem of conch

He similarly consecrates the lamp and grains of the altar and his bells, belt, rosaries, and drum (frame, hide, handle, drumstick) by citing the five directions from which each article comes: east, south, west, north, and center "above." Through these chants, Meme brings to life a scared yet tangible geography that centers around the patient's body and induces the patient to attend anew to this geography.

The rites of purification further realize the healing geography. Meme offers "incense" (*gtsang rab*, "sanrap") to the gods and goddesses of Helambu and neighboring lands, including Tibet and India. Beginning in the *sbas yul* ("beyul") or "hidden country" of Tibet, Meme tours "with his heartmind" the locales and shrines to the east of Helambu as they range south into the Kathmandu Valley and India. He then returns on a westerly route to climb back north to the Himalayas. After enumerating each set of deities, Meme requests the gods to "purify all that has been affected by pollution" (*pho pai drip ci bsangs*). The journey is quite lengthy and encompasses over four hundred sacred sites: from north to east, south, west, and north again.[67]

Meme locates the sacred geography within Helambu itself. The purificatory *gtsang rab* situates the divine among a range of "cliffsides, big rocks, and tall trees," as Meme spoke of the telluric haunts of his tutelary spirits. Speaking of Tamang versions of the lengthy recitation, Holmberg finds an "obsession to enumerate," a "maniacal urge" to repeat and parcel out lived experience so as to complete it.[68] Yet while Yolmo shamans are anxious to name and so keep on the safe side of all the gods, I have found that the litanies also serve as an introduction to trance. In this case, repetition is less obsession than technique. Meme's leitmotiv—focused, complete, and controlled—commands attention. As shamanic speech orchestrates the five directions, bodies become centered, alert, enraptured. By focusing on an extant geography, a foothilled expanse lodged in mountain and forest, spatial images draw the heartmind out of the body in a moment of ecstasis.

But what of the patient's body? What does Yeshi, supine beneath her shawl, sense of the shaman's songs? While patients often do not grasp the specifics of the opening chants, they do appear to sense their underlying poetics. The songs transform: all is purified, protected, replete with meaning. Constant and insistent, the cardinal points invoke an imaginative landscape for the ritual proceedings. As Meme mumbles his chant, cleansing Helambu's hills and forests, Yeshi catches snippets of meaning. The directional notation is clear: *shar . . . lho . . . nub . . . byang . . . dbus* repeatedly mark the five directions: east, south, west, north, center. Yeshi soon finds herself at the heart of the center, the four corners of the earth encircling her form. The articulation of place-names compels the patient to attend to and imagine specific locales—well-known hamlets and hillsides realized through a rapid, freeze-frame singsong.

So while Tibetans recover lost spirits by naming where they might have wandered to, Meme tries to recall Yeshi's spirit throughout an evening by chanting the places outside of her single-chamber home where she might have set foot. It may be that the articulation of this tangible expanse, which plays such a key role in how villagers make their livings, kindles attention and recalls healthy ways of moving the body.[69] A Tamang shaman flies within broad valleys because there "all the earth is opened up";[70] Meme's chants similarly open up a range of experiences. They draw Yeshi's heartmind out of her heavy body to dance through a rocky landscape, tracts of which she has walked, set foot upon, climbed, and bathed in: the underground spring below Khutumsang, the cliff above Melamchighyang, the northern forest, the southern valley, a natal home, village path, familiar lands, cremation grounds. The chants move on, resting nowhere, cleansing all the lands above, below, to the east and to the west.

From the opening drumbeats, Meme invokes a soulful presence. Common to this and other Himalayan chants is a flickery, place by place slide-show of perceptions that distracts, engages, and intrigues. Whether it be his healing geography, the lama's litany of the soul's haunts, or a Tibetan's invocation of the "here," spells of attention and presence work to remedy the sensory features of soul loss: listlessness, apathy, fatigue, distress. The calling of souls apparently has evolved in a such a way so as to "treat" the dysphoric sensibilities of soul loss, whatever the antecedents and parameters of these experience might be. The cure directly (but tacitly) confronts feelings of spiritlessness, crafting apathy into attentiveness and fatigue into vigilance. The near omnipresence of these rites in distant cultures—from Siberian flights to the curandero's balm for *susto*—suggests an ancient, panhuman base not only to a lack of vigor occasioned by lost souls, but to a means to recover lost vitality.

Kinesthesia

Meme's rites also enliven by attending to the sensory faculties of the body. The patient's body is a key player throughout a Yolmo healing, and this physiology takes center stage in the final hours. The acoustics of the soul-calling rite—Meme's "startled," bell-clanging body, the driving drumbeats, and shouts from the audience—maintain a high level of intensity throughout. The flicker of candles, the aroma of incense, and the taste of foods adds to the supple fusion of senses. Ritual sentience, by whetting the senses, helps to renew a villager's felt participation in the world.

With Yeshi's soul-hooking rite, a swastika of power and solidity "awakens" her limbs. Incense encircles her form to cleanse it of lingering harm. To "empower" her body, the *pathi* bowl filled with "life" (*tshe*) and "power" (*dbang*) is touched to her head, shoulders, chest, hands, and knees. The butter and magical "dagger" charge her forehead with renewed vitality. And the body recovers its vitality by consuming a "snow-flower" with an array of foods good to eat and think. Physically, sensorially, the body is cleansed, protected, and empowered. Meme presents images, actions, tastes, and sounds that speak directly to sensory experience, as if the body was the true audience and its language one of gesture, sense, and image.

The act of incorporating, brought home by sensate experiences, recurs. After Meme exorcises pains and impurities, Yeshi incorporates life, power, and vitality. The symbol of prosperity supporting her form, the touching of a vase to "all the parts of the body," and the butter affixed to the forehead touch off an integration of the values invested in these forms: prosperity, long life, and empowerment. Patients often underscore the displacement from outside to inside in telling of their experiences of the rites: power, life, and spirit, they stress, "enter inside the body."

With the *tshe grub* rite, a litany working to enhance Yeshi's life span, Meme attends to the body with a similar technology of sense. Image by image, he anticipates finite features of Yeshi's world: sole, calf, knee, heart, scalp. The body, with its crystal hips and golden stupas, becomes a cathedral of sacred icons. It assumes a hierarchy, for it aligns organs from foot to head as much as the cosmos layers demons and deities. And it grows complete, for the indexing of kneecaps, appendices, and golden flutes melds the body's fragments into a unified, healthy whole.

Matching the aesthetics of lunar vitality and repletion are those of corporeal balance and harmony. Earlier, Meme's travels through the five directions mapped a space of harmony and completion; now, the *tshe grub* rite unites the body within a cosmos of balance and integration. By weaving the distinct parts of the body within a tangible and balanced hierarchy (from foot to head), Meme articulates the bodily coordination so crucial for Yolmo health. In illness, the distinct functions of the body cease to communicate harmoniously with one another. But with stomach and heart now realized, disparate organs can work together once again.

The aesthetic themes of the song, namely, balance, harmony, and repletion, make themselves known through the most tactile of images, as if the "sensory pole" engaged by the rite worked to realize its "ideological pole."[71] In other words, by attending directly to the body, Meme taps into the most visceral of domains to get across his message of balance and integration. If successful, he engages a felt sense of change and harmony, such that the aesthetic values voiced by the song seem the natural, unquestioned steps toward renewed health. Yet since the values bodied forth by the song mesh with the vital political concerns of high status Lamas, a state of renewed health helps to further secure the rudiments of form (balanced hierarchies, bounded mosaics) that govern those values.

"When the spirit returns," says Nyima, using a rather modern idiom, "it feels like a jolt of electricity to the body." Bodies lighten. Eyes and heartminds brighten. A person wants to eat and walk and sleep again. Bad dreams are cut from the body. The potent blend of image and sensation intrinsic to Yolmo soul-callings, and the effect that this blend typically has on patients, suggests that shifts in how a patient thinks of his or her condition (the spirit has returned) or in the symbolic identity that defines that condition (renewed health, transformed contexts) can only partly explain how he or she might recover lost vitality. For healing to be effective, Meme must transform the felt quality, the sensory grounds, of a spiritless body. How does he do so? Our findings suggest that a less cerebral model than those above can explain Yolmo soul-callings: Meme attempts to change how a body feels by altering what it feels. "You need to touch all the parts of the body," he insists, and for good reason. His cacophony of music, taste, sight, touch, and wild, tactile images activates the senses and the imagination. This activation can "wake up" a patient, offer new ways of wielding the flesh, spark new sensibilities, and thus change how a person feels. The potential changes tie into the aesthetic qualities of sensory experience. Embodied aesthetics is a question of tact, of perception, of sensibility, and by adding to what Yeshi tastes, sees, touches, hears, and imagines, Meme tries to jumpstart a physiology.

9. Departures

By two in the morning, Yeshi lay asleep on a cot. After Meme rested from the soul-calling rites, he ended the healing by chanting a prayer of "departure" (*btang shag*, "*shyasal*") that asked the various deities to depart from the *gtor ma* altar and return to their respective "domains" (*dal*).

> Deities, to the domain of *lha*, depart
> Serpent-deities, to the domain of *klu*, depart
> Gods, to the domain of *jo*, depart
> Goddesses, to the domain of *jomo*, depart
>
> . . . The goddess of land, Sapsi Gyalmo, depart
> The goddess of sky, Gurumai Lhamo, depart
> One hundred thousand diseases (*nad pa*),
>   to the mountain peaks, depart
> Ten million, billion diseases,
>   to the ocean depths, depart

With deities departing and diseases banished, the healing came to a close. Meme turned each of the *gtor ma* cakes on its side, and Serki and I returned the rice to the storage bin and the dagger and bells to Meme's bag. The drum hung again from the central pillar. Each person received one of the *gtor ma* cakes. Tenzin served a final meal of chicken stew, which we ate along with the rice-dough figures.

Meme lay close to the hearth after eating and washing. With his bundled coat serving as a pillow, he rested where the altar previously lay. The rest of us sought warm places to lay our mats on the floor and tried to sleep until morning.

Yeshi rose before dawn, stoked the smoldering fire, and brewed a pot of tea. Others soon woke. After unhurried conversation, Meme blessed his fifty-rupee fee, collected his drum and bag, and walked out the door.

"Go carefully," Tenzin called out as Meme climbed up the mountain path with a sleepy, drum-toting apprentice trailing behind.

Efficacy

So far we have developed an account of the technology of Yolmo shaman-ism: how it works and its ability to effect change. But was Yeshi healed? To what extent did Meme's rites transform Yeshi's spiritlessness, her heavy body and dark dreams? The present chapter addresses these concerns. How effective are Meme's rites? When and why does he fail? What, in short, is the effect of ritual on experience? A failure to attend to these questions would reflect a weakness in the anthropological literature at large. Despite the wealth of studies on traditional medicine, only a few empirically question the efficacy of ritual healing.[1]

In this chapter, I want to discuss how well Meme's rites work to perhaps offer further insight into how they work. My strategy follows the attempt made in the last chapter to link specific techniques of healing to the ways in which patients tend to respond to the rites (e.g., a calling of souls alters the sensory grounds of a spiritless body). Csordas points out that we need to distinguish among three aspects of religious healing: "procedure" ("who does what to whom"), "process" ("the nature of the participants' experience"), and "outcome" ("the final dispositions of participants").[2] He also correctly notes that some studies tend to obfuscate or conflate the three elements. Yet once we make the distinctions, the next step is to sketch out, for a given healing practice, the interrelations among the different aspects: how procedures affect process and so, ideally, outcome. For Yolmo wa, a study of this sort involves the ways in which patients perceive healing (or failed healing) to occur, the words and imagery used to articulate the healing process, and the criteria on which perceptions of healing are based.

A focus on the effectiveness of Meme's rites rounds off our under-standing of the aesthetics of Yolmo experience, for, as we shall see, efficacy relates directly to aesthetic value. Efficacy is not a culture-free category; notions of what it means to be "healthy" are guided by cultural, political, and moral values.[3] A Western-styled "doctor" working in the clinic in Gulphubanyang might consider a man whom he treats for skin rash to be cured once the symptoms vanish, but that man might understand the underlying cause of that illness to be unresolved and seek a more "effective" remedy through a shaman. In discussing the question of efficacy, then, we must constantly bear in mind whose criteria we are using. For Yolmo wa, a healthy person lives with a sense of comfort, presence, protection, balance, and harmony. These sensibilities, which relate to political ideals, tie into an aesthetics of the everyday.

Experientialism

The way a person feels and dreams in the days after a rite typically "shows" whether or not he is healed. Often, the sensations are the main or sole criteria on which villagers judge the efficacy of healing. A young Tamang woman, for instance, suffered a deity's wrath late in her first pregnancy. She experienced lower back pains, stomach aches, fever, and an inability and unwillingness to sleep for five days prior to the healing. "When the god becomes angry and attacks," she said, "the god comes inside our body and causes the pain." A bombo was called to perform a small ritual offering (n. *puja*) to the neglected deity. The success of this rite was evinced by the woman's subsequent feelings and behavior. "At seven at night, the rite ended. By nine, I was asleep." The woman's newfound ability to sleep proved that the ritual offering appeased the god, a resolution confirmed by the cessation of pain subsequent to the rite. "While participating in the rite, I was in pain. After finishing, the pain left slowly, not immediately. Slowly, I could feel the pain leaving my body." For this woman, relief signaled the cure. The healing ceremony sparked feelings of well-being that were inter-preted as a full recovery.

Patients suffering from spirit loss mark the return of spirits on the basis of a similar experientialism. "I was so sick," Dawa said of a bout of spiritlessness. "My body felt dizzy, heavy. I kept fainting." Dawa dreamed of darkness, blackness, arriving at a stream, and wearing tattered clothes—all signs of a lost spirit. At first, however, his family was uncertain of the cause of his illness. "Some gods cannot be seen," he noted, referring to the possibility that a wrathful god was assaulting him. "We performed a small ritual offering, but it did not help. I went to see Temba Bombo, and through divination he saw that my spirit had gone above."

The renowned Temba, from the northwest of Helambu, summoned Dawa's spirit from the land of the dead. "When the spirit returned to my body," Dawa said, "I felt well. I felt happy, comfortable. I felt a little lighter by the next morning. Slowly, slowly, within ten, fifteen days, I was fine." Dawa's restored health was further signified by dreams that he witnessed after the healing: he dreamed of walking uphill and of seeing a bright, clear light.

Dawa's narrative, as an "illness story,"[4] embodied several of the core motifs of Yolmo experiences of illness and healing: the initial crisis of ill-formed malaise, the lack of knowledge, the failed first healing, the call of the shaman, and, finally, a successful healing marked by signs of health (good dreams, a slow release of pain, a gradual but steady recovery). Dawa's own story tells of a mythic movement from darkness to understanding, from illness to health, and from an imagery of death to one of life. His recovery was confirmed by an improved condition and auspicious dreams.

As in Dawa's case, dreams often count as experiential proof that health has been achieved. In everyday conversations, villagers tend to divide dreams into three categories: those which are "good" or auspicious (ascending a mountain, sighting a rising sun); those which are "bad" or inauspicious (descending a hill, spotting a fragmenting moon); and those which do not seem to bear significant import. Since dreams can reveal if a ghost has been exorcised before the body feels the benefits of the exorcism (e.g., pain leaving the body), villagers often turn first to their dreams to assess the effectiveness of a shaman's rites. Tattered clothes and decrepit houses, for instance, signify a diminished *tshe*. Similarly, if a dreamer walks along a river bed, visits a watermill, or comes on a river that proves difficult to cross or return on, it is a sign that the *bla* has quit the body. Health, conversely, is presaged through dreams of new houses, clothes, or hats; snow falling on the body; consuming "sweet" white foods such as milk; witnessing the rising of the sun, the waxing of the moon, or a bright, clear light; ascending into the Himalayas or crossing a river and being able to return on it—the flip side, that is, of omens of illness.[5]

Soon after I arrived in Helambu, I spoke with Pemba, an elderly Yolmo woman with a gently wrinkled smile, the morning after Meme's nephew, a shaman in his own right, performed a healing on Pemba's behalf at her brother-in-law Dawa's home. Exhausted from the night-long ceremony, Pemba said that for some time her dreams had been filled with visions of darkness, valley descents, and terrifying dead men. She subsequently had trouble sleeping at night and often felt feverish with "piercing" pains (*tsher ka*) throughout her body. Nominally a resident of Kathmandu, she traveled from her home in the city to Gulphubanyang to receive shamanic care. The shaman divined a few days before that a *shi 'dre* was afflicting her; the healing was an attempt to exorcise the ghost from her home and body.

When I asked Pemba if she felt better since the shaman played his drum, she said she still felt tired and sore but would have to see how she slept that night; in any event she "felt peace" in her heartmind. She said the bombo successfully exorcised "some, but not all" of the ghosts. When he played his drum, "It felt good in my heartmind, but the body was just okay.

There was no change. In my heart, there was a peaceful feeling that things would soon be okay, but my body does not feel good today. I still cannot sleep." Indeed, I thought she looked exhausted. "She seems very strained," I jotted in a notebook. "Perhaps from lack of sleep. Nor does she seem content."

The next day, Pemba stopped by my house on the way to collect firewood in a local forest with kin. Smiling from the doorsill, she said the bombo's work "went well." She slept well that night and dreamed of reaching a "pleasant place" in the Himalayas where she drank cold water.

"I'm fine now," she laughed, "the bad dreams have been lost."

Indeed, in contrast to the weariness I witnessed the morning before, Pemba seemed healthy, content, and full of energy. Two days later, she told me her dreams were going "well." A week later, she returned to Kathmandu. When I visited her there six months later, I found her in good health.

Recurrence

Although Pemba recovered from her ghostly pains, she was unsure whether or not she would remain healthy. She noted that the same shaman performed the exorcism for her "many times" before. And since he only exorcised "some, not all" of the ghosts afflicting her, he would probably need to play his drum again.

The recurrent nature of Pemba's malaise points to some limits of Yolmo shamanism. As a patient's sensibility (the way her body and heartmind feel) constitutes the criteria on which healing rites are judged efficacious or not, Meme's rites are often considered effective because they change, in a relatively lasting manner, the way a person feels. Yet while these changes suggest that the underlying causes of distress (a lost spirit, a wrathful deity) have been addressed, I have found that Meme's rites often work more to alter how body and heartmind feel without conclusively fixing the causes of malaise.

Lakpa, a middle-aged Yolmo woman who tended a tea shop in Gulphu-banyang while her husband farmed in the hamlet of Dhupchughyang to the north, experienced a recurrent illness similar to Pemba's. For several weeks in the spring of 1988, Lakpa was often nauseous, felt a sensation of "boiling rice" on the body and upper back, and suffered a "burning" pain in the legs and arms, particularly the shoulders. She dreamed at night of wandering through a cremation grounds where a corpse lay burning, and of seeing big, black men who frightened her away. During the day, she felt afraid of mysterious "clicking" noises in her house.

Lakpa went to see a doctor in Kathmandu soon after she fell ill in the hopes of addressing her physical pains. The hospital medicines did not cure her. "They didn't even touch my pains," she said. A month later, Lakpa's husband went to Meme's home and asked him to perform a divination. Meme did so and divined that a "nine-headed" demon lay at the root of Lakpa's malaise. For Lakpa, the demon caused vomiting, lack of appetite, and anger. Indeed, she linked her own "heart-pain" to "the greatest anger." "There may be a quarrel in the house," she told me. "If the demon goes into the beer [*chang*], it does not taste good. And we cannot finish our work on time. We need additional days."

Meme performed an elaborate ceremony to exorcise the demon from Lakpa's body and home. "Now, after performing the ceremony," Lakpa said, "those things don't happen." She considered the demon to be "thrown" from her body, for her body no longer hurt, her dreams improved, she wasn't angry as before, and she and her husband ceased their quarreling.

"I'm fine now," she said when I stepped up to her tea shop six months after the healing. "That illness was lost months ago."

Lakpa stressed that Meme's techniques, from exorcism to ritual cleansings, removed pain and illness from her body; "The burning pain left when the bombo bit me." She clarified that most, but not all, of her pain left at this time. "In some cases the illness leaves right away. But usually the illness is not gotten rid of immediately. It goes slowly day by day." Indeed, Lakpa said that a healer must perform a rite on several occasions for it to be truly effective and that Meme performed the exorcism "many times" for her in the past. The most recent rite, which treated identical symptoms, took place two years prior to the spring healing.

"It is like *chang*," Lakpa explained, referring to the addictive qualities of the sweet beer. "If I drink it today, I want to drink it tomorrow."

"Yes," her husband added, "We need to play the drum more than once, because the illness might come again."

Lakpa's malaise suggested a complex of social tensions and distress. She dreamed of fear and death, the family's inability to finish work on time hinted at a lack of social harmony, and the "sour" beer tasted of familial tensions. More directly, the demon sparked quarrels and Lakpa's anger.

This anger, significantly, was seen not as the cause, but as a symptom, of illness. By attributing her "greatest anger" to a demon, Lakpa was not held responsible for her distress. She and her family thus avoided the social stigma of uncontrolled anger. At the same time, her anger was objectified, talked about, and so molded into a symptom to be "lost." As with Kusang, the old man whose life span diminished because of a bad temper, Lakpa's anger required shamanic mediation. "To keep the peace in the country," she told me, "we need to call the police. In the same way, we need to call the gods when there is quarreling."

With the help of his gods, Meme cast anger and social tensions from Lakpa's house. His medicine took the form of an exorcism: explicitly, the "throwing" of the demonic from body and home; implicitly, it appears, a cleansing of social tensions. By attending to emotional conflicts, shamanic healing worked to exorcise a family's ill will embodied in one woman's pain.[6]

In Lakpa's case, the cure seemed effective, especially in comparison to the hospital care she received. Slowly the pain was cut, anger dissolved, quarrels ceased, the bad dreams were lost. Yet as Lakpa noted, Meme needed to play his drum repeatedly to stave off the demonic. The need for repeated healings suggests that Meme alleviated Lakpa's malaise but perhaps not the lingering causes of this distress. Lakpa suffered the same illness two years ago; anger, quarreling, and bodily distress could fall on her body and home in years to come. Villagers like Lakpa and Pemba are healed in the sense that their pains are alleviated, yet if the conflicts and tensions that occasion the pains recur, the pains often recur.

"If I Am to Die"

Meme's rites, save for his oracular divinations, thus tend to work more toward alleviating pain than toward addressing and eradicting its sources. And while a divination can show the sources of malaise (such as the causes of Yeshi's spiritlessness), divinations themselves have their own limitations that tie into the methods and constraints of shamanic knowledge. Meme assesses, through the conduit of his body, the somatic sensibilities of his patients to figure the nature and sources of malaise. Since these sensibilities tend to reflect the concerns and tensions of a person's social life (Yeshi's slumber, Mingma's fears), Meme is more adept at revealing and treating the sources of social malaise than the causes of pain rooted in specific biological disorders (a child's chronic diarrhea, tuberculosis). In fact, Meme's divinations tend to address the social and psychological concerns that cluster around moments of physical pain (a parent's worries over a stricken child) more than they do any biological sources of that pain. Yet while pain may not, at times, be amenable to interpretation and treatment, villagers expect it to be. Epistemic crises arise when shamans struggle to remedy pains that do not effectively respond to their ritual magic.

The history of Lopsang, a fifty-one year old man from Chumdeli, chronicles such a crisis. A healing ceremony performed on his behalf was one of the first I attended. Upon entering his home, I was struck by his visible suffering. He lay by the fire, flat against a mat, as Meme played the drum. A pain raged in his chest, swollen lymph nodes protruded from his neck. Skin collapsed against bone. Thin, gaunt, Lopsang was unable to stand on his own when Meme summoned his spirit from the land of the dead. His wife held him by the arms. He could not eat any food. Throughout the night a litany of pain issued from his lips. "*Ayo, ayo, ayo,*" he moaned. "[The pain] came, came, came."

Meme performed an elaborate ceremony on Lopsang's behalf: he threw "astrological plight" (n. *dasa graha*) from his body, cleansed him of pollution and pain, and attempted to recover his nine "life supports" (*srog*). Toward morning, the healing ended without any apparent improvement in Lopsang's condition. The litany continued. Meme set his drum on the floor, slouched his back, stared at the altar, and breathed heavily for several minutes.

"What could be done," he finally said, "I have done."

I interviewed Lopsang at his home four weeks later. He was still sick. He lay to the right of the hearth as his wife tended to his needs. He said he suffered from "gastric" illnesses for four years and had been severely sick for four months prior to the healing.

"We don't care to eat good food and, if we eat a lot, the stomach burns, and we vomit."

He also suffered from a "fire" in his chest, a piercing pain in his lower back, a bloated stomach, and a "sour watering" of his mouth. He dreamed of rivers, of walking in graveyards, and of police chasing him away.

Lopsang twice journeyed to Kathmandu to attend hospitals and spent over three hundred rupees (about fifteen U.S. dollars) on medicine, to no avail. "The doctor wanted me to go to India to have an operation," he explained, "but I thought I should show my wife my property first, in case I die, for she would not know where it is."

Lopsang returned to Helambu and called on Meme to perform a series of healing ceremonies. At different times, Meme interpreted Lopsang's symptoms and dreams to signify varying illnesses: the dreams of graveyards foretold that a ghost (*shi 'dre*) was afflicting him; a black serpent-deity (*klu*) was the cause of his bloated stomach; his nine life-supports were lost; he suffered from astrological plight (*dasa graha*). To "satisfy" the agents of illness, Lopsang sacrificed four goats and "so many" chickens. In addition to these expenditures, each healing cost Lopsang from forty to sixty rupees (about a week's salary).

"The illness was not lost," Lopsang said of the healing I attended; only his bloated stomach was ameliorated. "Nothing happened. I felt comfortable, but the god said I would die within four months. The bombo said I would die very soon. He was completely sure." The divination caused Lopsang significant distress: he despaired on learning his fate, his "passion" for life was "killed." At the same time, he questioned the veracity of the oracle.

"With this one always has doubt," he said of Meme's divination. "Some shamans say one will die, others say one will not die. Friends tell me such talk is like the wind."

Despite his doubts, Lopsang constantly expressed an unwavering fatalism. "Whatever god wants, he does. I don't know anything. If I am to die, I shall die."

I spoke with Lopsang nine months later. I found him sitting outside, in the sun. While he had gained some weight and looked generally healthier, he was still weak and frail. Since the healing I attended, Lopsang had returned to Kathmandu and received medical care because he did not feel significantly better after the shamanic healing. In the city, a doctor prescribed a host of Ayurvedic medicines and instructed Lopsang to follow a bland but nutritious diet. After telling me of this, Lopsang went into his house and returned with a plastic bag, dumping a dozen bottles of Ayurvedic medicine manufactured in India on the mat.

"Do you think these are good medicines?" he asked. "After using these medicines, I feel better. Now I'm getting well but have no energy, since I do not get the proper foods. Finding the right food is a problem here in the village."

Even with the medical care, Lopsang found that he was still afflicted with pain of a spiritual nature. "Sometimes, harm [*nad pa*] affects me. It makes the illness worse. At that time, if I eat the medicine, I feel worse. For treatment of that harm, I go to the bombo."

When I asked Lopsang if he now knew what ailed him, he explained that, though he had spent two thousand rupees in Kathmandu in the past year, "I haven't been able to decide what is really wrong with me." As for the shamanic divinations, "the bombo says it is a ghost, but hasn't been able to determine which one specifically." During our conversation, Lopsang alternatively named a ghost, a local goddess, and a diminished life as the source of his pain. Despite his uncertainty, he expressed confidence that he would not die.

"If I were to die," he reasoned, "I would have died already. But since I haven't, I believe I won't die. It seems that this is so, is it not?"

While Lopsang concluded that Meme's rites had failed to heal his illness, he said they were effective in other situations. "Sometimes the bombo's medicine doesn't work even if he is good. Sometimes it works just by touching the patient's body." Of interest here is the fact that, prior to the healing rite, Lopsang dreamed of rivers, walking in graveyards, and police who chased him away. After the healing, these dreams were "lost," suggesting that shamanic healing served to assuage his anxiety and fears toward ill health. And yet he did not witness auspicious dreams subsequent to the healing. Indeed, he later reported "bad" dreams of encountering policemen, bridges, and watermills, and climbing a tree only to fall from it.

On leaving Lopsang, I mentioned that I thought his medicines were good. While I climbed up the dusty trail leading from his home, he continued to gaze down on the pile of scattered "tablets."

Uncertainty and doubt marred the history of Lopsang's pains. As a shaman, Meme was expected to divine the nature, cause, and consequences of Lopsang's illness and thus to heal him. Groping for a meaning, Meme divined several causes for Lopsang's distress, but the pain continued with each diagnosis. Faced with Lopsang's lingering pain, Meme needed to discern the cause and course of the illness. But he also needed to explain why his healing efforts were failing. In admitting his inability to heal, two options were available to him: he could have said that the failed healings resulted from the limits of his own competence, or he could have declared that the patient's suffering was the work of the gods. For a lesser illness, Meme might have been more confident in his abilities. But I think that, with Lopsang, Meme sensed and feared ultimate failure. He therefore tried to avoid responsibility for Lopsang's continued suffering (and potential death) by divining that Lopsang was fated to die within four months.

While Meme despaired over diagnosing and healing Lopsang's illness, Lopsang despaired over Meme's diagnosis. Meme's divination effected more than cognitive dissonance; Lopsang thought he was going to die, a belief that killed his "passion" for life. Though Lopsang doubted Meme's divination from the start, taking comfort in a neighbor's suggestion that such talk was "like the wind," he also expressed unabated faith in what the gods decided. For Lopsang, it was not the gods who were to be doubted, but their spokesman; while a shaman may offer false information, the gods do not. Lopsang was thus torn between doubting the shaman and believing the gods. The problem was confounded by his inability to discern the cause of pain on his own. In contrast to the deities, he "didn't know anything," and so sought divination. But with Meme's continued failure to heal, Lopsang became further entrenched in uncertainty. Nine months later, he still could not decide what was "really" wrong, and his family still suffered the repercussions of his lingering distress.

Lopsang's continued malaise points to the nature and limitations of Yolmo knowledge. As a cultural construct, Yolmo divination works well in attending to some domains of experience—breaking the divine code, as it were, to inform the heartmind of the locus of distress. Yet there are limits to its powers. The shaman has trouble divining the causes of pain that bear little cultural meaning, nor can he assure that someone will be healed once a divination is performed. Consequently, patient and healer often waver between the realms of knowledge and uncertainty.

Peace of *Sems*

"Sometimes the bombo's medicine doesn't work even if he is good. Sometimes it works just by touching the body of the sick person." Lopsang's words suggest that shamanic and "hospital" medicine alternatively heal certain forms of distress but not others: the hospital remedies a burning chest and a poor diet; a shaman exorcises bad dreams and spiritual "harm." Other residents of Helambu evinced a similar sense of the bombo's variant efficacy in distinguishing between "inner" and "outer" bodily pains. "The bombo can cure outer illnesses," said one woman, "but not the inner engines. If the insides are broken, the healers cannot cure us, and so we go to the hospital." I found her view to be insightful, for villagers often express social malaise through the idioms of "hair" and "piercing" pains (*tashing nashing, tsher ka*). Witches (n. *boksi*) assault the body by inflicting sores and pains (n. *betha*) on the surfaces of the flesh (the bodily space most exposed to others); a diagnosis of witchcraft usually refers to social tensions.

Often both patient and healer display a subtle sense of whether lama, shaman, or "doctor" should be called based on the symptoms a person suffers from. Consequently, Meme often ends up treating outer illnesses (spirit loss, demonic affliction), while those bearing inner ailments (chronic wounds, internal injuries) go to the clinic. But this is not always the case: Tamang children die of dysentery while being treated for an affliction of a *sri* ghost; Lopsang called on the shaman for physical ailments caused by the wrath of gods.

In my estimation, the outer illnesses to which Yolmo wa refer often involve feelings of malaise tied to personal distress and social conflicts. An incident of spirit loss can be sparked by feelings of loss, and the assault of a witch can embody interfamilial conflicts. It is this sort of malaise—the somatic sensibilities borne of the communal exchanges of everyday life—that Yolmo shamans are most adept at healing. Of the thirty-odd patients whom I followed in the aftermath of shamanic healings (performed by Meme and other Yolmo, Tamang, and Gurung healers), patients who suffered from some kind of soul loss or ghostly affliction typically reported that pain was "lost" once the shaman recovered itinerant life-forces or exorcised ghosts. In contrast, what I took to be purely physical problems often lingered in the body even after repeated attempts by shamans to remedy the ailments. Villagers often arrived at the local clinic with ulcers, gastrointestinal problems, skin rashes, and respiratory disorders only after working with a local shaman for several months. The reluctance to visit the clinic earlier than this often frustrated the clinic staff. One Tamang man, who could not move his arms and felt severe pains in his joints, had to be carried by friends to the clinic to receive treatment. The medic, after diagnosing a case of severe arthritis, asked why the man waited three months become coming to the clinic. "We wanted to try the bombo first" was the man's response.

Yolmo wa often follow a similar strategy: I talked with one man who had a severe rash on his face, and another with a blistered foot. When asked if they had consulted the clinic, they said that, since deities had caused their discomfort, Meme was treating them instead. But from what I observed of clinic and ritual patrons, shamans usually failed to permanently alleviate such ailments.[7]

Yolmo shamans, then, are more adept at treating "outer" than "inner" pains. They can also heal the heartmind more readily than the body. Patients often reported that, while their bodily pains lingered in the hours and days following a healing rite, they variably felt "good," "content," "comfortable," and "happy" in the *sems*. For instance, while Pemba's pains lingered after the healing rite, she attained a certain peace of *sems*. As she put it, "It felt good in the heartmind, but the body was just okay." A shaman also failed to immediately soothe Pemba's body, but healed her heartmind. The healing of Pemba's body was later confirmed by dreams of a mountain ascent and the consumption of Himalayan waters.

In fact, I commonly found that only when a person experienced renewed spirits (and auspicious dreams) did the body's surface pains diminish. And when the pains do leave, they leave "slowly." Mingma, for instance, did not experience any significant improvement in his physical condition during or immediately after the healing performed by Meme on his behalf (Meme performed the elaborate *srog dgu mi* rite to separate Mingma's nine *srog* from the hands of "dead men"). "My body did not feel any different when the life-forces returned," Mingma said. "But in my heartmind, I felt my life-forces had returned and I thought I could live one or two more years to do the things I wished to do."

After Mingma's spirit was called, he returned to his bed and attempted to sleep, but his coughing and congested breathing persisted through the night. He later told me that he dreamed of crossing rivers and bridges and returning over them again (signifying a journey to, but also a return from, the land of the dead). His mood seemed to match his renewed spirit. I wrote in my notebook at the conclusion of the nightlong ceremony: "Postscript: Mingma seems in good spirits. Smiling, joking. More energy. Seems relieved and content."

It would appear that Mingma's healing assuaged the fear and anxiety surrounding his ill health. If Mingma's illness related to distress spawned by the death of two friends, particularly a private despair felt over his own imminent death, then Meme's rites effectively treated this distress. The cure could have been achieved by offering a sense of comfort and security, rescuing his life-forces from "the land of the dead," and staving death off for a few more years. And if the healing alleviated Mingma's despair, then the summer's funerals helped to soothe his grief. Two weeks after the July healing, Mingma attended the funeral for his deceased friend, Urgyen. He drank, danced, sang the funeral prayers, and appeared to enjoy himself immensely. On several occasions he sat with me to explain the funeral hymns. In the months after the healing rite until my departure the next spring, Mingma seemed, for a man of his age, healthy and at ease.

As with other villagers, Mingma benefited primarily from the peace and comfort that the healing offered. While it is impossible to specify which aspects of Yolmo shamanism effect the feelings of vitality, comfort, and contentment that patients often report, it appears that many of the techniques assessed in the chapters above are involved. The conviction that something is being done to relieve distress can reduce anxiety and give peace to the heartmind. The calling of souls invokes a sense of presence, vitality, and attentiveness. Rites of exorcism give the felt sense that pain is leaving the body. And the aesthetics enchanted throughout the healing (themes of balance, harmony, completion, integration, and purity) can create a sense of comfort, health, and propriety. These acts combine to lend peace to the heartmind, banish bad dreams, and ease pain. At times, however, these changes are not enough to effect lasting health; other transformations must occur.

"Slowly the Pain Was Lost"

Nyima, like Mingma, lost her spirit in the days following the death of Urgyen (see Table 2). She called a local shaman in late June to perform a small rite ("without playing the drum") to retrieve her spirit. The morning after, Nyima expressed confidence that she had recovered her vitality. When I asked why she thought this, she explained that, when the spirit returns, it feels like a jolt of electricity to the body. "I wouldn't feel this jolt if the spirit did not come back, would I?" I could not argue with her logic, for she claimed to feel better after the spirit returned. "Today," she said, "I feel a little better."

Several days later, Nyima still felt ill. From my perspective, she seemed worse than she had prior to the healing. I often found her sitting by herself in front of her doorsill, weary and ill at ease.

As Nyima continued to suffer a week later, her husband Latu called a second shaman. After participating in the more elaborate *srog dgu mi* rite (on the day of Lopsang's funeral), Nyima claimed her life-forces were retrieved from the haunts of deadly ghosts. The morning after the rite, I spoke with her as she sat in front of her house with her arms and legs tucked within a red shawl. She radiated energy and confidence and said she felt fine since the healing. "After the bombo called the spirit, I became well. When the bombo recalled the *bla*, I thought in my heartmind, 'My spirit is returning.' Afterward, my body felt light, I wanted to eat again, and could walk as well." Her main symptoms of spirit loss (insomnia, heavy body, lack of volition) were "cut" from her body the night of the second healing. Also "lost" were dreams of feeling afraid and of seeing streams, watermills, and policemen.

"Once the spirit returns," Nyima said in words reminiscent of Lakpa's empiricism, "it is placed on the head of the patient, who then becomes healthier day by day. But if the bombo does this falsely, the patient remains ill."[8] For Nyima, the return of lost life-forces achieved in the second healing was marked by a general comfort of body and mind. "When the spirit returned, the body felt good. After it returned, I could sleep well. Sleepiness came and I felt good in the heartmind." In turn, the secondary signs of her illness (the body's diffuse pains) diminished gradually. "When the spirit returned, the pain decreased slowly. Slowly the pain was lost and, in my mind, I thought I would be okay. Afterward, I did not see the bad dreams of before."

From what I observed, Nyima did not suffer distress subsequent to the second healing. In the days following the rite, she was cheerful, full of energy, and eager to talk. She remained healthy throughout the summer and during the fall, until the final funeral rites for Padma in December, when she fell ill once again.

Why did Nyima's second healing succeed where the first rite failed? Since double-blind clinical trials of indigenous healing practices have proven impossible to conduct,[9] an answer to questions of this sort might prove the closest we can come to an experimental study of traditional healing.

A different shaman conducted each of Nyima's two healings: she called a "Tamang" bombo from the valley to the east of Gulphubanyang for the first rite and a "Lama" shaman for the second. When I asked why she turned to a second shaman after the first healing failed, she said "We call whichever bombo is available." It is likely, however, that she lost faith in the first healer when she did not properly recover after the soul-calling rite and so called a second shaman. Her comment about a patient remaining ill if the bombo calls the spirit "falsely" probably referred to the failed first healing. At first, she was confident her spirit had returned, as evidenced by the "jolt of electricity" felt in her body, but this proved not to be the case in the days following the rite. Her continued malaise suggested that the *bombo* did not successfully heal. She therefore turned to a different shaman in the hopes of receiving better care. But the fact that she worked with two healers does not explain the discrepant outcomes of the two rites, for at the time of each healing she had "faith" she would be healed. While Yolmo wa often hold that a person must imagine that healing is, in fact, occurring for it to be effective ("You have to believe in the bombo's work," Dawa once said, "or else you will not feel better"), a lack of faith does not account for Nyima's failed first healing.[10] We must therefore seek another explanation.

The two healers performed different healing rites, based on different assessments of Nyima's malady. Can the distinct outcomes of the rites be explained by their contrasting nature? The first healer divined that Nyima's "spirit," which escaped when she stumbled into a stream, fell into the hands of a forest ghost (*ri shi 'dre*). He then performed a minor healing rite in which "the drum was not played." This suggests he tried to retrieve Nyima's spirit simply by calling out to it (as shamans often do when children lose their spirits), then returning it to her body.

The second healer divined a more serious cause for Nyima's spiritlessness: ghosts stole several of her nine "life supports" (*srog*) into the land of the dead. He then performed the elaborate *srog dgu mi* rite to retrieve the lost life-forces. As with Mingma, the shaman cut Nyima's nine *srog* (represented by nine white *gtor ma* cakes) from nine ghosts (represented by nine black *gtor ma* cakes), then returned the *srog* to Nyima's body and "threw" the ghosts over a hillside away from the house. It is possible that the second, more elaborate rite better assuaged Nyima's distress because it offered more drama and significance. It is also possible, however, that the second rite was more effective because of its ritual content. It is the second hypothesis, in conjunction with the first, that I wish to explore.

Earlier I proposed that Nyima's illness related to a complex of distress catalyzed by the deaths of Urgyen and Padma. Her reluctance to grieve, reinforced by Yolmo sensibilities, impeded her ability to attend to, and so alleviate, feelings of loss.[11] I believe this interpretation explains why Nyima's second healing succeeded where the first failed. As the first healing occurred a week prior to Padma's fifth-week funeral, the principle factors causing Nyima's distress continued to linger after the healing. The thought of Padma's imminent funeral caused Nyima great concern, for while she felt disturbed by his and Urgyen's death she did not wish to attend the respective mourning ceremonies. If her malaise related to the need but reluctance to grieve, then the first healing rite could not have resolved the no-win situation, for the factors causing the conflict remained: the funeral loomed one week ahead.

Nyima's changing sensations of health reflected her feelings of distress. She initially felt healed, as evidenced by the energy pulsing through her body. But in the days following the first rite, she felt worse than before. While she thought that the first healing failed because the Tamang bombo worked "falsely," it is likely that, with the conflict over Padma's funeral still unresolved, she continued to suffer distress over the mourning process and so continued to feel dispirited. In other words, the first healing succeeded in making her feel spirited again, but since the underpinnings of her spiritlessness were still at work, her body lost its vitality again in the days following the rite.

The two differing assessments of Nyima's malaise prove the value of a "truthful" divination: only the latter divination, which identified a deathly illness and called for an elaborate ceremony that combined soul calling with exorcism, led to renewed health. In contrast to the basic "spirit hooking" rite (*bla 'gug*), the *srog dgu mi* ("sok gumi") ceremony, with its ghosts, dramatic exorcism, and excursions into the "land of the dead," is ripe with death imagery. Death imagery similarly characterized the sensory grounds of Nyima's illness: she lost her spirit while "crossing a stream" on the way to one of Padma's weekly funerals; her spirit was captured by a "forest ghost"; a ghost caused her bodily pains; and local images of death (streams, forests) spooked her dreams.[12] To me, those images reflected the dynamics underlying Nyima's experience of soul loss: distress over the recent deaths of her uncles.

Only with the second healing, which took place on the day of Padma's funeral, did Nyima fully recover from her spiritlessness. It appears two changes had to occur before Nyima could recover her vitality: she needed to regain a sense of vitality, presence, and purity, and she needed to resolve the causes of her distress. The second healing, in contrast to the first, fulfilled both requirements. Since the healing took place in time with Padma's funeral, her anxiety over the mourning process was "lost" along with her bad dreams, spiritlessness, and dark ghosts.

One could argue that Nyima would have been cured without participating in the second healing, for, with Padma's funeral out of the way, she would no longer have suffered the acute distress that she felt prior to the funeral. But it seems to me that while Nyima could not be healed without eradicating the causes of her distress, nor could she be healed simply by avoiding the funeral process altogether. As noted above, anthropological research suggests that mourning ceremonies function the world over to relieve the tensions, anxieties, fears, and occasionally ambivalent feelings of the bereaved.[13] A person's reluctance to grieve or inability to participate in mourning ceremonies, in contrast, can lead to maladaptive grief reactions.[14] Lindemann discusses several clinical cases of this nature, and Reid writes of an Australian aboriginal woman who was deprived of the opportunity to participate and mourn in the mortuary ceremonies of a close kinsperson; her behavior subsequent to the mourning period suggested a pathological grief reaction similar to depression.[15]

I suspect that Nyima would not have been an exception to the apparent universal rule that human beings need to resolve their grief. If her distress related to a failure in the work of mourning, then avoidance of the funeral process altogether would not, in itself, constitute the alleviation of that distress. If she did not get rid of the ghosts haunting her, she would have continued to feel dispirited.

And yet the way in which Nyima eventually resolved her distress was far from Western psychoanalytic notions of an introspective "working through" of grief: the second healing offered a visceral means to cast off her distress without directly confronting it. What does Nyima's grief most mean to her? It means what it feels like: a heavy body, dreams of the deceased, and a visceral sense of loss.[16] The healing cut these feelings from Nyima's body. Just as the funeral cutting of souls separates the deceased from loved ones, and Meme's tiger sucked harm from Yeshi's flesh, so the shaman threw ghosts from Nyima's body. The cure related more to sensory kinesthetics than to cognitive reformations. The exorcism did not entertain a process of reflection or existential meaning-making in the face of death. Nor did it entail a process of "catharsis," which, while exorcistic in nature (from the Greek *kathairein* 'to cleanse' 'to purge'), belongs to a cultural tradition that lends priority to the psychological. Rather, it cut the ghostly reminders of death, and feelings of loss (its taste, touch, and smell), from the sensory grounds of her existence.

Shamanic healing thus worked for Nyima as an oblique "mourning" ceremony. While other villagers attended Padma's funeral to cut sorrow from their bodies, directly confronting their pain in ritual and song to transcend it, Nyima used the rites of exorcism as a way to get rid of the pains that she was either unable or unwilling to deal with head on. The creative use of shamanic ritual suggests the means taken by Yolmo wa to prevent distress from lingering among the bereaved: the second healing enabled Nyima to regain vitality as well as cleanse her body of ghosts. Only then, with the no-win situation resolved, was she cured.

Or "cured," that is, until distress of a similar form recurred in her life. It is of interest that Nyima claimed to repeatedly suffer from soul loss. She also became sick at the time of Padma's seventh-week funeral in early December—not from soul loss, but from a pained and feverish body. As with Lakpa and Pemba, when Nyima met with distress anew, her body hurt anew.

Yeshi

Yeshi's spiritlessness hinted at a similar pattern of limited healing. Meme performed a healing ceremony on her behalf in late May to recover a lost spirit. In early October, on the occasion of Kusang's healing, the gods still spoke of a diminished life span (*tshe nyams pa*) caused by tears, confusion, and Yeshi's inability to hold her heartmind.

Observations of Yeshi's life support the idea that she suffered continued distress. Though she recovered somewhat in the months following the May healing, losing some of her apathy and spiritlessness, she appeared to remain weary and disheartened throughout the summer and the fall, including the night of Kusang's healing. We could therefore infer that, whereas shamanic healing might have offered some relief by communicating distress and evoking a sense of vitality, Yeshi continued to suffer from soul loss because her living conditions did not improve much. And if there was no significant improvement in the circumstances underlying her distress (the stressful living situation, the heavy work load, two children dependent on her, the separation from family and natal village, the lack of female companionship, the hostility of husband and father-in-law), then Yeshi could not have recovered from her malaise in any significant fashion. Her case is similar to Nyima's in that spiritlessness lingered because the life situation did not change much.[17]

Perhaps through time Yeshi may unlearn her helplessness. Successive divinations may help to communicate her despair and temper Kusang's anger, events that may lessen her malaise. With the growth of children and the establishment of roots in her husband's village, she might achieve more security and independence. When her own children marry, she will obtain further power and develop lasting ties in the community. She can acquire more of a voice than she has held in her youth. Perhaps with and only with these changes will Yeshi permanently recover her spirit.

We may conclude that while Yolmo shamans often fail to successfully treat what appear to be strictly physical ailments (including amoebic dysentery, arthritis, tuberculosis, and gastrointestinal disorders), they are adept at healing illnesses related to personal distress or social conflicts (especially when compared with biomedical treatments). Most patients report the alleviation of so-called outer pains subsequent to healing rites performed on their behalf. The nature of this pain suggests that either social tensions, emotional distress, or a combination of both contribute to their malaise.

The strength of Yolmo shamanism thus lies in its ability to alleviate surface malaise, attend to social conflicts, and alter a person's felt sense of body and spirit. Meme's various technologies of healing, assessed above, work toward these goals. Faith or "suggestion" is an important and perhaps necessary part of healing but not enough in itself: other changes must occur. These changes do not entail any overarching symbolic transformations or singular changes in a patient's worldview (one picture for another), but rather involve a collage of diverse but distinct brushstrokes that ultimately change how a person feels and goes about his or her life. With this collage, Meme relies on a kitchen sink approach to healing, drawing on a variety of techniques in the hope that one will hit on lasting change. Many of these techniques attend directly to the sensory faculties of the body (to the extent that Meme seems unable to heal without "touching" the body, to quote Lopsang). The soul-calling rites jumpstart body and heartmind. The kinesthesia of exorcism, working with rudiments of form, brushes the body free of "harm." The aesthetics of healing create the embodied sense of balance, harmony, completion, integration, and purity. In turn, oracular divinations offer an indirect forum to mediate social tensions and communicate sentiments of anger, grief, and despair. There are limits to healing, and Meme often fails to heal, but given the protean nature of his tasks, he works magic. Ritual can transform experience.

These transformations conform to Yolmo aesthetics of the everyday, for a person typically comes to assume a healthy, politically ideal, form: bounded, integrated, the body exudes a sense of harmony, purity, and the capacity for restraint. Yolmo notions of "efficacy," in other words, are tinged with political value. Yolmo shamans work to fashion an ideology of felt experience as much as they alter felt experience. And since the values bodied forth by a healing rite mesh with the vital political concerns of high-status lamas, a state of renewed health legitimates the seemingly natural sensibilities of well-being and so further secures the political forms (balanced hierarchies, bounded mosaics) that govern those sensibilities.

There is one significant qualification to the shaman's magic. Lakpa, Pemba, and Nyima repeatedly fall ill with similar pains, and Yeshi lived without vitality for several months because her living situation continued to spawn frustration and despair. The fact that malaise so often recurs suggests that, while Meme's rites can alleviate some of the sensibilities of distress (and so, for Yolmo wa, are quite efficacious), illness returns if villagers experience distress again in their lives. For others, a series of healings may be necessary to fully alleviate distress. Indeed, there can even be an "addiction" to shamanic cures. Lakpa, for instance, longs for healing as she does sweet beer.

Both the need for repeated healings and the reasons for the addiction relate to certain limitations intrinsic to Yolmo ways of being. For instance, while specific cultural constraints and tensions contributed to Nyima's and Yeshi's distress, shamanic healing offered a partial resolution of those tensions. We have seen, then, that tensions between aesthetic sensibilities and personal desire, or between different strands of a society's spectrum of values, can, under certain conditions, spark conflicts leading to illness. The forms of malaise that many Yolmo healings address often relate, at least in part, to these conflicts.

For Yolmo wa, some forms of distress relate to tensions intrinsic to their corporate ways of life. The major threats to Yolmo bodies, households, and villages are those of fission, fragmentation, and dispersal. In the southwest of Helambu, it looks as if the threats are becoming a reality. Due to a variety of political and economic factors, the tenuously composed mosaics of families and villages appear, at times, to be on the verge of breaking apart, and the dominant sensibilities of pain are those of loss and *tsher ka*. Indeed, new social configurations and sensibilities, which value personal achievements over social harmony, might soon come to the fore. Meme's rites apparently address these larger historical tendencies. The shaman is a healer of form, and his rites work to shore up fragmenting mosaics, be they made of flesh, stone, or social bonds. They also seem to recall and embody a particular way of life. Thus, to be effective, the *tshe grub* litany must be chorused by all the participants of the healing, as if Meme's chant works to secure the social body as much as the patient's own form. Yet I wonder how effective the prayer can ultimately be. Meme's is an aging voice, and his song one night's magic against a historical tide.

10. Afterwords

"When Karma hears this," Latu held a tape cassette in his hand, "tears will come to his eyes."

"Please speak again, grandfather?" I asked, stepping up to his trailside shop.

"When my nephew hears this," Latu put the cassette into his recorder, then pointed at his tearduct, "tears will come to his eyes."

It was the morning after Karma first arrived in Gulphubanyang. When I introduced him to Latu, Latu spoke of his friendship with Karma's father, who died three years before.

Latu played a section of the tape, which sounded several male voices chorusing a Buddhist chant.

"Listen," he cupped his ear. "The deeper voice is his father's."

Karma walked down the trail and stepped up to Latu's porch. "Hello," he said to Latu and Nyima, then stood still and listened to the ongoing recording.

Karma heard his father's voice, turned, and jumped off the porch. He walked to a clearing at the edge of the village and stood with his right hand over his eyes.

I stepped off the porch and began to walk over to Karma.

"Don't follow him, Meme," Latu said to me. "Stay here."

It was apparent that Karma was crying.

"Stay, Meme."

I did not know what was going on, or what to do, so I stepped back on the porch. I felt confused and angry and unsure of Latu's motives.

Karma stood alone in the clearing for several minutes, then walked back to Latu's shop. Latu had put away the tape recorder and was busy with some farmers who wanted to buy some cloth.

"Oh nephew," Latu asked, "how about some tea?"

"Please, uncle," Karma smiled.

Since Latu invoked the memory of Karma's father in December 1988, I have yet to make complete sense of his actions. I am not quite sure why Latu acted as he did. Nor do I know what Karma made of the event or how he felt in response to hearing his father's voice. Neither Karma nor Latu spoke of the event after it occurred, and, since one does not heedlessly inquire into the feelings or motives of another in Helambu, it would have been improper for me to ask.

Until now, I have written as little of the incident as I have spoken of it. The interaction possessed such a surplus of meaning that I could not fit it into any of my tidy discussions of Yolmo lives. "You have to put that in," a colleague said when I told her my memory of the event. "It says so much about the people you're writing about." I agreed, but when I tried, the implications of Latu's and Karma's actions exceeded the logic of sentences much like a river overflows its banks.

And yet the question lingers: How can an interaction that "says so much" about a people still elude ethnographic analysis? For me, the answer lies in the fact that what is said through the actions of Karma and Latu is immediate to those actions and so cannot readily be translated into a symbolic code, a depth psychology, or a set of structural relations. Much like a ritual, the implications of the event far exceeds our ability to portray those implications.[1]

I now want simply to present my memory of the event rather than to transpose it onto a larger ethnographic grid. In so doing, we can perhaps appreciate the interaction on its own terms, much as one approaches the vitalities of a story. My understanding of the event remains limited, but since ambiguity is common to many encounters in Helambu, uncertainties enhance our involvement. I suggested at the outset that every social interaction brings with it an air of flux and ambiguity, and we must carry this ambiguity over into the world of our readers so that they can begin to sense what might be at stake in a given interaction. This is how the negative capability of an ethnographer ties into the art of storytelling, for a successful tale "claws" its way into a reader (Beckett) through its gaps and inferences—as much through its connotations as through its adverbs and adjectives. The experience of a story (rather than its telling) comes together in the body of a listener, if and when images create "hooked atoms" (Coleridge) of similitude and anticipation. The human sciences, some have argued, proceed through this act of felt recognition or empathy.[2]

And yet to go that far, to become engaged in any significant way, requires a great deal. What is required is an understanding of what is meant by appreciating an interaction "on its own terms." If we were to encounter the above interaction cold, without any nuanced feel for Yolmo society, neither the significance nor the implications of Latu's actions would be comprehensible. The art of a story builds on sensibilities, common to teller and audience, that explain why people act the way they do and what those actions imply. Since aesthetic values often do not transcend cultural traditions, we can only appreciate what took place between Latu and Karma by learning, from scratch, the sensibilities that governed their actions.

Indeed, Yolmo sensibilities are what the incident apparently "says" so much about. While we cannot know what Latu or Karma felt that wintery morning, why they acted as they did seems to correlate with many of the concerns central to this book. Memories of the dead can evoke feelings of pain and are therefore best avoided; Karma quickly leaves Latu's shop. Villagers try to "hide" their hearts in the company of others; Karma stands for several minutes on the outskirts of the village. Yolmo wa struggle to cleanse their hearts of pain and maintain smooth facades when interacting with others; Karma recovers his smile when he returns to Latu's home and his response to the tape recorder goes unmentioned. It is inappropriate to inquire into another's feelings of distess, so Latu calls me back. And since constraints on the communication of emotional distress make it difficult to show one's empathy for another's plight through direct, verbal means, Latu plays a tape recording of Karma's father to convey, perhaps, that he cares for Karma, that he understands what Karma feels, and that he too grieves the loss of Karma's father. By evoking the memory of Karma's father, Latu might have sought to create a "bond of love" between Karma and himself— in spite of, or precisely because of, the pain it caused. Since these sensibilities were specific to the residents of Helambu, I reacted with anger and bewilderment because my rather American sensibilities differed and because I did not understand Latu's motives. At the same time, I had, by December, acquired a bit of Yolmo common sense and thus obeyed Latu, because to have done other would have created undue social tension. My uncertainty became further entrenched when I was unable to talk later with Karma or Latu.

The forces of harmony, purity, and restraint common to Yolmo lives seem intrinsic to the encounter, but implicitly so. The interaction says so much, yet eludes translation, precisely because it realizes a way of being in the world that belongs more to the senses than to the written word. The irony and wonder of such moments is that we turn to words, often quite successfully, to learn what lies beyond words.

"To some extent," Nelson Goodman tells us in his attempt to show how emotions function cognitively in aesthetic experiences, "we may feel how a painting looks as we may see how it feels. The actor or dancer—or the spectator—sometimes notes and remembers the feeling of a movement rather than its pattern, insofar as the two can be distinguished at all. Emotion in aesthetic experience is a means of discerning what properties a work has and expresses."[3] I have been trying to make a similar point: that we may feel how a culture "looks" as we may see how a people feels. That is, our understanding of a people's ethos is not necessarily limited to analytic insights. We can also begin to sense, through nonverbal, visceral means, something of a people's sensibilities by attending to the patterns, orientations, and concerns that commonly impact on their lives. How an ethnographer might go about developing felt understandings in living with a people, and how he or she might try to convey this knowledge in writing, have been two of the concerns of the present work.

Indeed, I find that it is by attending to local aesthetic sensibilities, rather than any symbolic actions, structural relations, or deep psychic processes, that we can best understand what took place between Karma, Latu, and myself. We cannot foresake a study of discourse and meaning, but only because words and images are one of the key means through which people learn and express sensibilities. Geertz, for one, also speaks of "sensibilities," and some of his most engaging work articulates a people's ethos—"the tone, character, and quality of their life, its moral and aesthetic style and mood," to use his words.[4] For instance, his writings on the "quietistic" style of life in Java or his contention that Balinese "live in spurts"[5] suggests that he would be one of the first to admit that we may feel how a culture works. However, Geertz, like others, fails, in my opinion, to develop a theoretical framework that would account for the nature, force, and impact of cultural sensibilities. The failure seems due, in part, to his commitment to a semiotic view of culture, which builds on the representational approaches of Cassirer and Langer.[6]

The limitations inherent in Geertz's semiotics of culture are evident in the ways he talks about art and ritual in his later, more programmatic essays. By studying aesthetics as a "semiotic system," and thus attending primarily to what works of art or social performances "mean" and "are about,"[7] Geertz neglects to consider how a story, funeral, or ritual is experienced. Consequently, while he focuses on the meanings and qualities perceived in paintings, plays, and cockfights, he does not show how these "things," as he calls them, affect their participants. The significance of the cockfight, for example, lies for Geertz in its bounded meaning, not in how it might disturb, engage, or delight its participants: it is tellingly seen as something "disquietful"[8] rather than as something "disquieting." To speak of art primarily in terms of symbolic form, perception, and interpretation (as do Cassirer, Langer, and Geertz), rather than in terms of performance, sentience, and experience (as do Dewey, Dufrenne, and Iser), entails a great deal.[9] It means, basically, that we are not dealing with aesthetic experiences or with felt immediacies but simply with meaning and interpretation. When art is reduced to signs and symbols, when *Hamlet* is diluted to a singular "meaning," a great deal is left out.[10]

The same goes for an aesthetics of the everyday. We cannot make sense of a culture if we limit ourselves to a semiotic model. Nor can we understand how sensibilities impact on particular individuals if we stay at the level of either cognition or public meanings. To speak, when talking of Latu's and Karma's actions, of symbolic meanings only, of allegories in action, does not go far enough. We must know a twitch from a blink, as Geertz puts it,[11] but we must also consider why one blinks, the sensibilities that lend value to that act, and the effect the act might have on its participants. The ethnographer in Geertz seems to appreciate all this, but the theorist in him fails to account for it.[12] What is needed is a nonsemiotic, phenomenological theory of felt sensibilities to better account for the ethnography. Since much of interpretive anthropology has served as a model of and for Geertz's own work, the need is a pervasive one.

Practice-oriented theories such as Garfinkle and Bourdieu do ask, at times, why a person blinks,[13] but focus more on the ways and means of social interactions rather than on the sensibilities that drive them. In 1967, Garfinkle defined ethnomethodology as the study of practical actions "as contingent ongoing accomplishments of organized artful practices of everyday life."[14] We now know a great deal about the practices of everyday life, such that we can parse a streetside conversation for its political import. But we have yet to fully consider if the practices are, in fact, "artful" ones, and, if so, what this implies.

The conclusion we can draw from Helambu, at least, is that everyday actions are rooted in local sensibilities; this rootedness forces us to rethink how we talk of moralities, bodies, pain, healing, and politics. For Yolmo wa, the aesthetic values that govern how a person dresses in the morning or talks with a neighbor constitute a tacit moral code, such that ethics and aesthetics are one. In Helambu, values of presence, balance, and harmony are embodied, sensible ones, and thus contribute to the force and tenor of human sentience. Yolmo sensibilities influence how and why villagers fall ill, how they heal, and what moments of pain and comfort feel like. At the same time, they are borne of enduring political concerns and thus reflect and add to the social history of "the Lama people." In all, an understanding of the aesthetics of the everyday is crucial for investigations into other aspects of Yolmo experience.

"A sensibility (as distinct from an idea)," writes Susan Sontag, "is one of the hardest things to talk about. . . . To snare a sensibility in words, especially one that is alive and powerful, one must be tentative and nimble."[15] While Sontag expresses the sensibility of high "Camp" through a series of impressions, I seek to convey Yolmo sensibilities by developing an archaeology of feeling, a phenomenology of embodied aesthetics that attends to local senses of pain, loss, and comfort. And since the ways of being, feeling, and knowing that contribute to these sensibilities are specific to Yolmo lives, I try to comprehend them not by applying wholesale any Western categories of body, speech, or mind, but by working from the ground up to grasp their varied influence on bodily experience and the charge of the relationship between them. And I have done so, in part, to question how such ways of being, like the inner walls and walkways of a city, either hinder or facilitate the lives of villagers and thus contribute to the loss or recovery of a body's vitality.

To make sense of Yolmo sensibilities, we must consider the presence of bodies. We have found that much of Yolmo experience turns on what a body feels, and so knows, in everyday life. The pain of separation wears out a body, Meme divines the pulse of a family, and Nyima recovers a lost spirit by sensing, through direct, visceral means, its return. Seremetakis tells us that "Ethnological theory transforms the body (*soma*) into a sign (*sema*),"[16] but such an alchemy must be questioned to its bones. A generation of anthropologists has worked under the guiding assumption that culture consists of networks of symbols, of webs of significance, such that ethnographers now consider bodies as texts, emotions as discourses, and healings as symbolic. But do these orientations, which derive from central tenets of Western literary traditions, have much validity in a place where women, men, and children spend much of their time working in fields, collecting firewood, sowing millet, walking, dancing, eating, drinking, hurting, and healing?

Our brief review of Yolmo concerns suggests that any theoretical orientation that values representation over presentation, or discourse over felt experience, can only take us so far in explaining what life (and death) is like for these people. From the outset, I wagered that we must consider Yolmo actions from the plane of the body. Our finding that Yolmo wa feel their bodies more than they "read" or "write" them proves the utility of that stance. Of course, we often know of others only by what they say of their experiences. But to say that we should not consider the experiences themselves because we cannot know them for sure (or worse, because they are illusory)[17] is a mistake. We must rely on words to approximate the stench of pain or the pleasures of sleep. Always a patchy translation, I agree, but a necessary one. Without considering, if only conjecturally, the effects of touch or image on human sentience, we would be at a loss to explain how Meme's rites heal or Yolmo songs of pain soothe. And since Yolmo spells of grief or spiritlessness appear to be deeply felt experiences, we must try to understand not only how these afflictions "read," but what they feel like.

A few heretics have thrown stones at the Western literary canon. Nietzsche condemned "the despisers of the body," and sought, like Schopenhauer before him and Merleau-Ponty after, to ground philosophy within physiology.[18] Joyce's *Ulysses* searched for words to celebrate desires and digestions.[19] Artaud created a theater of "cruelty," where feeling was prior to signification and sentience prior to thought.[20] Sontag faults any criticism that abstracts "a shadow of meanings" from our felt experience of art.[21] Feminist writers have sought ways in which they can speak from their own bodily experience.[22] And George Steiner urges a return to the tactile presence of words.[23] Despite these outcries, Western ways of reading the world have dominated our accounts of other peoples and other sensibilities, such that a return to the sentient body now seems needed.[24] Indeed, an emergent anthropology of the senses is answering this call, and we now have ethnographies of taste and smells in a range of valleys.[25]

Yet as I stress above, we cannot assume that human sentience is the same everywhere, as if bodily sensations offer an esperanto of lived experience, to be collected like souvenirs. Since it is the aesthetic sensibilities of a people that make sense of, and give force to, human sentience, we need to situate any study of feeling within the local play of values. This entails an analysis of the social histories, rudiments of form, and embodied aesthetics common to a people. Felt sensations are always sensible ones and so demand less a natural than a cultural history. We cannot know what a shaman knows simply by dreaming, touching, or "shaking" when he does. But we can gain a fair sense of what he and his neighbors commonly experience through a lengthy dialogue, gleaning what they sense of the gods by comparing, and sensing, the differences between sensibilities.

At its best, this sort of hermeneutics involves a reflexive participation in the give and take of everyday life. Since the first chapter of this work, observations on my own interactions with the residents of Helambu have obstensibly remained offstage. Yet many of the interpretations voiced above result from a bodily engagement with Yolmo ways of being. For instance, the sense that Yolmo experiences are founded on a play between interiors and exteriors, ingress and egress, grew out of my shamanic fumblings. My body, in beseeching the gods to "fall" within it and in feeling hot water slapped against legs, back, and arms, began to sense new ways of wielding and construing its varied organs. I also began to embody a schema of value that taught me the proper, sensible ways to greet Meme, walk through a village, or eat a bowl of rice. These and other novel patterns of experience led to a sensory appreciation of the need for harmony, restraint, and presence in the foothills of Helambu, and a sense, I believe, of what it might feel like for Mingma or Nyima to lose a spirit, grow old, or be healed. My share in this conversation was always an awkward, hesitant one, like a child learning to walk. The awkwardness was, at times, a welcome, instructive one. The confusions, tensions, and insights sparked by the clash of differing sensibilities began to haunt the gait of my sandles to the extent that my feet seemed to assimilate, in a partial, reflexive way, Yolmo ways of being. When I left Nepal, I could not shake off the sensibilities that helped me get about Helambu, and found, when I tried to speak with friends or buy a pair of sneakers, that I had lost the knack for being American. Indeed, the relation between my felt sense of Yolmo lives and the portrait sketched here is of such an affinity that I find the portrait to be an entirely sensible one, the basic tenets of which I can outgrow as easily as I can step outside my body.

As with the fieldworker, so with the reader: I made sense of the felt flow of Yolmo life through the everyday actions of my body and try, in writing, to engage the reader's body in that flow (as I have come to understand it). Linking sense to image, I have sought much of this engagement through tactile means, such that the portent of an experience is not so much bound to print as, ideally, it becomes patterned within the body of the reader. The reader thus begins to feel, or so I am suggesting, how a culture works. This way of writing ethnography, which relies deeply on a reader's response to words, meets with several difficulties. To begin with, while I discuss the semantics of Yolmo "heartaches" in several analytic passages, I agree with Armstrong that emotional experience "can be denoted but not presented discursively."[26] I have therefore tried to convey a sense of *sems pa tsher ka* by seeking its "objective correlative" in several scenes common to Yolmo life: a dead man's unseen footsteps, a daughter's farewell. The term comes from T. S. Eliot, who proposed that "The only way of expressing emotion in the form of art is by finding an 'objective correlative'; in other words, a set of objects, a situation, a chain of events which shall be the formula of that *particular* emotion; such that when the external facts, which must terminate in sensory experience, are given, the emotion is immediately evoked."[27]

Although Eliot's maxim might hold true for Western representational art, it quickly runs into trouble in ethnographic writing. While the external features of a situation may evoke emotions, it is questionable whose emotions are being evoked. Eliot took it to be the reader's (and so the protagonist's), but with cross-cultural accounts this becomes problematic: what Karma feels in grief and the import of his feelings are significantly at odds from what most Americans know of the experience. An author's portrait becomes a question of cultural translation: he or she must not only convey felt immediacies, but contextualize the grounds, nature, and significance of differing experience. The reader is thus drawn into a hermeneutic circle, always needing to interpret the significance of events for the cultural actor, yet always questioning the validity of those interpretations. For me, writing ethnography is an exercise in cultural translation—to express not only what we can know of Karma and Latu but also to learn the limits of this knowledge and the constraints of ethnographic presentation.

These constraints begin and end with language itself. In writing, I try to draw on Yolmo idioms, images, and metaphors to give a feel for the cultural realities in question. Tactile images map the rocky terrain of Yolmo experiences, Nyima's hesitant speech nods toward the anxiety of spirit loss, and portraits of healing meter the rhythm of Meme's chants. Yet I find that the sentences, to be intelligible to audiences outside Helambu, must be marked by Western idioms, and the English language, Whorf notes, implies a specific linguistic universe.[28] The words "ghost," "heartache," and "I lost my spirit" create a world of associations distinct from the ones in which Yolmo live. Likewise, the hunger for personal pronouns (I, you, me) in the English language requires a grammar that would annoy Yolmo ears. A more radical attempt at fidelity would dispense with pronouns, English grammar, and modern American idioms, but earlier experiments of mine suggest that, devoid of a familiar context, the language veers toward unintelligibility. I have therefore settled for a middle ground, hoping to convey the experiential fabric of Yolmo lives to a non-Yolmo audience by sketching the "rudiments of form" and "imaginative force," if not the specific territory and content, of those lives. But this ground, like my "shamanic" visions and the embodied knowledge that they apparently realized, lies at best in a no-man's-land, betwixt and between cultures. As with any conversation, understanding is never direct or total.

And so there are limits to the knowledge sown by the narrative stance authored here. Yeshi's pain lingers in silence, Nyima's grief takes on an oddly Western slant, Mingma's wistful smile continues to ask "Who am I?" These uncertainties, it should be stressed, result not from writing narrative per se, but from portraying different experiential realities, and therefore color all attempts at ethnographic writing. Many anthropologies try to ferret out the "real" toads (depression, political economies) from patches of another people's "imaginary" garden (soul loss, sacred cows). We must, however, constantly question the reality of the toads we find, how well we understand another society's ways of beings, and our motives for doing so. This is not to argue that anthropology, a chaser of windmills, should close up shop. Rather: our understandings are borne of an uncertain dialogue between cultural traditions. With this dialogue, "one can never know," we have learned, "what lies within another's heart." But this need not be cause for despair. We begin to know one another most through the doubts, awkward greetings, and frail truths owned by any conversation.

Notes

Chapter 1: Imaginary Gardens with Real Toads

1. Clarke, 1980a, 1980b, 1980c, 1983, 1985, 1990; Clarke and Manandhar, 1988.

2. See Clarke (1980a, 1980b, 1980c, 1983, 1985, 1990) and Clarke and Manandhar (1988) for a more complete account of a historical process that here has been presented only in outline.

3. See Levine, 1987.

4. Clarke (1980a) sketches out the similarities and differences in aspects of social organization between Yolmo and Tamang families in Helambu.

5. See Clarke, 1990.

6. Clarke (1980a:79) writes of the term Helambu, "Locally this name is held to derive from a combination of the Tibetan names of two of the main upland crops: from *he*, potato, and *la-phug*, radish, comes the compound *he la-phug*, literally 'potatoes and radishes.'"

7. Evans-Wentz, 1974:235. Noted in Clarke, 1980a:79.

8. The term Tamang is used to refer to variously related peoples with Tibetan ancestry (see March 1979; Holmberg 1989; Peters 1981). In other parts of Nepal, Tamang groups refer to themselves as "lama" (see Holmberg 1989), but in and around Helambu, the term typically applies to lineages of Yolmo wa.

9. See Clarke (1980c) for a discussion of local variation in kinship practices and some of their implications.

10. The Yolmo term *bombo* itself relates to the Tibetan word *bon po*, which apparently refers to the practioners of the Tibetan *Bon* religion.

11. See Clarke, 1980a, 1980c.

12. Clarke, 1980a, 1980b.

13. See Paul, 1976.

14. Graham Clarke (personal communication) finds that the lower villages to the east of Helambu, and the pastoral settlements to the north, always have been and still are shamanic.

15. Deren, 1970; Peters, 1981.

16. Harner, 1980; Taussig, 1987.

17. Deren, 1970:10;257.

18. Peters, 1981:37.

19. Ibid.: 53.

20. Taussig, 1987:435–46.

21. Ibid.: 406.

22. Harner, 1980:1–19.

23. Geertz, 1973:49.

24. See Bateson, 1972:166–76.

25. I use "conversation" in the strong sense of the term, as spelled out by Rorty (1979), who proposes that Western philosophy should no longer be seen as a tribunal of pure reason, but as a way of continuing the conversation that defines our history.

26. Bateson, 1975.

27. Watkins, 1976.

28. Moore, 1935.

29. Singer and Pope, 1978; Zieg, 1982; Noll, 1985; Wilbert, 1985; Desjarlais, 1989.

30. Watkins, 1976; Achterberg, 1985.

31. Jung, 1969.

32. Bogoras, 1928.

33. See Wengle, 1984.

34. I later learned that Sumjok was involved in a difficult family situation: several years before, her husband had married a younger and wealthier woman, and Sumjok became the less favored wife.

35. Levy, 1984.

36. Bourdieu, 1977; Rosaldo, 1984:192–93.

37. See Paul, 1970:77–78.

38. With Foucault's "archaeology of knowledge" (1972), there is nothing beneath the surface to know. With the present archaeology of feeling, experiences lie beneath the pale of words, though we are hard-pressed to know them directly.

39. Turner and Bruner, 1986; Jackson, 1989; Kleinman and Kleinman, 1991.

40. Bateson, 1972:319.

41. See Douglas, 1970; Bourdieu, 1977; Scheper-Hughes and Lock, 1987.

42. The stress falls on the "particular": if I spoke with women more than men, my perceptions would likely be different.

43. Ironically, the body has often been the cultural object approached through the most intellectual of means. Connerton (1989:104), for instance, comments on the "cognitive tilt" apparent in studies of the body: "Frequently what is being talked about is the symbolism of the body or attitudes towards the body or discourses about the body; not so much how bodies are variously constituted and variously behave."

44. Steps toward such an orientation have recently been taken by Stoller (1989), Jackson (1989), and Csordas (1990), all influenced by Merleau-Ponty's (1962) phenomenology of the lived body.

45. Bourdieu, 1977:2.

46. Lévi-Strauss, 1969.

47. Fernandez, 1987.

48. I agree with Csordas (1990) that we should think of images as being multisensory, involving taste, touch, sound and smell as well as sight. But as such images must be conveyed through print, their representation often involves visual imagery. Until we include scratch and sniff fliers within our ethnographies, we must let words convey our smelling for us.

49. Barthes, 1970; Iser, 1978.

50. Eliot, 1932.

51. See Mattingly, 1988; Good, n.d.

52. Marsella, 1985:292–94.

53. Geertz, 1988:145.

54. See Bruner (1986) for an interesting discussion of how a skillful eth-nographic account and Joyce's "Araby" affect a reader differently: the short story's ability to highlight subjective states and alternative possibilities enables its meaning to take more vivid, "subjunctive" form in the mind of the reader.

55. Plessner, 1970.

56. My intent to write from the level of the body leads me to think that, for the purposes of this book, the uses of "I," "he," and "she" might be better replaced with the phrases "my body," "his body," and "her body." While I stick with the English pronouns (which curiously seem to refer more to the minds than the bodies of agents), the reader might want to keep the bodily locus of the pronouns in mind.

57. Yeats, (1970) 1907:38.

58. See Stoller, 1989; Jackson, 1989; Howes, 1991; and, in a related vein, Steiner, 1989.

59. See Obeyesekere, 1981, 1990.

60. Bourdieu, 1989:18.

61. Hallowell, 1955.

62. Bateson, 1972.

63. The terms come from Tambiah (1990).

64. Merwin, 1980:viii.

65. Jackson, 1989; Stoller, 1989:144–45.

66. Dewey, (1980) 1934:32.

67. Iser, 1978. Bruner, 1986. As Margulies (1984) notes, Keats's "negative capability" parallels Merleau-Ponty's ideal of the phenomenological reduction: both strategies attempt to approximate the inner experience of another by "putting the world between brackets," reducing the world to pure perception, to stave off the precepts of one's a priori knowledge.

68. In Kunitz, 1985:51.

69. Geertz, 1983:58.

70. Kohut, 1977:306.

Chapter 2: Body, Speech, Mind

1. See Lévi-Strauss, 1967.

2. My use of the term "rudiments of form" thus compares to what Kluck-hohn (1941) means by the term "pattern": the "structural regularities" that pattern, for example, the arrangement of items in a Navajo arrow or the ways Navajo dance. "Such conceptions are necessarily conscious constructs, abstractions," Kluckhohn writes (1941:112). Rudiments of form, on the other hand, are more molecular than cultural patterns, and are therefore not necessarily cognized.

3. See, for instance, Wikan, 1991; Kleinman, 1991; Howes, 1991. The term

"experience-near," coined by the psychoanalyst Heinz Kohut, entered into anthropological circles with Geertz's work (1983:57). Yet in recent years, "experience-near" has come to mean not simply what an informant understands, but what anybody, including an ethnographer, "sees" and "feels." "The study is not experience-near enough," one often hears these days in anthropology departments, suggesting that the study in question does not include enough local color.

4. Hence Ackerman's nonanthropological title, *A Natural History of the Senses* (1990).

5. See White and Kirpatrick, 1985.

6. Johnson, 1987.

7. Ibid., xxxvii.

8. Ibid., 1987:14, italics in original.

9. The *rnam shes* is the soul-like "consciousness" of Tibetan lore that departs at death and endures through successive rebirths until one attains enlightenment. In Helambu, this force implies both consciousness and sensory experience, and death occurs when this life-sustaining "soul" separates from the body (cf. Tucci 1980:193). "If the *rnam shes* is gone, you're finished," one woman assured me in slicing her finger through her throat. After death, the *rnam shes* is thought to wander around the countryside for up to forty-nine days, at which time lamas help it to ascend into "heaven" to be reborn in another earthly body.

10. Beyer, 1973:441,436,456.

11. Gibson, 1950:228; cited in Hallowell, 1955:184.

12. Clarke (1991) also discusses the hierarchies implicit in the seating arrangments of lamas and laymen.

13. Tucci, 1966:46.

14. Bourdieu, 1977:89.

15. Clarke, 1980c:115.

16. Stein (1972:240) tells of the great lama Mila Repa's tutorship on "the art of 'moving house' [transferance, *pho-ba* and *gnas-spo*]" to a man reborn as a dried-dung worm. Latu's analogy is not an idiosyncratic one. As one young shaman explained, in order to invoke the "forest shaman" (*ri bombo*) into the body during possession, a bombo must "open up all the doors and windows, calling to the five cardinal directions." In Tibet, the house represents both body and cosmos (Stein 1957, 1972; Tucci 1980). Through meditation, Tibetan adepts visualize their bodies "as a divine mansion" and "a tent of white silk" in an attempt to abolish the samsaric illusion of the "residence and its residents": body and soul as dual (Beyer 1973).

17. Beyer, 1973:77.

18. Tucci, 1980:190.

19. Compare to Hardman, 1981:167.

20. See Desjarlais (1991a), for further discussions of Yolmo dreaming.

21. McHugh, 1989; Ortner, 1978; March, 1979; Hardman, 1981.

22. Clarke, 1980a, 1980b, 1985, 1990. The next few pages owe much to Clarke's meticulous work on Yolmo social and political organization.

23. Clarke, 1980b, 1983; Clarke and Manandhar, 1988.

24. Clarke, 1980b.

25. I say "corporatelike" because, strictly speaking, a household cannot be a corporate group as Maine (1861) initially defined the term. "Corporations never

die," Maine wrote (1861:122–23), because they do not consist of distinct individuals but of continuing legal and jural claims (see Fortes 1969:292). Following Clarke (1980a), then, we can speak of Yolmo lineages and extended families, but not of households, as being strictly corporate in nature, because a household does not possess any political-jural status beyond the status of its immediate members (indeed, Yolmo wa are keenly aware of the fact that households and bodies can, in fact, "die"). However, as we shall see, Yolmo households, families, villages, and even bodies are all "collective" in nature, and I wish to underscore these commonalities.

26. For further discussion of Yolmo "households," see Clarke (1980c:250–67).

27. Clarke, 1980c:269.

28. Clarke (1980a, 1990) offers poignant examples of the tactical uses of kinship by Yolmo wa to elevate their status.

29. See Clarke, 1990.

30. See Clarke, 1980a.

31. Clarke, 1980b; 1991:57.

32. See Clarke, 1980c:268.

33. As Clarke (1985:197) notes, "All Lama villagers may be seen as equals together, in contrast to the lower level peoples." The latter peoples are predominantly Tamang.

34. Clarke, 1985:197. Both Clarke (1980b, 1985) and Ortner (1989) suggest that the contradiction between notions of hierarchy and equality have shaped the cultural histories of Tibetan peoples. While I find this interpretation to be accurate for the descent of Lamaist lineages and hence large-scale historical tendencies, I find the tension between values of autonomy and interdependence to be more important in the everyday life of Yolmo villagers.

35. Clarke, 1980b.

36. I prefer the term "relational self" to others previously applied to ethnographic contexts. Marriot (1976), for instance, considers Indian persons as being "dividual"—divisible, that is, in contrast to the individual (indivisible) notion of personhood common in the modern West. The term "dividual" would not do justice to the strong notion of autonomy characterizing Yolmo understandings of personhood. Shweder and Bourne (1984), in turn, use the term "sociocentric" to distinguish nonwestern concepts of self from the more "egocentric" ones found in the modern West. Yet "sociocentric" could be applied to many societies and situations (including some in the West) and does not get at the specific qualities of Yolmo relatedness. Such relatedness compares, in significant ways, to concepts of personhood reported among other South Asian groups, such as Gurung of Nepal (McHugh 1989) and Indian Tamil (Daniel 1984, Trawick 1990), wherein individuals are embedded in networks of familial relationships and draw much of their identity from their position within those networks.

37. The degree to which Yolmo wa experience their lives in relation to others is suggested in local dream imageries. Many dreams predict an event that will affect, in waking reality, not the dreamer himself, but those around him: Yolmo epistemologies of self embrace the lives of others. If a person experiences a "bad dream" foreseeing illness, it can have consequences for another. When a person envisions his upper teeth falling out, one of his relatives will fall ill; if the lower teeth, one of his immediate family. Seeing objects being broken or the sun set also denotes that

another person is falling ill. And the bad dreams visited on shamans never refer to themselves but to their patients.

38. *Bān*, a Nepali word, refers to a magical "arrow" that can cause illness and paralysis when used against another person.

39. See Clarke, 1990:173.

40. See Ortner, 1978; March, 1979.

41. Johansson, 1970:23.

42. Das, 1987:1276; Tucci, 1980:58–67.

43. Clarke, 1980a:81.

44. Clarke, 1980a:82.

45. See Clarke (1990) for an extensive discussion of Yolmo festivals of *na rag*.

46. Douglas, 1970; Bourdieu, 1984.

Chapter 3: An Aesthetics of Experience

1. Schieffelin, 1976; Chernoff, 1979; Feld, 1982; Kapferer, 1983; Herzfeld, 1985; Brenneis, 1987; Laderman, 1991; Roseman, 1991.

2. See Kapferer (1983) and Roseman (1988:816), for instance.

3. Michael Herzfeld's "poetics" of Glendiot manhood also focuses on the everyday (1985:10–19). But Herzfeld is concerned more with "performative excellence," in which "the self is not presented within everyday life so much as in front of it" (1985:11), than with the mundane or with acts conducted in solitude (as I am here).

4. See, for instance, Geertz (1983), Shweder and Bourne (1984), White and Kirpatrick (1984), and Marsella, Devos and Hsu (1985).

5. See Shweder and Bourne, 1984.

6. See Kleinman and Kleinman, 1991.

7. Wikan, 1989; Geertz, 1973.

8. Richards, 1952:16–17.

9. Dewey, (1980) 1934:3.

10. Ibid.: 12–13.

11. See Langer, 1953:36, for instance.

12. Wittgenstein, (1967) 1922, 6.421.

13. Kupfer, 1983.

14. Dewey, (1980) 1934:35–57.

15. Kupfer, 1983:4–6.

16. Dewey, (1980) 1934:14–15.

17. Bourdieu, 1984.

18. Ibid.: 190, 466.

19. Ibid.: 190.

20. Ibid.: 474.

21. Bateson and Mead, 1942; Bateson, 1972; Bateson, 1975.

22. Bateson, 1975.

23. See Bateson, 1975:63.

24. Nietzsche, (1964) 1895.

25. Ricoeur, 1979a; Geertz, 1983.

26. Nichter, 1981; Good and Good, 1982; Obeyesekere, 1990.

27. The present study thus builds on the insights of several cultural anthropologists who sought to develop a study of cultural values (see Kluckhohn 1951, Kroeber 1949, Kroeber and Kluckhohn 1952:171–174, Opler 1945).

28. Iser, 1978:70.

29. Becker, 1979.

30. Compare to Nader, 1990.

31. Bishop, 1973.

32. The imagery of integration and fragmentation reflects motifs common to many Himalayan bodies (see Tucci 1980; Beyer 1973).

33. Introduced into Tibet in the fifth century (Clifford 1984:52), the Ayurvedic system disseminated throughout the plateau from the eighth until the seventeenth century (Chandra 1984:xviii).

34. Filliozat, 1964:28.

35. Caraka, 1949:267.

36. Burang, 1974:89.

37. Clifford, 1984:96.

38. Ibid.: 1984.

39. Ibid.: 1984:133.

40. See Levine, 1981:114.

41. In Bateson and Mead (1942:7), an essay that can be read as initiating an anthropology of embodied aesthetics.

42. March, 1979:372.

43. Lichter and Epstein, 1983.

44. See Tucci, 1980.

45. Clarke, 1990:172.

46. Clarke (1990) chronicles several ways in which Yolmo wa attempt to increase their "merit," through virtuous actions or by receiving "blessings" (*byin rlabs*) from lamas.

47. See Spiro, 1967.

48. Clarke, 1985, 1990:174.

49. Eliade, 1964.

50. Devereux, 1980:34.

51. Foucault, 1988:16–18.

52. See Canguilhem, 1978; Foucault, 1966; Devereux, 1980; Marsella and White, 1982; Kleinman, 1988.

53. See Good, Good, and Moradi, 1985.

54. Campbell, 1959.

55. Martin, 1987.

56. Geertz, 1983.

57. Obeyesekere, 1990.

Chapter 4: Pain Clings to the Body

1. The Yolmo funerary process generally consists of seven ceremonies (*bdun tshigs*) performed after the cremation of the body, including a merit-making ceremony (*dge ba*) for the deceased after the third or fifth week, and the final *sbyang par*

rite held, ideally, on the forty-ninth day (cf. Skorupski, 1982). An anniversary rite (*nebar*) is held one year after the death. Padma's funerals were distinct in that the *sbyang par* rites were performed at the time of the fifth-week *dge ba* ceremonies (July 4), with a final, larger funeral performed in early December, in fair weather, so many mourners could attend (see Table 2, Chapter 5).

2. See Hertz (1960), Van Gennep (1960), and Huntington and Metcalf (1979).

3. Holmberg, 1989:194. For similar approaches to the social dimensions of funerary rites, see Hertz (1960), Van Gennep (1960), Huntington and Metcalf (1979), and Bloch and Parry (1982).

4. See Becker (1979) for a discussion of the contextual relations involved in Javanese Shadow Theatre, and Fox (1974) for an analysis of the semantic links between dyadic sets of words in Rotinese ritual language.

5. Bakhtin, 1984:208.

6. See Ortner, 1978.

7. Kligman, holding the Durkheimian (1965 [1912]) view that expressions of grief should be treated as "social facts," looks at Romanian funeral laments as "expressions of cosmology and social relations" (1988:152), and Urban (1988) argues that "ritual wailing" in Amerindian central Brazil conveys a "desire for sociability." Schieffelin (1979) and Feld (1982) explain how the metaphoric and aesthetic dimensions of Kaluli funerary songs "move men to tears," Trawick (1986) explores notions of "iconicity" in Paraiyar "crying songs," and Abu-Lughod (1986) demonstrates how folk poetry among Egyptian Bedouin serves as an alternative discourse to the dominant ideology of honor and autonomy.

8. Lutz and Abu-Lughod, 1990.

9. Beeman, 1985; Crapanzano, 1989; Abu-Lughod, 1990:28.

10. See Irvine, 1982:34.

11. Abu-Lughod and Lutz, 1990:12; Abu-Lughod, 1990:41.

12. Abu-Lughod, 1990:28. This point apparently follows Foucault's precept that discourse should be seen as consisting "not of signs (signifying elements referring to contents or representations) but as practices that systematically form the objects of which they speak" (1972:49).

13. Mishler, 1986:160, citing Jameson, 1972.

14. Abu-Lughod, 1990.

15. See Irvine, 1982; Devereux, 1967; Kleinman and Kleinman, 1991.

16. I am reminded of the Ethiopian woman Emawayish's response to the suggestion by Michel Leiris (1934) that she record some love songs for him: "Does love exist in France?" she asked Leiris. Renato Rosaldo (1984) takes a position similar to my own in discussing the tendency to "eliminate the emotions" in anthropological studies of death and mourning.

17. Or, as Susanne Langer puts it, "What art expresses is *not* actual feeling, but ideas of feeling; as language does not express actual things and events but ideas of them" (1953:59). Yet it is also important to acknowledge that art can *evoke* feelings (Dufrenne 1973).

18. In eliciting *tsher glu* from villagers, I seldom found significant variance in the wording of couplets, and often listeners could readily recite the second line on

hearing the first. But while individual couplets are more or less standardized, each song is improvised out of a series of couplets and is thus a unique creative achievement. In fact, villagers consider much of a song's artistry to be based on the cohesiveness, subtlety, and ingenuity of its lyrics as chosen by its composer(s).

19. Crapanzano, 1989:79.

20. Jaschke, 1949:451,577; Das, (1987) 1902:1031,1276.

21. See Rahula, 1959:16–17; Bowker, 1970:240; Smith, 1991:101.

22. Lutz, 1988:148.

23. In an earlier paper (1991b), I glossed *tsher ka* as "sadness," but have since found that this translation admits to some unnecessary connotations. The word is therefore better translated as "pain" and *sems pa tsher ka* as "heartache."

24. See O'Flaherty (1980:122–24) on Hindu *viraha*. *Tsher ka* thus compares to the Polish *tesknota*, which Wierzbicka (1986) glosses as "the pain of distance" and "sadness caused by separation."

25. See Clarke, 1983; Holmberg, 1989.

26. Simply put, the Four Noble Truths, as stated in the First Sermon of the Buddha at Benares, are that: life is suffering; the cause of suffering is "thirst" or desire; the cessation of suffering is the extinction of desire; and the Path leading to the cessation of suffering is the Noble Eightfold Path: right view, right thought, right speech, right action, right livelihood, right effort, right mindfulness, right concentration (from the *Dhammacakkappavattanasutta*; cited in Bowker, 1970:238).

27. Obeyesekere, 1985.

28. Levy, 1973; 1984.

29. Consider a Yolmo epistemology of politics. As the political ethos of Nepal in the 1980s was one of status hierarchies and deferential respect, village communities, careful to stay on good terms with the central government, put more effort into maintaining peaceful relations than demanding change. Thus, when a government official toured the outlying regions of Nepal, village problems were swept under the rug of outer appearances. As a Hollywood stage set hides the vacant lot behind it, so the politician "only saw what's right in front of him," as one man put it. To please the king, the man explained, amiable villagers dressed in their finest clothes, tailored fields and houses to beauty, and replenished defunct water taps with just enough water to last through the visit. When the politician left, the scenery was brought down, villagers grumbled anew over lasting problems, and the well ran dry once again.

30. Notions of epistemic interiors and exteriors find their way into Tibetan culture as well. Tucci (1980:123), for instance, notes that various kinds of liturgical objects can be classified as outer, inner, and secret. Such a geometry of knowledge is also figured in *The Tibetan Book of the Dead*, which divides the "signs of death" into six classes: external, internal, secret, distant, near, and miscellaneous (Beyer 1973:368–73). It is likely that the particular spatial form of Tibetan and Yolmo knowledge relates to the architecture of the house and thus of cosmos and body.

31. See Levine, 1981.

32. Studies suggest that the tendency to avoid emotional distress pervades many Western and non-Western societies (Levy 1973, Wikan 1989).

33. Once, while visiting another village to the north of Helambu, I stayed in a

lodge run by an elderly Yolmo couple. Early one morning, several Nepali policemen came to the home of an acquaintance and arrested him on the suspicion that he stole some sheep. On waking, my hosts told me of this occurrence and suggested that I go to my friend's home to witness the events. When I expressed my reluctance to do so (more from a desire not to get involved than anything else), the wife knowingly replied, "Oh yes, if you go there, then it will hurt in the heartmind." Neither I nor my hosts left the room.

34. See Lutz, 1985; D'Andrade, 1987:143; Lakoff and Kovecses, 1987; and Wellankamp, 1988.

35. Peters, 1981:90.

36. Abu-Lughod (1986) develops a similar argument for the Egyptian Bedouin, for whom folk poetry serves as an alternative discourse of emotionality and intimacy to the dominant ideology of honor and emotional restraint.

37. See March (1984) for a comparable tension among Tamang women.

38. *sDong po* is a type of forest plant.

39. A *mala* or "rosary" is composed of a series of beads with silver ornaments intermittently interposed.

40. Tousignant and Maldonado (1989:900), building on Schieffelin (1985).

41. See Trawick, 1988; Warren and Bourque, 1985; Scott, 1990.

42. *Kalde*, an alpine tree, is the habitat of the *jolmo*, a high-altitude bird that migrates to the valleys in winter.

43. Here I think that Abu-Lughod (1986) and others (Lutz and White 1986: 421) have underemphasized how poetic discourses serve not only to reflect personal distress but to structure it as well.

44. Geertz, 1973:123.

45. Bourdieu, 1977; Comaroff, 1985.

46. Beyer, 1973:77. Paul (1970:98) and Ortner (1970:163) find a similar duality present among Solu Khumba Sherpa.

47. Tucci, 1980:260.

48. *Bar do* is the intermediate state of existence between reincarnations, usually lasting forty-nine days (see Evans-Wentz, 1960).

49. Evans-Wentz, 1960:161.

50. The mind-body duality continues, finally, into death, for the resulting loss of life-forces causes the body to be greatly devalued. When the body is imbued with life, it is sacrosanct, but when the "soul" (*rnam shes*) departs, it is thought of as being "empty," a mere "bundle of discarded clothes," as Karma put it. While cremating a corpse, then, Yolmo wa treat it without undue reverence, handling it less like a sacred temple than a hollow bag-of-bones. They drink tea by its side, tug clothes off its frame, and carry it roughly to the cremation hill—where flesh and bones are "stuck" into the ground.

51. Bateson, 1972; Iser, 1978.

52. Iser, 1978:85.

53. Freud, (1956) 1917.

54. The term comes from Coleridge's definition of poetry in his *Biographia Literaria* (1817): "The synthetic and magical power" of imagination "reveals itself in the balance or reconcilement of discordant qualities . . . a more than usual state of

emotion with more than usual order." Coleridge's formula for beauty, in turn, is "multeity in unity . . . or that in which the many, still seen as many, becomes one."

55. The idea that emotions possess narrative form derives, in part, from Dewey: "Emotions are qualities," he writes, "of a complex experience that moves and changes. . . . The intimate nature of emotion is manifested in the experience of watching a play on the stage or reading a novel. It attends the development of a plot; and a plot requires a stage, a space, wherein to develop and time in which to unfold" (1934:41–42).

56. Gadamer, 1975:133.

57. Abu-Lughod, for instance, uses the term sentiment rather than emotion "to signal the literary or conventional nature" of Bedouin responses to various life crises through folk poetry (1986:34). Lutz (1988), in turn, considers emotions as akin to rational thoughts.

Chapter 5: Soul Loss

1. Gillin, 1948; Kiev, 1968.

2. Rubel, O'Nell, and Collado-Ardon, 1984.

3. Bolton, 1981.

4. Lutz, 1985.

5. Ortner, 1984.

6. See Weiss and Kleinman, 1987:199.

7. Geertz, 1983:73, citing Wittgenstein, 1953:8.

8. Kleinman, 1986; Good, n.d.

9. Good and Good, 1982.

10. Shweder, 1985:194.

11. See, for instance, Tucci 1980:190, Watters 1975:143, Stein 1972:226, and Poree-Maspero 1951. See also Roseman (1991) for soul loss in Indonesia.

12. See Stein (1972:227) for the Tibetans.

13. Kennedy (1973) argues that depression provoked by loss may be more prevalent in societies with an emphasis on social cohesion than those without strong interpersonal bonds. He suggests that the closer the ties between individuals, the deeper the grief will be when those ties are ruptured.

14. Gaines and Farmer, 1986.

15. Freud, (1956) 1917.

16. Gorer, 1965; Kennedy, 1978; Marsella, 1980:272; Schieffelin, 1985.

17. Rosenblatt, Walsh, and Jackson, 1976.

18. Keyes, 1985.

19. Ibid, 1985:163.

20. Lindemann, 1944; Gorer, 1965; Reid, 1979; Parkes, 1972.

21. Lindemann, 1944:143.

22. See Parkes, 1982.

23. Gorer, 1965.

24. Schutz, 1970:253–55.

25. The behavior recalls the penchant of Balinese children to fall asleep when

confronted by pain or distress, as is promised in a tooth-pulling rite (Bateson and Mead 1942).

26. Aziz, 1978; Bennett, 1983.

27. See Obeyesekere, 1981.

28. Yeshi's story, as I have interpreted it, bears close affinities with two recent anthropological studies of "depression" in traditional societies (Schieffelin 1985a; Wellenkamp, n.d.).

29. Kleinman, 1984.

30. Cheung et al. (1981), for instance, argue that depressed Chinese patients communicate their distress via a "somatic *facade* [that] *concealed* the depressive-ridden state of mood" (cited in Kleinman, 1986:53, with emphasis added here).

31. Shweder, 1988:489.

32. Kleinman, 1984.

33. Kirmayer, 1984:249.

34. Western psychologies, in contrast, often take depression to be first and foremost a kind of psychological distress, with the "somatization" of depression a secondary (and often pathological) phenomenon.

35. Nancy Levine, personal communication. My understanding of Helambu Tamang is that they are more often concerned with the assault of ghosts, deities, and witches than with the loss of life-forces. Some ethnic groups, such as Gurung, talk often of lost souls (see Pignede 1966; McHugh 1989; and Mumford 1989:168). For discussions of "soul loss" in other Himalayan communities, see Nebesky-Wojkowitz 1956; Tucci 1980:190; Watters 1975:143; Holmberg 1989:154; Peters 1981: 71; and Karmay 1987.

36. See Bowker (1970, 1991) for a review of Buddhist perspectives on suffering and death, and Obeyesekere (1985) and Keyes (1983) for anthropological accounts of Buddhist theology.

37. Beyer, 1973:390; Karmay, 1987:118.

38. Tucci, 1980:192; Karmay, 1987.

39. Stein, 1972:222–23; Lichter and Epstein, 1983:240.

40. Tucci, 1980; Nakazawa, 1986.

41. Bogoras, 1928; Eliade, 1964.

42. O'Flaherty, 1973:45; Beck, 1976:223; Bennett, 1983:287.

43. MacDonald, 1980.

44. Pandolfi, 1990; Kleinman and Kleinman, n.d.

45. Obeyesekere, 1990.

Chapter 6: The Art of Knowing

1. Meme's drum, like those of other Yolmo shamans, is the double-headed, single-handled *dhyangro* (n) used by many Tamang, Sherpa, and Limbu healers.

2. At the base of the winnowing tray rest several ritual implements: to the left, a candle (*mar men*) and a thigh-bone trumpet (*rkang gling*, "leg-flute"); in the middle, an egg; to the right, a handful of uncooked rice kernals (*sergi*). Behind the tray, five green stems of an incense plant rest against the far wall such that they rise

above the *gtor ma* altar enshadowed before them. These plants, known as "the god curtain" (*lha dal*), stand for the ancestral trees from the five directions. To the left of the winnowing tray sits a copper bucket (*pāthi*; normally used to measure grains) filled with "grains" (*chhene*) of maize. Set upright within this bowl is the bombo's magical *phurba* dagger, a small, hand-held sickle (*chhenchya*; which "clears the path"), a small, circular mirror (*me long*) facing out from the altar, and three colored cloth (*rtags dar*) banners—white, red, and blue—set on a rod.

3. See Tucci (1980), Stein (1972), and Clarke (1985, 1991) for further discussions of the tripartite structure of Tibetan and Yolmo universes. As noted above, Yolmo lamas occasionally speak of more esoteric Buddhist notions, such as the karmic wheel of life, but villagers do not bring up these notions in conversation.

4. This relationship is of such importance that Yolmo shamans cannot heal without the assistance of the gods. In the monsoon month of Saun, bombos refrain from performing healing ceremonies because their divinities go on retreat at that time. "If the gods are not there to accept offerings," Meme said of the furlough, "we cannot heal." The absence of the deities' protection and thus the shaman's inability to heal explains the prevalence of illness during the rainy season.

5. Derrida, 1981.

6. See Tucci, 1980:173; Clifford, 1984:97.

7. Parker, 1988; Stone, 1976.

8. For studies on the relation between knowledge and power, see Foucault (1972) and Fardon (1985). Although both shaman and lama can divine in Helambu, what the former "sees" is different from what the latter knows. As "one who knows," a lama uses a complex divinatory calender to "calculate" (*rtsis*) moments of personal fortune and misfortune, from auspicious days of travel to the vigor of one's "life span." A shaman develops a more finite knowledge of the world and its vicissitudes through oracular communications with the gods. The lama's knowledge is rational and general; the bombo's, ecstatic and particular. And while the lama's codices appear to be a surer bet than the shaman's inner musings, the sick primarily call on shamans to divine because they can ascertain the specific cause of a patient's illness and what needs to be done to cure it. See Ekvall (1963, 1964) and Mumford (1989) for comprehensive discussions of Lamaist astrology and divination, and Holmberg (1989) for an analysis of the relation between shaman and lama in the Tamang "ritual field."

9. Peters (1981:81) describes a comparable relationship between a Tamang shaman and his "internal guru."

10. See Hofer and Shrestha, 1973:55; Daniel, 1984:182–224.

11. Asking the first of many questions, such as "Are you a *shi 'dre* that lives in the forest?," the diviner takes a pinchful of rice grains and places it within a metal plate. He then counts out the first set of grains to determine whether they number odd or even. Once counted, he takes a second set and goes though the same calculations. What is important is whether the successive countings come out even or odd: like a die that comes up odd five times in a row, if the next five (sometimes seven) countings of rice all turn out to be odd (the first set holding 7 grains, the second 9, the third 11, the fourth 9, the fifth 7), then the answer is "yes" and it is clear that the *shi 'dre* is to blame. Five even sets (6, 8, 12, 10, 8), on the other hand, prove a

"no" answer. If a string of odd or even sets is broken before the fifth counting, such as three odds followed by an even set (7, 11, 9, 8), the answer is inconclusive and Meme begins the process again with a new question. Once a healer conclusively reveals the identity of the malevolent force, he ask other questions (where it came from, what it wants) until he gathers all necessary information.

12. See Höfer 1974:177, Peters 1978:69, and Holmberg 1989:135–36, 159. This manner of purifying and so appeasing the gods of one's habitat has its roots in the ancient folk religion of Tibet (Tucci 1980:167–68).

13. The way in which the gods "fall" into a body, and the effect this act typically has on Yolmo shamans, parallels the oracular possessions of Tibetan spirit mediums (see Nebesky-Wojkowitz 1956, Stein 1972).

14. Yolmo wa define *sri* as any "recurring harm" or misfortune: recurring quarrels within a household, misfortunes within a village, or a series of illnesses or deaths within a family are the effects of *sri*. Most often, *sri* denotes the ghost of a deceased person that enters into the body of a close relative (such as a sibling) and causes that person to wither away. "It is as if one is dying," Latu explained. "One gets very thin, and may become as if everything is binding together. The body turns in on itself, and becomes very weak."

The latter symptomology refers to the *sri* of young infants, for villagers understand that, when a child dies, its spirit can reenter the mother's womb on her next pregnancy. The invading *sri* drains the mother of blood and strength, making her thin, weak, and prone to illness. When the mother gives birth, the *sri* enters into the newborn infant's body and "eats" away at that child. If the child dies, the *sri* returns to the mother's womb to begin the process anew. It is therefore necessary to stop a *sri*'s onslaught before it causes irrevocable harm. Indeed, several healings that I witnessed worked to exorcise a *sri* from a frail infant (who, in my view, occasionally suffered from dysentery).

15. Patron(s) denotes the host(s) of the healing ceremony, usually the patient and his or her extended family.

16. *Ding ding*: feeling "heavy," congested, suffocated in consciousness; the sensation of blacking out when in fever.

17. That is, in order to retrieve the patient's lost "life."

18. In this context, *tsher ka* refers to stabbing pains felt internally, having the sensation of piercing—like a nerve being pinched, or muscle cramps.

19. *Dolakha Mai* and *Dolakha Bhinsen* are apparently two Hindu deities located in the village of Dolakha.

20. Yurung Bon is one of the five primordial shamans who serve as tutelary spirits for Yolmo healers.

21. *Tsabu tsubu*: restlessness, uneasiness, anxiety; also a feeling of "suffocation."

22. *Tashing nashing*: series of pain sensations felt on the surface of the skin; as felt from heat, a thorn, etc.

23. Undecipherable. Probably a place name or pilgrimage site.

24. *Yarpe marpe*: literally, to go up, to go down, to change position continuously: anxiety, confusion.

25. *Sems pa len ni mi 'dug*: implies that one cannot hold or "catch" one's heart and so contain one's feelings within the body.

26. *Ginda*, a supernatural affliction, is "set" like a trap is set.

27. Bachelard, 1964:225.

28. Mumford, 1989:120–21.

29. Holmberg, 1989:163.

30. Sagant, 1976:81.

31. March, 1979; Peters, 1981. See also Turner, 1967; Lewis, 1971; Harris, 1978; Boddy, 1989.

32. Holmberg writes of shamanic divinations among Tamang: "At the inception of a revelatory sequence, one bombo, for instance, chants that the sponsor is under assault from all manner of harmful agents and in a state of fearful helplessness. He declares that she is frozen in fear (*thom-thom*), stumbling about in a dark haze (*rhi-rhi*), and vigorously shaken; 'her body is helpless; her heartmind is riven with anxiety'" (1989:166). As in Helambu, we find an emphasis on emotional distress: hazy feelings of fear, anxiety, and helplessness. Holmberg concludes that, for Tamang, "The revelatory sequence is performed to bring order to these inchoate states" (1989:166). But I would suggest that Yolmo divinations serve less to order a patient's subjectivity than to articulate it.

33. See Lévi-Strauss, 1950; Ricouer, 1970.

34. Lewis, 1971; Skorupski, 1976.

35. Nietzsche, 1967:327.

36. Joyce, (1964) 1916.

37. Gadamer, 1975:133.

38. Armstrong, 1971.

39. See Iser, 1978; Bruner, 1986.

40. I find it interesting, in this regard, that divination is achieved in numerous societies by permitting the body to "speak" through its varied gestures, from Navajo "hand trembling" (Levy, Neutra, and Parker 1987) to the "automatic writing" of European spiritualists and surrealists, to Mayan divinations based on a sense of "lightening" pulsing through the body (B. Tedlock 1981; D. Tedlock 1990).

41. Bateson, 1972:319.

42. I doubt that Bateson would disagree with these phrasings. See Bateson and Bateson, 1987.

Chapter 7: Metamorphoses

1. See Geertz (1973) and Skorupski (1976), respectively, for exemplary rationales for investigations into the meanings and beliefs of ritual practices.

2. See Ortner, 1978; Paul, 1979; and Kapferer, 1983.

3. See Ortner, 1978:98.

4. Bourdieu (1976), Skorupski (1976), Comaroff (1983), and Jackson (1989) point out the problems that emerge when anthropologists try to abstract semantic meanings out of nonverbal ritual performances.

5. Jackson (1989), Csordas (1990), and Stoller (n.d.) similarly attend to the bodiliness of ritual performances.

6. Geertz (1968:108) reports that anthropologists cannot get "phenomeno-

logically accurate descriptions of religious experience" for they must rely on detached analysis. See Poole (1982) for a response to Geertz.

7. See Bourdieu (1977:3) and Jackson (1989:125–27) on the ineffability of ritual performance.

8. Stroll, 1988.

9. Meme's rites of "binding" compare to the invocations performed by Brahman priests of central Nepal at the onset of ghost exorcisms (Gray 1987; Höfer and Shrestha 1973:69).

10. Höfer, 1981:32.

11. Höfer, 1981:47–48.

12. Tucci, 1980:237, 244; Höfer, 1974:181.

13. Jaschke, 1949:117.

14. See Beyer, 1973; Tucci, 1980.

15. Bourdieu, 1977.

16. Bourdieu, 1977:116.

17. March, 1979; Holmberg, 1989.

18. Watters, 1975:150.

19. Ortner, 1978:93.

20. See Tucci, 1980:177; Höfer, 1981:23,111; Beyer, 1973:330,416; Nebesky-Wojkowitz, 1956:367, 516.

21. Artaud, 1958; Sontag, 1966.

22. Ortner, 1973; Turner, 1967; Dow, 1986; respectively.

23. Ortner, 1978.

24. Paul, 1979.

25. See Skorupski, 1976.

26. Freud, (1950) 1913:62.

27. Plessner, 1970.

Chapter 8: A Calling of Souls

1. Meme noted that, for the *tshe grub* rite to be most effective, the patient must "visualize" (*sgom*) that the sun is beginning to rise from the crest of the head, and that the *tshe*-flower is descending from the heavens. Other villagers suggested that one may envision "snow falling and covering all over the body." For Latu, a person should liken his or her body to a mountain covered with snow, "from first being bare to becoming brighter and brighter."

2. *Snang ba mtha' yas* ("nangpa thaye") denotes the name and heavenly locale of a Buddha. *Rter tshugs* ("tsertshug") is the immaterial space that tops the fontanel.

3. Yu, 1981, 1987.

4. Stein, 1972:226.

5. Stein, 1972:226–27. See also Karmay, 1987:102, and Bawden, 1962:83.

6. Hence a Tibetan "wind horse" bears the wish "May life-force, body and strength increase like the waxing moon" (Stein 1972:223). And while Buddhist artists complete portraits of deities to aid in ritual visualization, "The painting must be made in phase with the increasing moon, capturing its increase" (Beyer 1973:460).

7. See Höfer (1981:20) and Holmberg (1989:289) on Tamang *Bon*, who parallel the primordial shamans of Yolmo wa.

8. *Dbus rnam par snang mdsad* denotes the celestial home of Vairocana, a Buddhist deity who resides in the "center-sky" (*dbus*, "ui").

9. Yolmo wa also use these Buddhist symbols during marriage ceremonies and the lama's consecration of long life. Clarke (1990:177–78) finds that the swastika and *dorje*, as well as other offerings in this context, represent worldly material fortune (*rten 'brel*, "tendil"). When I asked Meme about these images, he said that they embody "the sacred part of the earth. We should have the patient sit in this part of the pure earth." He later added that they served "to wake up the patient, to bring the spirit down, to give a firm foundation for the patient."

10. See Tucci (1980:237, 244) on the *khyung* of Tibetan mythology.

11. Compare to Rappaport, 1979.

12. These are by no means the only positions. Csordas and Kleinman (1990), for instance, note the existence of at least four models of "therapeutic process," which attribute therapeutic efficacy to either "structural," "clinical," "social," or "persuasive" elements. In my estimation, however, the most influential orientations toward ritual healing are the "intellectualist" or "symbolist" positions.

13. Skorupski, 1976.

14. Frank, 1974.

15. Malinowski, (1965) 1948.

16. See Dow (1986), Kleinman (1988). I use the term "symbolist" in a broader fashion than does Skorupski (1976).

17. Lévi-Strauss, (1967) 1950.

18. Dow, 1986.

19. Kleinman, 1988:131–33.

20. Kapferer, 1983:180.

21. Ibid.: 179–226.

22. Kleinman, 1988:134.

23. Csordas, 1983.

24. Kleinman and Song, 1979.

25. See Kleinman and Song (1979), Csordas (1988), Bourguignon (1976), Finkler (1983, 1985), and Kleinman and Gale (1982) for studies on the efficacy of religious healing.

26. Kapferer, 1983; Schieffelin, 1985b; Laderman, 1987; Roseman, 1991.

27. Schieffelin, for instance, contends that the participants of Kaluli curing seances "co-create a new reality that recontextualizes particular problematic social circumstances and enables action to be taken in regard to them" (1985b:707). Roseman, in turn, finds that songs performed by Senoi Temiar effect cures by "moving the heart to longing," an act which creates a balanced intimacy between humans and the spirit world (1991:169, 173).

28. My attention to the sensory dimensions of ritual healing builds upon recent work devoted to an emergent anthropology of the senses (Jackson 1989, Stoller 1989, Howes 1991), as well as cultural analyses of embodiment (Csordas 1990). Earlier research focused on the ability of ritual stimuli (such as drumming and hallucinogens) to excite sympathetic and parasympathetic nervous systems (Lex 1970, Joralemon 1984).

29. Hitchcock, 1967:157.
30. Mumford, 1989:170–75.
31. Holmberg, 1989:164; Peters, 1978:72; March, 1979:231.
32. Watters, 1975:146.
33. Eliade, 1964:415.
34. Allen, 1974:8.
35. Holmberg, 1989:164–65.
36. Eliade, 1964; Frazer, 1935.
37. Rubel, O'Nell, and Collado-Ardon, 1984:42.
38. Eliade, 1964:217.
39. Yu, 1981.
40. Hawkes, 1959:101–14.
41. Lessing, 1951:272.
42. Ibid.: 253.
43. See Olson's essay on "Projective Verse" in his *Human Universe* (1951).
44. Ricoeur, 1979b: 149–50.
45. Ibid.: 150.
46. See Lévi-Strauss, 1950; Fernandez, 1986.
47. Ricoeur, 1979b:149.
48. Brooks and Warren, 1961:272.
49. Baker, 1957.
50. Baker, 1957:195–96.
51. Benjamin, (1968) 1936:240.
52. Ibid.: 240.
53. Ibid.: 240.
54. Iser, 1978.
55. Ricouer, 1981.
56. Laderman, 1987:301; Turner, 1967.
57. Schieffelin, 1985b:721.
58. Ibid.: 721.
59. Ibid.: 721.
60. Hitchcock, 1976:170.
61. Ibid.: 170.
62. Lessing, 1951:273.
63. Bawden, 1962:95.
64. Hawkes, 1959.
65. Collected by the Tibetan encyclopedist *Kong sprul* from some "exorcists" in late 19th century; as cited in Martin (n.d.). Bawden (1962:102) and Mumford (1989:169) report similar litanies of the "here."
66. The winnowing tray within which the *gtor ma* cakes rest itself bears the five directions, with the side closest to Meme pointing east. When shamanizing, Meme envisions himself to be seated within the "center" (*dbus*) of the altar. These cardinal points serve as a map of Helambu, proposing a "minature replica" of its sacred geography. "It's like bringing together all the gods and goddesses," Meme said, "but placed in their proper directions."
67. Holmberg, 1989:136–37, citing Lévi-Strauss, 1981.

68. See Schieffelin (1976), Feld (1982), and Roseman (1991) for discussions of parallel uses of geographical imagery in Kaluli and Temiar curing rites.

69. Holmberg, 1980:304.

70. See Turner, 1967:28.

Chapter 9: Departures

1. Jilek, 1974, 1982; Kleinman and Song, 1979; Ness, 1980; Kleinman and Gale, 1982; Finkler, 1983, 1985.

2. Csordas, 1988.

3. Kleinman and Song (1979) and Csordas (1988) discuss how notions of "efficacy" are culturally constituted.

4. Price, 1987.

5. Much of this dream imagery, both auspicious and inauspicious, parallels Tibetan understandings, where "Of all the categories of divination, that of dreams is invested with the greatest degree of religious authority" (Ekvall 1964:272; see also Lessing 1951:275, Nebesky-Wojkowitz 156:465, Wayman 1967, Beyer 1973:370, and Desjarlais 1991a).

6. See Harris, 1978. March (1979) offers several poignant examples of how shamanic rituals among Solu-Khumbu Sherpa attend to social conflicts within and between families.

7. These findings bear out the general tenor of research on therapeutic efficacy in traditional societies, which suggests that folk healers are most effective in alleviating malaise spawned by psychological and social distress (see Bourguignon 1976:16; Kleinman 1988:131; Kleinman and Song 1979; Kleinman and Gale 1982; Jilek 1974, 1982; Ness 1980; and Finkler 1983, 1985).

8. "Falsely" here refers to the suspicion that a bombo can sincerely perform a healing without actually retrieving the patient's spirit. While Yolmo rarely consider healers to be charlatans, they occasionally question the effectiveness of their rites.

9. Kleinman, 1988:131.

10. See Kennedy, 1967:191.

11. Freud, (1956) 1917.

12. The water imagery coursing through many Yolmo dreams probably ties to the fact that when a corpse is cremated its ashes are deposited into a nearby stream.

13. See Kennedy, 1978; Osterweis, Solomon, and Green, 1984.

14. Gorer, 1965; Rosenblatt et al., 1976.

15. Lindemann, 1944; Reid, 1979.

16. To better appreciate the visceral force of Yolmo *sdug*, we might want to recall the etymology of the English word "grief": from the Latin *gravis* 'heavy', something immobile, serious, to be reckoned with (see Lewis 1960:75).

17. This observation parallels Kleinman and Gale's (1982:411) unexpected finding that both medical and folk healers in Taiwan experienced difficulty in treating patients with somatized psychiatric diseases because, the researchers concluded, the patients' "psychological and social situations had not been much changed even if symptoms were somewhat improved."

Chapter 10: Afterwords

1. Bourdieu, 1977.

2. Gadamer (1975), for instance, contends that the human sciences are distinct from the natural sciences because the truths they advance can only be understood in light of the histories of those perceiving the truths.

3. Goodman, 1968:248.

4. Geertz, 1973:89.

5. Geertz, 1960; 1973:391–98.

6. Cassirer, 1953; Langer, 1953.

7. Geertz, 1983:99, 101.

8. Geertz, 1973:444.

9. Cassirer, 1953; Langer, 1953; Geertz, 1983:94–120; Dewey, (1980) 1934; Dufrenne, 1973; Iser, 1978.

10. See Iser, 1978:3–19; Steiner, 1989.

11. Geertz, 1973:6–7.

12. Part of the failure might be due, along with his focus on semiotics, to Geertz's unwillingness to speak of the personal experiences of his informants in anything but a remote fashion. "Whatever sense we have of how things stand with someone else's inner life, we gain it through their expressions, not through some magical intrusion into their consciousness. It's all a matter of scratching surfaces" (1986:373).
    While others have successfully turned a knack for scratching surfaces into various models of experience (see Dewey 1934, Merleau-Ponty 1962, and Ricouer 1970 on Freud), Geertz depends on the truth of his statement to rule out any anthropological studies of experience, save for the most abstract and nonexperientialist of sorts (see his 1986 essay, "Making Experience, Authoring Selves," for instance). This aversion to talk of "experiences" relates to his failure to consider, in theoretical terms, either the play between culture and bodily experience, how works of art might affect their participants, or the possibility of private meaning. In the end, Geertz's call for epistemic surefootedness is achieved at the expense of a more subtle, if less certain, outlook.

13. See Garfinkle, 1967; Bourdieu, 1977.

14. Garfinkle, 1967:11.

15. Sontag, 1966:275–76.

16. Seremetakis, 1991:177.

17. On the idea that we cannot know someone else's inner life for sure, see note 12 above; on the idea that these inner lives might be illusory, see Abu-Lughod and Lutz (1990).

18. Nietzsche, 1967.

19. " 'Among other things,' he [Joyce] said, 'my book is the epic of the human body. . . . In my book, the body lives in and moves through space and is the home of a full human personality. The words I write are adapted to express first one of its functions then another. In *Lestrygonians* the stomach dominates and the rhythm of the episode is that of the peristaltic movement.' 'But the minds, the thoughts of the characters,' I began. 'If they had no body they would have no mind,' said Joyce" (Budgen, 1960:21).

20. Artaud, 1958.

21. Sontag, 1966.

22. See Jacobus, Keller, and Shuttleworth, 1990.

23. "The arts are most wonderfully rooted in substance, in the human body, in stone, in pigment, in the twanging of gut or the weight of wind on reeds" (Steiner 1989:227).

24. Scott Lash (1988) observes that a turn from discourse to images, and from interpretation to sensation, is evident in postmodern aesthetics.

25. See Stoller (1989) and the collection of essays in Howes (1991).

26. Armstrong, 1971:75.

27. Eliot, 1932.

28. Whorf, 1956.

Glossary of Terms

Words of Tibetan origin unless otherwise noted.

bān (n.)	harm-inflicting magical "arrow"
bar chad	spiritual "hindrance"
behos (n.)	fainting; "unconsciousness"
betha (n.)	harms; sores and pains
bidyā (n.)	learning, science
bla ("la")	spirit
bla 'khyer zin (?) ("la kelzin")	spirit loss
bla 'gug	hooking, summoning the spirit (ritual)
bla ma ("lama")	Buddhist priest
boksi (n.)	witch
bon	primordial shaman
bon po ("bombo")	shaman
chang	corn beer
chos ("cho")	order, customary way, dharma
dasa graha (n.)	astrological plight; "ten planets"
dbang ("wang")	power; empowerment, "initiation"
dge ba ("gewa")	"merit"; third or fifth week "merit"-making funeral
dgon pa ("gonpa")	lamaist temple
dmigs pa ("mikpa")	imagining
gtsang rab ("sanrap")	purification offering
gtor ma ("torma")	votive cakes
Helambu (n.)	Nepali name for Yolmo region
jo, jo mo	local god, goddess
khyung	mythical Garuda bird
klad pa ("lepa")	brain
klu ("lu")	serpent-deity
lam bstan ("lamten")	white funereal banner "showing the road" to heaven

las ("le") — karma; "work"

lha — deity

lo gsar ("losar") — Tibetan New Year

lus ("li") — body

mkhas pa ("keba") — artist

mi kha — gossip; "human talk"

mo — divination

nebar — anniversary funerary rite

nad pa ("nepa") — "harm"; pain, disease

'on pa — mute

phur ba — ritual "dagger"

puja (n.) — ritual offering

ri bon po ("ri bombo") — forest shaman

rnam shes ("namshe") — consciousness; "soul"

rter tshugs ("tsertshug") — an incorporeal entryway into the body above the fontanel

sbas yul ("beyul") — hidden country

sbyang par ("changpar") — "purification paper"; seventh week funerary rite to burn the "purification paper" and so transmigrate the soul (*rnam shes*)

sdig pa ("dikpa") — vice

sdug ("dhuk") — sorrow

sems ("sem") — heart-mind

sems khral (semghal) — worry, anxiety

sems pa sdug po ("sempa dhukpu") — sorrow

sems pa tsher ka ("sempa tsherka") — heartache

sgom ("gom") — meditation, contemplation

sgrib ("tip") — pollution

shi 'dre ("shindi") — ghost; spirit of a person who has not received a proper funeral

shi yul — land of the dead

skyid po ("kipu") — happiness; "comfort," warmth

sman ("men") — medicine

smyon pa ("nyonpa") — madness

snying ("nying") — organic heart

sri ("si") — recurrent misfortune; often, ghost of a dead child that recurrently afflicts a mother and her later children

srog ("sok")	life support(s)
srog dgu mi ("sok gumi")	nine men of the srog (ritual); also, name of affliction that requires this ritual
srung ga ("srunga")	protective amulet
Tamang	ethnic group of Tibetan descent
tashing nashing	"hair-pain" felt on the surfaces of the skin
thang ka	Lamaist paintings
trongba	household
tshab ("sob")	effigy of the deceased
tshe	life; life span
tshe grub ("tshe dup")	enhancing the life (ritual)
tshe nyams pa	diminished, weakened life span
tsher ka ("tsherka")	pain; pain of separation
tsher glu ("tsherlu")	song(s) of pain in separation
Yol mo wa ("Yermuwa")	ethnic group of Tibetan descent

References

Abu-Lughod, Lila. 1986. *Veiled Sentiments: Honor and Poetry in a Bedouin Society*. Berkeley: University of California Press.

———. 1990. Shifting Politics in Bedouin Love Poetry. In *Language and the Politics of Emotion*, edited by C. Lutz and L. Abu-Lughod, pp. 24–45. New York: Cambridge University Press.

Abu-Lughod, Lila, and Catherine A. Lutz. 1990. Introduction: Emotion, Discourse, and the Politics of Everyday Life. In *Language and the Politics of Emotion*, edited by C. Lutz and L. Abu-Lughod, pp. 1–23. New York: Cambridge University Press.

Ackerman, Diane. 1990. *A Natural History of the Senses*. New York: Random House.

Achterberg, Jeanne. 1985. *Imagery in Healing: Shamanism and Modern Medicine*. Boston: Shambala.

Allen, Nicholas. 1974. The Ritual Journey, a Pattern Underlying Certain Nepalese Rituals. In *Contributions to the Anthropology of Nepal*, edited by C. Von Furer-Haimendorf, pp. 6–22. Warminster, England: Aris and Phillips.

Armstrong, Robert Plant. 1971. *The Affecting Presence*. Urbana: University of Illinois Press.

Artaud, Antonin. 1958. *The Theatre and Its Double*. New York: Grove Press.

Aziz, Barbara N. 1978. *Tibetan Frontier Families*. New Durham: Carolina Academic Press.

Bachelard, Gaston. 1964. *The Poetics of Space*. Boston: Beacon.

Baker, James V. 1957. *The Sacred River: Coleridge's Theory of the Imagination*. New Orleans: Louisiana State University Press.

Bakhtin, Mikhail. 1984. *Problems of Dostoevsky's Poetics*. Minneapolis: University of Minnesota Press.

Barthes, Roland. 1970. *Writing Degree Zero*. Boston: Beacon Press.

Bateson, Gregory. 1972. *Steps to an Ecology of the Mind*. New York: Ballantine.

———. 1975. Some Components of Socialization for Trance. *Ethos* 3:143–56.

Bateson, Gregory, and Margaret Mead. 1942. *Balinese Character: A Photographic Essay*. Special Publication of the New York Academy of Sciences, Vol. 11. New York: Ballantine.

Bateson, Gregory, and Mary Bateson. 1987. *Angel's Fear: Towards an Epistemology of the Sacred*. New York: Macmillan.

Bawden, C. R. 1962. Calling the Soul: A Mongolian Litany. *Bulletin of the School of Oriental and African Studies* 25:81–103.

Beck, A. T. 1976. The Symbolic Merger of Body, Space and Cosmos in Hindu Tamil Nadu. *Contributions to Indian Sociology* 10:213–243.

Becker, A. L. 1979. Text-Building, Epistemology, and Aesthetics in Javanese Shadow Theatre. In *The Imagination of Reality*, edited by A. L. Becker and A. A. Yengoyan, pp. 211–243. Norword, NJ: AbLEX.

Beeman, William O. 1985. Dimensions of Dysphoria: The View from Linguistic Anthropology. In *Culture and Depression*, edited by A. Kleinman and B. Good, pp. 216–43. Berkeley: University of California Press.

Benjamin, Walter. 1968. The Work of Art in the Age of Mechanical Reproduction. In *Illuminations*, edited by H. Arendt, pp. 217–51. New York: Schocken Books.

Bennett, Lynn. 1983. *Dangerous Wives and Sacred Sisters: Social and Symbolic Roles of High-Caste Women in Nepal*. New York: Columbia University Press.

Berglie, Per-Arne. 1976. Preliminary Remarks on Some Tibetan "Spirit Mediums" in Nepal. *Kailash* 4:85–108.

Beyer, Stephan. 1973. *The Cult of Tara*. Berkeley: University of California Press.

Bishop, John. 1973. *Music of a Sherpa Village*. New York: Ethnic Folkway Records.

Bloch, Maurice, and Jonathan Perry, eds. 1982. *Death and the Regeneration of Life*. Cambridge: Cambridge University Press.

Boddy, Janice. 1989. *Wombs and Alien Spirits: Women, Men and the Zar Cult in Northern Sudan*. Madison: University of Wisconsin.

Bogoras, Waldemar. 1928. The Shamanistic Call and the Period of Initiation in Northern Asia and Northern America. In *Proceedings of the 23rd International Congress* (New York), pp. 441–44. Nendeln/Liechtenstein; Kraus-Thomson.

Bolton, Ralph. 1981. Susto, Hostility, and Hypoglycemia. *Ethnology* 20:261–76.

Bourdieu, Pierre. 1977. *Outline of a Theory of Practice*. Cambridge Studies in Social Anthropology. Vol. 16. Cambridge: Cambridge University Press.

———. 1984. *Distinction*. Cambridge, MA: Harvard University Press.

———. 1989. Social Space and Symbolic Power. In *In Other Words: Essays Towards a Reflexive Sociology*, pp. 123–39. Stanford, CA: Stanford University Press.

Bourguignon, Erica. 1976. The Effectiveness of Religious Healing Movements: A Review of the Recent Literature. *Transcultural Psychiatric Research Review* 8:5–21.

Bowker, John. 1970. *Problems of Suffering in Religions of the World*. Cambridge: Cambridge University Press.

———. 1991. *The Meanings of Death*. Cambridge: Cambridge University Press.

Brenneis, Donald. 1987. Performing Passions: Aesthetics and Politics in an Occasionally Egalitarian Community. *American Ethnologist* 14:236–50.

Brooks, Cleanth, and Warren, Robert Penn. 1961. *Understanding Poetry*, 3rd Ed. New York: Holt, Rinehart and Winston, Inc.

Bruner, Jerome. 1986. *Actual Minds, Possible Worlds*. Cambridge, MA: Harvard University Press.

Budgen, Frank. 1960. *James Joyce and the Making of Ulysses*. Bloomington: Indiana University Press.

Burang, Theodore. 1974. *The Tibetan Art of Healing*. Translated by Susan Macintosh. London: Robinson and Watkins.

Campbell, Joseph. 1959. *Primitive Mythology*. The Masks of God. Vol I. Middlesex, England: Penguin.

Canguilhem, Georges. 1978. *The Normal and the Pathological*. Dordrecht, Holland: D. Reidel.

Caraka. 1949. *Caraka Samhita, v. Jannayar*. India: Shree Gulpkunverba Ayurvedic Society.

Cassirer, Ernst. 1953–57. *Philosophy of Symbolic Forms*. 3 Vols. Translated by Ralph Manheim. New Haven: Yale University Press.

Chandra, Lokesh. 1984. Introduction. In *Tibetan Buddhist Medicine and Psychiatry: The Diamond Healing*, by Terry Clifford. York Beach, ME: Samuel Weisner.

Chernoff, John M. 1979. *African Rhythm and African Sensibility: Aesthetics and Social Action in African Musical Idioms*. Chicago: University of Chicago Press.

Cheung, F., et al. 1981. Somatization among Chinese Depressives in General Practice. *International Journal of Psychiatry in Medicine* 10:361–74.

Clarke, Graham E. 1980a. Lama and Tamang in Yolmo. In *Tibetan Studies in Honor of Hugh Richardson*, edited by Michael Aris and Aung San Suu Kyi, pp. 79–86. Warminster, England: Aris and Phillips.

———. 1980b. A Helambu History. *Journal of the Nepal Research Centre* 4:1–38.

———. 1980c. *The Temple and Kinship Among a Buddhist People of the Himalaya*. Ph.D. Dissertation, University of Oxford.

———. 1983. The Great and Little Traditions in the Study of Yolmo, Nepal. In *Contributions on Tibetan Language, History and Culture*, edited by Ernst Steinkellner and Helmut Tauscher, vol. 1, pp. 21–37. Vienna: Arbeitskreis Fur Tibetische und Buddhistische Studien, University of Vienna.

———. 1985. Equality and Hierarchy among a Buddhist People of Nepal. In *Contexts and Levels: Anthropological Essays on Hierarchy*, edited by R. H. Barnes, D. de Coppet, and R. J. Parkin, pp. 193–209. Oxford: JASO Occasional Papers, no. 4.

———. 1990. Ideas of Merit (*bsod-nams*), Virtue (*dge-ba*), Blessing (*byin-rlabs*) and Material Prosperity (*rten-'brel*) in Highland Nepal. *Journal of the Anthropological Society of Oxford* 21:165–84.

———. 1991. Nara (*na-rag*) in Yolmo: A Social History of Hell in Helambu. In *Festschrift für Geza Uray*, edited by M. T. Much, pp. 43–62. Vienna: Arbeitskreis fur Tibetische und Buddhistische Studien, Universitat Wien.

Clarke, Graham E., and Manandhar, Thakurlal. 1988. A Malla Copper-Plate from Sindu-Palchok. *Journal of the Nepal Research Centre* 8:105–39.

Clifford, Terry. 1984. *Tibetan Buddhist Medicine and Psychiatry: The Diamond Healing*. York Beach, ME: Samuel Weisner.

Coleridge, S. T. 1967 [1817]. *Biographic Literaria*. London: Oxford University Press.

Comaroff, Jean. 1983. The Defectiveness of Symbols or the Symbols of Defectiveness? On the Cultural Analysis of Medical Systems. *Culture, Medicine and Psychiatry* 7:3–20.

———. 1985. *Body of Power, Spirit of Resistance: The Culture and History of a South African People*. Chicago: University of Chicago Press.

Connerton, Paul. 1989. *How Societies Remember*. Cambridge: Cambridge University Press.

Crapanzano, Vincent. 1989. Preliminary Notes on the Glossing of Emotions. *Kroeber Anthropological Society* 69–70:78–85.

Csordas, Thomas. 1983. The Rhetoric of Transformation in Ritual Healing. *Culture, Medicine and Psychiatry* 7:333–76.

————. 1988. Elements of Charismatic Persuasion and Healing. *Medical Anthropology Quarterly* 2:121–42.

————. 1990. Embodiment as a Paradigm for Anthropology. *Ethos* 18:5–47.

Csordas, T., and A. Kleinman. 1990. The Therapeutic Process. In *Medical Anthropology: A Handbook of Theory and Method*, edited by T. M. Johnson and C. Sargent, pp. 11–25. New York: Greenwood Press.

D'Andrade, Roy. 1987. A Folk Model of the Mind. In *Cultural Models in Language and Thought*, edited by D. Holland and N. Quinn, pp. 112–50. Cambridge: Cambridge University Press.

Daniel, E. V. 1984. *Fluid Signs: Being a Person the Tamil Way*. Berkeley: University of California Press.

Das, Chandra. 1987 [1902]. *A Tibetan-English Dictionary*. Kathmandu, Nepal: Ratna Pustak Bhandar.

Deren, Maya. 1970. *Divine Horsemen: The Voodoo Gods of Haiti*. New York: Delta.

Derrida, Jacques. 1978. *Writing and Difference*. Chicago: University of Chicago Press.

————. 1981. *Dissemination*. Translated by Barbara Johnson. Chicago: University of Chicago Press.

Desjarlais, Robert. 1989. Healing Through Images: The Magical Flight and Healing Geography of Nepali Shamans. *Ethos* 17:289–307.

————. 1991a. Dreams, Divination and Yolmo Ways of Knowing. *Dreaming* 1:211–24.

————. 1991b. Poetic Transformations of Yolmo "Sadness." *Culture, Medicine and Psychiatry* 15:387–420.

————. 1992. Yolmo Aesthetics of Body, Health and "Soul Loss." *Social Science and Medicine* 34:1105–1117.

Devereux, George. 1967. *From Anxiety to Method in the Behavioral Sciences*. The Hague: Mouton.

————. 1980. *Basic Problems in Ethnopsychiatry*. Chicago: University of Chicago.

Dewey, John. 1980 [1934]. *Art as Experience*. New York: Perigee Books.

Douglas, Mary. 1970. *Natural Symbols*. New York: Vintage.

Dow, James. 1986. Universal Aspects of Symbolic Healing: A Theoretical Synthesis. *American Anthropologist* 88:56–69.

Dufrenne, Michel. 1973. *The Phenomenology of Aesthetic Experience*. Evanston, IL: Northwestern University Press.

Durkheim, Emile. 1965 [1912]. *The Elementary Forms of the Religious Life*. New York: Free Press.

Ekvall, Robert B. 1963. Some Aspects of Divination in Tibetan Society. *Ethnology* 2:31–39.

————. 1964. *Religious Observances in Tibet: Patterns and Function*. Chicago: University of Chicago Press.

Eliade, Mircea. 1964. *Shamanism: Archaic Techniques of Ecstasy*. Princeton: Princeton University Press.

Eliot, T. S. 1932. *Selected Essays: 1917–1932*. London: Faber and Faber.

Evans-Wentz, W. Y. 1960. *The Tibetan Book of the Dead*. London: Oxford University Press.

———. 1974. *Tibet's Greatest Yogi, Mila Repa*. Oxford: Oxford University Press.

Fardon, Richard. 1985. *Power and Knowledge: Anthropological and Sociological Approaches*. Edinburgh: Scottish Academic Press.

Feld, Steven. 1982. *Sound and Sentiment*. Philadelphia: University of Pennsylvania Press.

Fernandez, James. 1986. *Persuasions and Performances: The Play of Tropes in Culture*. Bloomington: Indiana University Press.

———. 1987. The Argument of Images and the Experience of Returning to the Whole. In *The Anthropology of Experience*, edited by V. Turner and E. Bruner, pp. 159–87. Urbana: University of Illinois Press.

Filliozat, Jean. 1964. *The Classical Doctrine of Indian Medicine*. Translated by Dev Raj Chana. Delhi: Munshiram Manoharlal.

Finkler, Kaja. 1983. *Spiritualist Healers in Mexico*. New York: Praeger.

———. 1985. Symptomatic Differences Between the Sexes in Rural Mexico. *Culture, Medicine and Psychiatry* 9:27–57.

Fortes, Meyer. 1969. *Kinship and the Social Order*. Chicago: Aldine Publishing Company.

Foucault, Michel. 1966. *Madness and Civilization*. New York: Mentor.

———. 1972. *The Archaeology of Knowledge*. New York: Harper Colophon.

———. 1988. Technologies of the Self. In *Technologies of the Self*, edited by L. H. Martin, H. Gutman, and P. Hutton, pp. 16–49. Amherst: University of Massachusetts Press.

Fox, James. 1974. "Our Ancestors Speak in Pairs": Rotinese Views of Language, Dialect and Code. In *Explorations in the Ethnography of Speaking*, edited by R. Bauman and J. Sherzer, pp. 65–88. Cambridge: Cambridge University Press.

Frank, Jerome. 1974. *Persuasion and Healing: A Comparative Study of Psychotherapy*. New York: Schocken Books.

Frazer, James. 1935. *Taboo and the Perils of the Soul*. New York: Macmillan.

Freud, Sigmund. 1950 [1913]. *Totem and Taboo*. New York: Norton.

———. 1956 [1917]. Mourning and Melancholia. In *Collected Papers*, edited by J. Strachey, Vol. IV, pp. 152–70. London: Hogarth Press.

Gadamer, Hans-George. 1975. *Truth and Method*. New York: Crossroads.

Gaines, Atwood, and Paul Farmer. 1986. Visible Saints: Social Cynosures and Dysphoria in the Mediterranean Tradition. *Culture, Medicine and Psychiatry* 10:295–330.

Garfinkle, Harold. 1967. *Studies in Ethnomethodology*. Englewood Cliffs, NJ: Prentice-Hall.

Geertz, Clifford. 1960. *The Religion of Java*. Glencoe, IL: The Free Press.

———. 1968. *Islam Observed*. New Haven: Yale University Press.

———. 1973. *The Interpretation of Cultures*. New York: Basic Books.

———. 1983. *Local Knowledge*. New York: Basic Books.

———. 1986. Making Experience, Authoring Selves. In *The Anthropology of Experience*, edited by V. Turner and E. Bruner, pp. 373–80. Urbana, IL: University of Illinois.

———. 1988. *Works and Lives*. Palo Alto: Stanford University Press.

Gibson, James. 1950. *Perception of the Visual World*. Boston: Houghton Mifflin.

Gillin, John. 1948. Magical Fright. *Psychiatry* 11:387–400.

Good, Byron. n.d. *Medicine, Rationality and Experience: An Anthropological Perspective*. Cambridge: Cambridge University Press. Forthcoming.

Good, Byron, and Mary-Jo Good. 1982. Toward a Meaning-Centered Analysis of Popular Illness Categories: "Fright Illness" and "Heart Distress" in Iran. In *Cultural Conceptions of Mental Health and Therapy*, edited by A.J. Marsella and G. White, pp. 141–66. Boston: D. Reidel.

Good, B., Good, Mary-Jo, and Robert Moradi. 1985. The Interpretation of Iranian Depressive Illness and Dysphoric Affect. In *Culture and Depression*, edited by A. Kleinman and B. Good, pp. 369–428. Berkeley: University of California Press.

Goodman, Nelson. 1968. *Languages of Art*. Indianapolis: Bobbs-Merrill.

Gorer, Geoffrey. 1965. *Death, Grief, and Mourning in Contemporary Britain*. London: Cresset Press.

Gray, John. 1987. Bayu Utarnu: Ghost Exorcism and Sacrifice in Nepal. *Ethnology* 26:179–99.

Hallowell, A. Irving. 1955. The Self in Its Behavioral Environment. In *Culture and Experience*, pp. 75–110. Philadelphia: University of Pennsylvania Press.

Hardman, Charlotte. 1981. The Psychology of Conformity and Self-Expression among the Lohorung Rai of East Nepal. In *Indigenous Psychologies: The Anthropology of the Self*, edited by P. Heelas and A. Lock, pp. 161–79. London: Academic.

Harner, Michael. 1980. *The Way of the Shaman*. San Francisco: Harper and Row.

Harris, Grace G. 1978. *Casting Out Anger: Religion Among the Taita of Kenya*. Cambridge: Cambridge University Press.

Hawkes, David. 1959. *Ch'u Tz'u: The Songs of the South*. Oxford: Clarendon Press.

Hertz, Robert. 1960. *Death and the Right Hand*. Glencoe, IL: Free Press.

Herzfeld, Michael. 1985. *The Poetics of Manhood: Contest and Indentity in a Cretan Mountain Village*. Princeton: Princeton University Press.

Hester, Marcus B. 1967. *The Meaning of Poetic Metaphor*. The Hague: Mouton.

Hitchcock, John T. 1967. A Nepalese Shamanism and the Classic Inner Asian Tradition. *History of Religions* 7:149–58.

———. 1976. Aspects of Bhujel Shamanism. In *Spirit Possession in the Nepal Himalayas*, edited by J. T. Hitchcock and R. L. Jones, pp. 165–96. Warminster, England: Aris and Phillips.

Höfer, Andras. 1974. Is the "Bombo" an Ecstatic? Some Ritual Techniques of Tamang Shamanism. In *Contributions to the Anthropology of Nepal*, edited by C. Furer-Haimendorf, pp. 168–82. Warminster: Aris and Phillips.

———. 1981. *Tamang Ritual Texts, I: Preliminary Studies in the Folk-Religion of an Ethnic Minority in Nepal*. Wiesbaden: Franz Steiner.

Höfer, Andras, and Bishnu P. Shrestha. 1973. Ghost Exorcism among the Brahmans of Central Nepal. *Central Asiatic Journal* 17:51–77.

Holmberg, David. 1980. Lama, Shaman, and Lambu in Tamang Religious Practice. Ph.D. Dissertation, Cornell University.

———. 1989. *Order in Paradox: Myth, Ritual and Exchange among Nepal's Tamang*. Ithaca: Cornell University Press.

Howes, David, ed. 1991. *The Varieties of Sensory Experience: A Sourcebook in the Anthropology of the Senses*. Toronto: University of Toronto Press.

Huntington, Richard, and Peter Metcalfe. 1979. *Celebrations of Death: The Anthropology of Mortuary Ritual*. Cambridge: Cambridge University Press.

Irvine, Judith. 1982. Language and Affect: Some Cross-Cultural Issues. In *Contemporary Perceptions of Language: Interdisciplinary Dimensions*, edited by Heidi Byrnes, pp. 31–47. Washington, D.C.: Georgetown University Press.

Iser, Wolfgang. 1978. *The Act of Reading: A Theory of Aesthetic Response*. Baltimore: John Hopkins University Press.

Jackson, Michael. 1989. *Paths Towards a Clearing*. Bloomington: University of Indiana Press.

Jacobus, Mary, Evelyn Fox Keller, and Sally Shuttleworth. 1990. *Body/Politics: Women and the Discourses of Science*. New York: Routledge.

Jameson, Frederic. 1972. *The Prison-House of Language*. Princeton, N. J.: Princeton University Press.

Jaschke, Heinrich A. 1949. *A Tibetan-English Dictionary*. London: Routledge and Kegan Paul Ltd.

Jilek, Wolfgang. 1974. *Salish Indian Mental Health and Culture Change*. Toronto: Holt, Rinehart and Winston.

———. 1982. *Indian Healing*. Surrey: Hancock House.

Johansson, R. E. A. 1970. *The Psychology of Nirvana*. Garden City, NY: Doubleday/Anchor.

Johnson, Mark. 1987. *The Body in the Mind*. Chicago: Chicago University Press.

Joralemon, Donald. 1984. The Role of Hallucinogenic Drugs and Sensory Stimuli in Peruvian Ritual Healing. *Culture, Medicine and Psychiatry* 8:399–430.

Joyce, James. 1964 [1916]. *Portrait of the Artist as a Young Man*. New York: Viking Press.

Jung, C. G. 1969. The Psychology of Transference. In *The Collected Works of C. G. Jung, Volume 16: The Practice of Psychotherapy*. Princeton, NJ: Princeton University Press.

Kapferer, Bruce. 1983. *A Celebration of Demons: Exorcism and the Aesthetics of Healing in Sri Lanka*. Bloomington: Indiana University Press.

Karmay, S. G. 1987. L'âme et la turquoise: un rituel Tibetain. *L'Ethnographie* 83:97–130.

Kennedy, John. 1967. Nubian Zar Ceremonies as Psychotherapy. *Human Organization* 26:185–94.

———. 1973. Cultural Psychiatry. In *Handbook of Social and Cultural Anthropology*, edited by J. Honigmann, pp. 1119–98. Chapel Hill: University of North Carolina.

———. 1978. Death Ceremonies. In *Nubian Ceremonial Life*, edited by John G. Kennedy, pp. 224–44. Berkeley: University of California Press.

Keyes, Charles. 1983. Merit Transference in the Karmic Theory of Popular Theravada Buddhism. In *Karma: An Anthropological Inquiry*, edited by C. Keyes and E. V. Daniel, pp. 261–86. Berkeley: University of California Press.

———. 1985. The Interpretive Basis of Depression. *Culture and Depression*, edited by A. Kleinman and B. Good, pp. 153–74. Berkeley: University of California Press.

Kiev, Ari. 1968. *Curanderismo: Mexican-American Folk Psychiatry*. New York: Free Press.

Kirmayer, Lawrence. 1984. Culture, Affect and Somatization, parts 1 and 2. *Transcultural Psychiatric Research Review* 21(3):159–88, (4):237–62.

Kleinman, Arthur. 1984. Somatization. *Referential Journal of Psychiatry* (China) 2:65–68.

———. 1986. *Social Origins of Distress and Disease: Depression, Neurasthenia and Pain in Modern China*. New Haven: Yale University Press.

———. 1988. *Rethinking Psychiatry*. New York: Free Press.

Kleinman, Arthur, and L. H. Song. 1979. Why do Indigenous Practitioners Successfully Heal?: A Follow-up Study of Indigenous Practice in Taiwan. *Social Science and Medicine* 13O:7–26.

Kleinman, Arthur, and J. Gale. 1982. Patients Treated by Physicians and Folk Healers: A Comparative Outcome Study in Taiwan. *Culture, Medicine and Psychiatry* 6:405–23.

Kleinman, Arthur, and Joan Kleinman. 1991. Suffering and Its Professional Transformation: Toward an Ethnography of Experience. *Culture, Medicine and Psychiatry* 15:275–301.

———. n.d. Remembering the Cultural Revolution: Alienating Pains and the Pain of Alienation/Transformation. Paper Presented to the Association for Asian Studies Annual Meeting, April, 1991, New Orleans.

Kligman, Gail. 1988. *The Wedding of the Dead: Ritual, Poetics, and Popular Culture in Transylvania*. Berkeley: University of California Press.

Kluckhohn, Clyde. 1941. Patterning as Exemplified in Navajo Culture. In *Language, Culture, and Personality*, edited by L. Spier, A. I. Hallowell, and S. Newman, pp. 109–30. Menasha, WI: Sapir Memorial Publication Fund.

———. 1951. Values and Value-Orientation in the Theory of Action. In *Toward a General Theory of Action*, edited by T. Parsons and E. Shils, pp. 388–433. Cambridge, MA: Harvard University Press.

Kohut, Heinz. 1977. *The Restoration of the Self*. New York: International Universities Press.

Kroeber, A. L. 1949. Values as a Subject of Natural Science Inquiry. *Proceedings of the National Academy of Sciences* 35:261–64.

Kroeber, A. L., and Clyde Kluckhohn. 1952. Culture: A Critical Review of Concepts and Definitions. *Papers of the Peabody Museum of American Archaeology and Ethnology, Harvard University*. Vol. 47, no. 1.

Kunitz, Stanley. 1985. *Next to Last Things*. Boston: Atlantic Monthly Press.

Kupfer, Joseph. 1983. *Experience as Art: Aesthetics in Everyday Life*. Albany: State University of New York.

Laderman, Carol. 1987. The Ambiguity of Symbols in the Structure of Healing. *Social Science and Medicine* 24:293–301.

———. 1991. *Taming the Wind of Desire: Psychology, Medicine, and Aesthetics in Malay Shamanistic Performance*. Berkeley: University of California Press.

Lakoff, George, and Zoltan Kovecses. 1987. The Cognitive Model of Anger Inherent in American English. In *Cultural Models in Language and Thought*, edited by D. Holland and N. Quinn, pp. 195–221. Cambridge: Cambridge University Press.

Langer, Susanne. 1953. *Feeling and Form*. New York: MacMillan.

Lash, Scott. 1988. Discourse or Figure? Postmodernism as a "Regime of Signification." *Theory, Culture and Society* 5:311–36.

Leiris, Michel. 1934. *L'Afrique fantome*. Paris: Gallimard.

Lessing, Ferdinand. 1951. Calling the Soul: A Lamaist Ritual. *Semitic and Oriental Studies* 11:263–84.

Levine, Nancy. 1981. Perspectives on Love: Morality and Affect in Nyinba Interpersonal Relationships. In *Culture and Morality*, edited by A.C. Mayer, pp. 106–25. Delhi: Oxford University Press.

———. 1987. Caste, State, and Ethnic Boundaries in Nepal. *Journal of Asian Studies* 46:71–88.

Lévi-Strauss, Claude. 1967 [1950]. The Effectiveness of Symbols. In *Structural Anthropology*, pp. 167–85. New York: Basic Books.

———. 1967. *Structural Anthropology*. New York: Basic Books.

———. 1969. *The Raw and the Cooked*. New York: Harper and Row.

———. 1981. *The Naked Man*. New York: Harper and Row.

Levy, Jerrold, Raymond Neutra, and Dennis Parker. 1987. *Hand Trembling, Frenzy Witchcraft, and Moth Madness*. Tucson: University of Arizona Press.

Levy, Robert. 1973. *Tahitians: Mind and Experience in the Society Islands*. Chicago: University of Chicago Press.

———. 1984. Emotion, Knowing and Culture. In *Culture Theory: Essays on Mind, Self and Emotion*, edited by R. Shweder and R. Levine, pp. 214–37. Cambridge: Cambridge University Press.

Lewis, C. S. 1960. *Studies in Words*. Cambridge: Cambridge University Press.

Lewis, I. M. 1971. *Ecstatic Religion: An Anthropological Study of Spirit Possession and Shamanism*. Harmondsworth: Penguin.

Lex, Barbara. 1979. The Neurobiology of Ritual Trance. In *The Spectrum of Ritual: A Biogenetic Structural Analysis*, edited by E. G. Di'Aquili, C. D. Laughlin, Jr., and J. McManus, pp. 117–51. New York: Columbia University Press.

Lichter, David, and Lawrence Epstein. 1983. Irony in Tibetan Notions of the Good Life. In *Karma: An Anthropological Inquiry*, edited by C. Keyes and E. V. Daniel, pp. 223–59. Berkeley: University of California.

Lindemann, Erich. 1944. Symptomology and Management of Acute Grief. *American Journal of Psychiatry* 101:141–48.

Lutz, Catherine. 1985. Ethnopsychology Compared to What? Explaining Behavior and Consciousness Among the Ifaluk. In *Person, Self, and Experience: Exploring Pacific Ethnopsychologies*, edited by G. M. White and J. Kirpatrick, pp. 35–79. Berkeley: University of California Press.

———. 1988. *Unnatural Emotions*. Chicago: University of Chicago Press.

Lutz, Catherine, and Geoffrey White. 1986. The Anthropology of Emotions. *Annual Review of Anthropology* 15:405–36.

Macdonald, A. W. 1980. Creative Dismemberment Among the Tamang and Sherpas of Nepal. In *Tibetan Studies in Honor of Hugh Richardson*, edited by M. Aris and A. San Suu Kyi, pp. 199–208. Warminster: Aris and Phillips.

Maine, Sir Henry. 1861. *Ancient Law*. London: Murray.

Malinowski, Bronislaw. 1965 [1948]. *Coral Gardens and Their Magic*. Bloomington: Indiana University Press.

March, Kathryn S. 1979. The Intermediacy of Women. Ph.D. Dissertation, Cornell University.

———. 1984. Weaving, Writing and Gender. *Man* 18:729–44.

Margulies, Alfred. 1984. Toward Empathy: The Uses of Wonder. *The American Journal of Psychiatry* 141:1025–33.

Marriot, McKim. 1976. Hindu Transactions: Diversity without Dualism. In *Transaction and Meaning*, edited by Bruce Kapferer, pp. 109–42. Philadelphia: Institute for the Study of Human Issues.

Marsella, Anthony. 1980. Depressive Experience and Disorder across Cultures. In *Handbook of Cross-Cultural Psychology*, edited by H. Triandis and J. Draguns, Vol. 6, pp. 237–90. Boston: Allyn and Bacon.

———. 1985. Culture, Self and Mental Disorder. In *Culture and Self: Asian and Western Perspectives*, edited by A. Marsella, G. Devos, and F. Hsu, pp. 281–308. New York: Tavistock.

Marsella, Anthony, George Devos, and Francis Hsu, eds. 1985. *Culture and Self: Asian and Western Perspectives*. New York: Tavistock.

Marsella, Anthony, and Geoffrey White. 1982. *Cultural Conceptions of Mental Health and Therapy*. Boston: D. Reidel.

Martin, Dan. n.d. Calling, Hooking and Ransoming: Popular Tibetan Rituals for Recovering Lost Souls. Unpublished Paper.

Martin, Emily. 1987. *The Woman in the Body: A Cultural Analysis of Reproduction*. Boston: Beacon Press.

Mattingly, Cheryl. 1988. Thinking With Stories: Story and Experience in a Clinical Practice. Ph.D. Dissertation, Massachusetts Institute of Technology.

McHugh, Ernestine. 1989. Concepts of the Person among the Gurungs of Nepal. *American Ethnologist* 16:75–86.

Merleau-Ponty, Maurice. 1962. *The Phenomenology of Perception*. London: Routledge and Kegan Paul.

Merwin, W. S. 1980. *Selected Translations: 1968–1978*. New York: Atheneum.

Mishler, Eliot G. 1986. *Research Interviewing: Context and Narrative*. Cambridge, MA: Harvard University Press.

Moore, Marianne. 1935. *Selected Poems*. New York: Macmillan.

Mumford, Stanley. 1989. *Himalayan Dialogue*. Madison: University of Wisconsin Press.

Nader, Laura. 1990. *Harmony Ideologies: Justice and Control in a Zapotec Mountain Village*. Stanford: Stanford University Press.

Nakazawa, Shinichi. 1986. The Zero Logic of Disease: A Critique of Violence. *Monumenta Serindica* 15:117–66.

Nebesky-Wojkowitz, Rene de. 1956. *Oracles and Demons of Tibet*. The Hague.

Ness, Robert C. 1980. The Impact of Indigenous Healing Activity: An Empirical Study of Two Fundamentalist Churches. *Social Science and Medicine* 14:167–80.

Nichter, Mark. 1981. Idioms of Distress. *Culture, Medicine and Psychiatry* 5:379–408.

Nietzsche, Friedrich. 1964 [1895]. *Nietzsche Contra Wagner*. New York: Russell and Russell.

———. 1967. *The Will to Power*. New York: Vintage.

Noll, Richard. 1985. Mental Imagery Cultivation as a Cultural Phenomenon. *Current Anthropology* 26:44–61.

Obeyesekere, Gananath. 1981. *Medusa's Hair: An Essay on Personal Symbols and Religious Experience*. Chicago: University of Chicago Press.

———. 1985. Depression, Buddhism, and the Work of Culture in Sri Lanka. In *Culture and Depression*, edited by A. Kleinman and B. Good, pp. 134–52. Berkeley: University of California Press.

———. 1990. *The Work of Culture*. Chicago: University of Chicago Press.

O'Flaherty, Wendy. 1973. *Asceticism and Eroticism in the Mythology of Siva*. London: Oxford University Press.

———. 1980. *Women, Androgynes and Other Mythical Beasts*. Chicago: University of Chicago Press.

Olson, Charles. 1951. *Human Universe*. New York: Grove Press.

O'Nell, Carl W. 1975. An Investigation of Reported "Fright" as a Factor in the Etiology of Susto, "Magical Fright." *Ethos* 3:41–63.

Opler, Morris. 1945. Themes as Dynamic Forces in Culture. *American Journal of Sociology* 51:198–206.

Ortner, Sherry. 1970. Food for Thought: A Key Symbol in Sherpa Culture. Ph.D. Dissertation, University of Chicago.

———. 1973. Sherpa Purity. *American Anthropologist* 75:49–63.

———. 1978. *Sherpas Through their Rituals*. New York: Cambridge University Press.

———. 1984. Theory in Anthropology since the Sixties. *Comparative Studies in Society and History* 26:126–66.

———. 1989. *High Religion: A Cultural and Political History of Sherpa Buddhism*. Princeton: Princeton University Press.

Osterweis, Marian, Frederic Solomon, and Morris Green, eds. 1984. *Bereavement: Reactions, Consequences and Care*. Washington: National Academy Press.

Pandolfi, Mariella. 1990. Boundaries Inside the Body: Women's Sufferings in Southern Peasant Italy. *Culture, Medicine and Psychiatry* 14:255–73.

Parker, Barbara. 1988. Ritual Coordination of Medical Pluralism in Highland Nepal: Implications for Policy. *Social Science and Medicine* 27:919–25.

Parkes, Colin Murray. 1972. *Bereavement: Studies in Grief in Adult Life*. New York: International Universities Press.

Paul, Robert. 1970. Sherpas and Their Religion. Unpublished Ph.D. Dissertation. University of Chicago.

———. 1976. The Sherpa Temple as a Model of the Psyche. *American Ethnologist* 3:131–46.

———. 1979. Dumje: Paradox and Resolution in Sherpa Ritual Symbolism. *American Ethnologist* 6:274–304.

Peters, Larry. 1978. Psychotherapy in Tamang Shamanism. *American Ethnologist* 7:397–418.

———. 1981. *Ecstasy and Healing in Nepal: An Ethnopsychiatric Study of Tamang Shamanism*. Malibu, CA: Undena Publications.

Pignede, Bernard. 1966. *Les Gurungs*. Paris: Mouton.

Plessner, Helmuth. 1970. *Laughing and Crying: A Study of the Limits of Human Behavior*. Evanston, IL: Northwestern University Press.

Poole, Fitz John Porter. 1982. The Ritual Forging of Identity: Aspects of Person and Self in Bimin-Kuskusmin Male Initiation. In *Rituals of Manhood*, edited by G. Herdt, pp. 99–154. Berkeley: University of California.

Porée-Maspero, Eveline. 1951. La Cérémonie de l'Appel des Esprits Vitaux. *Bulletin de l'École Francaise d'Extrême-Orient* 45:145–69.

Price, Laurie. 1987. Ecuadorian Illness Stories: Cultural Knowledge in Natural Discourse. In *Cultural Models in Language and Thought*, edited by D. Holland and N. Quinn, pp. 313–42. Cambridge: Cambridge University Press.

Rahula, Walpola. 1959. *What the Buddha Taught*. New York: Gordon Fraser.

Rappaport, Roy. 1979. *Ecology, Meaning and Religion*. Richmond, CA: North Atlantic Books.

Reid, Janice. 1979. A Time to Live, A Time to Grieve: Patterns and Processes of Mourning Among the Yolngu of Australia. *Culture, Medicine and Psychiatry* 3:319–46.

Richards, I. A. 1952. *Principles of Literary Criticism*. New York: Harcourt, Brace and Co.

Ricoeur, Paul. 1970. *Freud and Philosophy: An Essay on Interpretation*. New Haven: Yale University Press.

———. 1979a. The Model of The Text: Meaningful Action Considered as a Text. In *Interpretive Social Science*, edited by P. Rabinow and W. Sullivan, pp. 73–101. Berkeley: University of California Press.

———. 1979b. The Metaphorical Process as Cognition, Imagination, and Feeling. In *On Metaphor*, edited by S. Sacks, pp. 141–57. Chicago: University of Chicago Press.

———. 1981. *Hermeneutics and the Social Sciences: Essays on Language, Action and Interpretion*. Edited by J. Thompson. Cambridge: Cambridge University Press.

Rorty, Richard. 1979. *Philosophy and the Mirror of Nature*. Princeton: Princeton University Press.

Rosaldo, Renato. 1984. Grief and a Headhunter's Rage: On the Cultural Force of Emotions. In *Text, Play, and Story: The Construction and Reconstruction of Self and Society*, edited by E. Bruner, pp. 178–95. Washington, D.C.: American Ethnological Society.

Roseman, Marina. 1988. The Pragmatics of Aesthetics: The Performance of Healing Among Senoi Temiar. *Social Science and Medicine* 27:811–18.

———. 1991. *Healing Sounds from the Malaysian Rainforest*. Berkeley: University of California Press.

Rosenblatt, Paul, R. Patricia Walsh, and Douglas Jackson. 1976. *Grief and Mourning in Cross-Cultural Perspective*. Washington: HRAF Press.

Rubel, Arthur J., Carl W. O'Nell, and Rolando Collado-Ardon. 1984. *Susto, A Folk Illness*. Berkeley: University of California Press.

Sagant, Philippe. 1976. Becoming a Limbu Priest: Ethnographic Notes. In *Spirit Possession in the Nepal Himalayas*, edited by J. T. Hitchcock and R. L. Jones, pp. 56–99. Warminster, England: Aris and Phillips.

Scheper-Hughes, Nancy, and Margaret Lock. 1987. The Mindful Body: A Prolegomenon to Future Work in Medical Anthropology. *Medical Anthropology Quarterly* 1:6–41.

Schieffelin, Edward L. 1976. *The Sorrow of the Lonely and the Burning of the Dancers*. New York: St. Martin's Press.

————. 1979. Mediators as Metaphors: Moving a Man to Tears in Papua, New Guinea. In *The Imagination of Reality: Essays in Southeast Asian Coherence Systems*, edited by A. L. Becker and A. A. Yengoyan, pp. 127–44. Norwood, NJ: Ablex Publishing Corporation.

————. 1985a. The Cultural Analysis of Depressive Affect: An Example from New Guinea. In *Culture and Depression*, edited by A. Kleinman and B. Good, pp. 101–33. Berkeley: University of California Press.

————. 1985b. Performance and the Cultural Construction of Reality. *American Ethnologist* 12:704–24.

Schutz, Alfred. 1970. *On Phenomenology and Social Relations*. Edited by H. R. Wagner. Chicago: University of Chicago Press.

Scott, James C. 1990. *Domination and the Arts of Resistance: Hidden Transcripts*. New Haven: Yale.

Seremetakis, Nadia. 1991. *The Last Word: Women, Death, and Divination in Inner Mani*. Chicago: University of Chicago Press.

Shweder, Richard A. 1985. Menstrual Pollution, Soul Loss, and the Comparative Study of Emotions. In *Culture and Depression*, edited by A. Kleinman and B. Good, pp. 182–215. Berkeley: University of California Press.

————. 1988. Suffering in Style. *Culture, Medicine and Psychiatry* 12:479–98.

Shweder, Richard, and Edmund Bourne. 1984. Does the Concept of the Person Vary Cross-Culturally? In *Culture Theory: Essays on Mind, Self and Emotion*, edited by R. A. Shweder and R. A. Levine, pp. 158–99. London: Cambridge University Press.

Singer, Jerome, and K. S. Pope, eds. 1978. *The Power of the Human Imagination: New Methods in Psychotherapy*. New York: Plenum Press.

Skorupski, John. 1976. *Symbol and Theory: A Philosophical Study of Theories of Religion in Social Anthropology*. Cambridge: Cambridge University Press.

Skorupski, John. 1982. The Cremation Ceremony According to the Byang-Gtar Tradition. *Kailash* 9:361–76.

Smith, Huston. 1991. *The World's Religions*. New York: Harper Collins.

Sontag, Susan. 1966. *Against Interpretation*. New York: Anchor.

Spiro, Melford. 1967. *Burmese Supernaturalism*. New Jersey: Prentice-Hall.

Stein, Rolf A. 1957. L'habitat, le monde et le corps humain en Extrême-Orient et en Haute-Asie. *Journal Asiatique* 245:37–74.

————. 1972. *Tibetan Civilization*. Standford, CA: Stanford University Press.

Steiner, George. 1989. *Real Presences*. Chicago: University of Chicago Press.

Stoller, Paul. 1989. *The Taste of Ethnographic Things*. Philadelphia: University of Pennsylvania Press.

————. n.d. The Sorcerer and His Body. Unpublished Paper.

Stone, Linda. 1976. Concepts of Illness and Curing in a Central Nepal Village. *Contributions to Nepalese Studies* 6:55–80.

Stroll, Avrum. 1988. *Surfaces*. Minneapolis: University of Minnesota Press.

Sustruta. 1963. *Susruta Samhita*, Vol. II. Edited and translated by K. L. Bhisagratne. Chowkhamba Sanskrit Series Office, Varanasi I.

Tambiah, Stanley. 1990. *Magic, Science, Religion, and the Scope of Rationality*. Cambridge: Cambridge University Press.

Taussig, Michael. 1987. *Shamanism, Colonialism and the Wild Man: A Study in Terror and Healing*. Chicago: University of Chicago Press.

Tedlock, Barbara. 1981. *Time and the Highland Maya*. Albuquerque: University of New Mexico Press.

Tedlock, Dennis. 1990. *Days From a Dream Almanac*. Urbana: University of Illinois Press.

Tousignant, Michel, and Mario Maldonado. 1989. Sadness, Depression and Social Reciprocity in Highland Ecuador. *Social Science and Medicine* 28:899–904.

Trawick, Margaret. 1986. Iconicity in Paraiyar Crying Songs. In *Another Harmony: New Essays on the Folklore of India*, edited by A. K. Ramanujan and S. Blackburn, pp. 294–344. Berkeley: University of California Press.

———. 1988. Spirits and Voices in Tamil Song. *American Ethnologist* 15:193–215.

———. 1990. *Notes on Love in a Tamil Family*. Berkeley: University of California Press.

Tucci, Giuseppe. 1966. *Tibetan Folk Songs*. Ascona: Artibus Asiae.

———. 1980. *The Religions of Tibet*. Translated by Geoffrey Samuel. University of California Press.

Turner, Ralph L. 1965 [1931]. *A Comparative and Etymological Dictionary of the Nepali Language*. London: Routledge and Kegan Paul.

Turner, Victor. 1967. *The Forest of Symbols*. Ithaca: Cornell University Press.

Turner, Victor, and Edward Bruner, eds. 1986. *The Anthropology of Experience*. Urbana: University of Illinois Press.

Urban, Greg. 1988. Ritual Wailing in Amerindian Brazil. *American Anthropologist* 90:385–400.

Van Gennep, Arnold. 1960. *The Rites of Passage*. London: Routledge and Kegan Paul.

Warren, Kay, and Susan Bourque. 1985. Gender, Power and Communication. In *Women Living Change*, edited by S. C. Bourque and D. R. Divine, pp. 255–86. Philadelphia: Temple University Press.

Watkins, Mary. 1976. *Waking Dreams*. New York: Harper and Row.

Watters, David. 1975. Siberian Shamanistic Traditions among the Kham-Magars of Nepal. *Contributions to Nepalese Studies* 2:123–68.

Wayman, Alex. 1976. Significance of Dreams in India and Tibet. *History of Religions* 7:1–12.

Weiss, Mitchell, and Arthur Kleinman. 1987. Depression in Cross-Cultural Perspective: Developing a Culturally Informed Model. In *Health and Cross-Cultural Psychology: Toward Applications*, edited by P. R. Dasen, J. W. Berry, and N. Sartorius, pp. 179–206. Newbury Park, CA: Sage Publications.

Wellenkamp, Jane. 1988. Notions of Grief and Catharsis Among the Toraja. *American Ethnologist* 15:486–500.

———. n.d. Love Magic and Depression: A Case Study from Toraja. Paper Presented at the 88th Annual Meeting of the American Anthropological Association.

Wengle, John. 1984. Anthropological Training and the Quest for Immortality. *Ethos* 12:223–43.

White, Geoffrey M., and John Kirpatrick, eds. 1985. *Person, Self, and Experience*. Berkeley: University of California Press.

Whorf, Benjamin. 1956. *Language, Thought and Reality: The Selected Writings of Benjamin Lee Whorf.* Cambridge, MA: MIT Press.

Wierzbicka, Anna. 1986. Human Emotions, Universal or Culture-Specific? *American Anthropologist* 88:584–94.

Wikan, Unni. 1989. Managing the Heart to Brighten Face and Soul: Emotions in Balinese Morality and Health Care. *American Ethnologist* 16:294–312.

———. 1991. Toward an Experience-Near Anthropology. *Cultural Anthropology* 6:285–305.

Wilbert, Johannes. 1985. The House of the Swallow-Tailed Kite: Warao Myth and the Art of Thinking in Images. In *Animal Myths and Metaphors in South America*, edited by G. Urton, pp. 145–82. Salt Lake City: University of Utah.

Wittgenstein, Ludwig. 1953. *Philosophical Investigations.* New York: Macmillan.

———. 1963 [1922]. *Tractatus Logico-Philosophicus.* Translated by D. F. and B. F. McGuinness. London: Routledge and Kegan Paul.

Wylie, T. V. 1959. A Standard System of Tibetan Transcription. *Harvard Journal of Asiatic Studies* 22:261–67.

Yeats, W. B. 1970 [1907]. *Discoveries: A Volume of Essays.* Shannon, Ireland: Irish University Press.

Yu, Ying-Shih. 1981. New Evidence on the Early Chinese Conception of Afterlife. *Journal of Asian Studies* 41:81–85.

———. 1987. "O Soul, Come Back!" A Study in the Changing Conceptions of the Soul and Afterlife in Pre-Buddhist China. *Harvard Journal of Asiatic Studies* 47:363–95.

Zeig, Jeffrey, ed. 1982. *Ericksonian Approaches to Hypnosis and Psychotherapy.* New York: Brunner/Mazel.

Index